WHAT PARISH
ARE YOU FROM?

WHAT PARISH ARE YOU FROM?

A Chicago Irish Community and Race Relations

EILEEN M. McMAHON

THE UNIVERSITY PRESS OF KENTUCKY

Editorial and Sales Offices: The University Press of Kentucky
663 South Limestone Street, Lexington, Kentucky 40508-4008
www.kentuckypress.com

The Library of Congress has cataloged the hardcover edition as follows:

McMahon, Eileen M., 1954–
   What parish are you from? : A Chicago Irish community and race
relations / Eileen M. McMahon.
          p.   cm.
   Includes bibliographical references and index.
   ISBN 0-8131-1877-8 (alk. paper)
   1. St. Sabina's (Church : Chicago, Ill.). 2. Chicago (Ill.)—
Church history. 3. Irish Americans—Ethnic identity.
4. Catholics—Illinois—Chicago. 5. Race relations—Religious
aspects—Catholic Church. 6. Chicago (Ill.)—race relations—Case
studies. 7. Irish Americans—Illinois—Chicago—Case studies.
8. Parishes—Illinois—Chicago—Case studies. 9. Catholic Church—
Illinois—Chicago—Case studies. I. Title.
BX4603.C5S785   1995
305.6′2077311—dc20   94-24300

Paper ISBN-10: 0-8131-0894-2
Paper ISBN-13: 978-0-8131-0894-0

This book is printed on acid-free recycled paper meeting
the requirements of the American National Standard
for Permanence in Paper for Printed Library Materials.

∞ ✪

Manufactured in the United States of America.

Member of the Association of
American University Presses

Contents

Maps and Tables

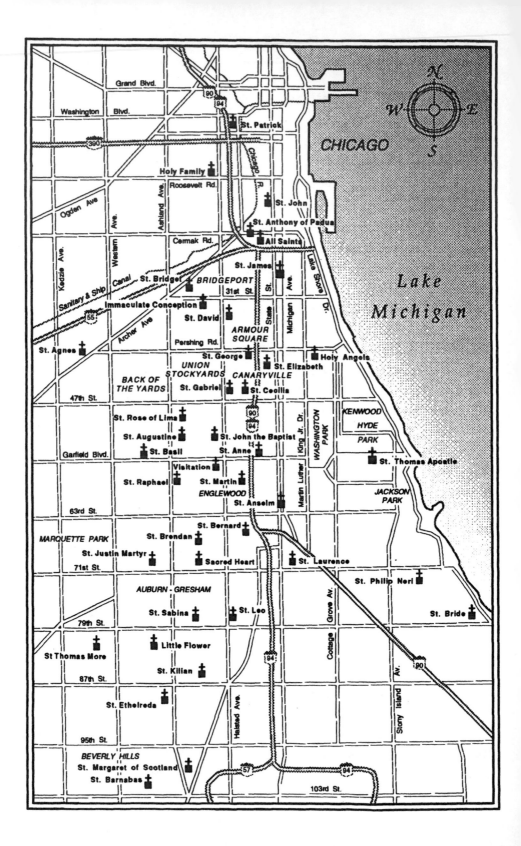

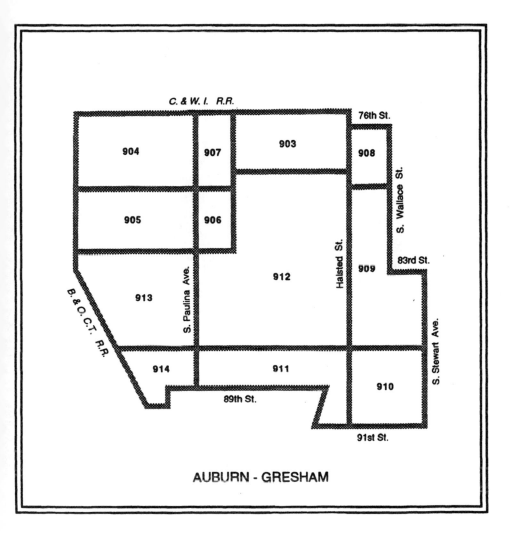

C. & W. I. R.R.

76th St.

904

907

903

908

S. Wallace St.

905

906

Halsted St.

912

83rd St.

909

913

S. Paulina Ave.

B. & O. C. T. R.R.

S. Stewart Ave.

914

911

910

89th St.

91st St.

AUBURN - GRESHAM

To my father,
JOSEPH A. MCMAHON,
in memory

Acknowledgments

When I was growing up in St. Linus's parish, I never suspected that parish life had historic significance. It was simply the way in which we lived our lives. The church steeple stood as a sentinel above the neighborhood and all the Catholic children attended the parish school. I remember thinking when I was young that others not of the parish must belong to the public religion because they went to the public school. We weren't above teasing them for having to go to school on holy days. In a generic sense, we considered ourselves American. But the everyday world, as far as we could discern, was divided between Catholics and Protestants. Our Irishness was something we brought out on St. Patrick's Day when we'd dye our milk green, listen to Bing Crosby sing "Did Your Mother Come From Ireland?" and wear green ribbons in our hair. As we got older, my friends and I debated whether we were American or Irish. We never resolved this question, in part because we knew precious little about our heritage.

As I grew older and left the world of the parish, I began to understand its singularity in urban America and have come closer to answering the question the companions of my youth and I pondered. In my quest to do so, I have become indebted to many people. I would like to especially thank Lawrence J. McCaffrey for encouraging me to pursue Irish studies with him at Loyola University of Chicago. I am grateful to William Galush for his thoroughness and encouragement as he directed me through this study and for sharing his knowledge of ethnic and Catholic America. Special thanks are also due Lewis Erenberg and Kathleen McCourt for their helpful suggestions. Thanks to Ellen Skerrett for introducing me to St. Sabina's.

Several other people assisted me in researching this work. Archie Motley and the staff at the Chicago Historical Society and John Treanor and his staff at the Archdiocese of Chicago Archives were very helpful in making their collections available to me. Sister Toman at the Sinsinawa Dominican Archives provided gracious assistance with their records. Special thanks are due to Msgr. John J. Egan for making his personal papers readily available to me. I also wish to thank the staffs at the Chicago Municipal Reference Library, Northwestern University's Deering Library, Mundelein College Resource Learning

Center, De Paul University Library, the Regenstein Library of the University of Chicago, and Loyola University of Chicago's Cudahy Library.

I am especially appreciative of the warm welcome I received from the people of St. Sabina's. Rev. Michael Pfleger and his very gracious assistant, Ann Gaskin, and the rest of the staff made their records available to me and made the many hours I sat in the rectory dining room very pleasant. I am also indebted to all the people whose lives were touched by St. Sabina's and who were willing to share their experiences with me. Without them, this book would not exist. I have often been asked whether I am related to any of the McMahons mentioned in the text. Our only linkage appears to be our common ancestor, Brian Boru, high king of Ireland.

Projects such as this also rely on financial assistance. The Graduate School of Loyola University facilitated my work through the granting of a University Fellowship for the 1985-86 academic year, which I greatly appreciate.

Finally, I am very grateful to my husband, Ted, for his unfailing support and encouragement. He never seemed to tire of hearing about St. Sabina's. I also want to thank Teddy and Joey for taking long naps.

Introduction

It began as a typical summer afternoon in August 1965. Seventeen-year-old Frank Kelly and his buddies headed over to St. Sabina's after their ball game to meet up with some of the girls from the parish. They had all graduated from the Catholic grade school and had spent many hours in the community center gym playing sports and roller skating. Now that they were in high school, they had the privilege of attending the popular Sunday night dances. The school and the parish, however, had changed since the days when the children had donned their uniforms for first grade. African Americans were buying homes and moving into the apartments and flats nearby. This made many Irish-American parishioners apprehensive. They did not have a history of amiable relations with blacks, with whom they had competed for employment and housing in overcrowded neighborhoods. Sometimes their associations erupted into violence. The pastor, Msgr. John McMahon, reassured the people of the neighborhood that parish life could continue as usual. He had even enlisted the community organizer, Saul Alinsky, and other local leaders to form an organization to work for neighborhood stability while integration occurred. Indeed, so far it seemed to be working.

What happened that August afternoon, however, convinced St. Sabina parishioners that this experiment was a failure. While Frank and his friends stood across the street from the community center, three black teenagers appeared around the corner. The boys exchanged insults. Two of the black youths drew guns and fired into the group. A sixteen-year-old girl was shot in the leg. Frank was shot in the chest and died minutes later as Father White administered the last rites of the Church. In the months that followed, hundreds of white families sold their homes and moved to the suburbs. St. Sabina's became a predominantly African-American community.

At this time, when scores of neighborhoods were changing in Chicago and other northern cities, St. Sabina's reaction to this inter-racial conflict appeared to be no different from that of other white communities facing integration. However, Catholic ethnics defined neighborhood and community differently than other whites did. Dan Rostenkowski, the noted Illinois Congressman, reminisced on this

sense of community. He stated that "church spires . . . were the bea-
cons of Chicago—the exact centers of neighborhoods, the symbols of
our ethnic heritage."[1] To these Catholics the parish defined the center
and parameters of their community. Their neighbors were people who
shared a common ethnic tradition and Catholic heritage. This shaped
their unique reaction to others who did not fit into their world.

Parishes were the center of a vital Catholic subculture. These
neighborhood churches became more important to Catholic ethnics in
America than they had been in Europe. Back in the old country,
religion and culture had been so intertwined that the local church was
but one avenue among many for Catholics to partake of their faith. Yet,
when European Catholics emigrated to America they found themselves in a society that professed to be secular but was, in practice,
heavily influenced by Protestantism. Catholic immigrants used the
parish as the main avenue for the expression of their faith and as the
nucleus for a "ghetto culture." While Catholics did not form the only
ghetto culture in America, John Cogley asserts that theirs "became the
best organized and most powerful of the nation's subcultures."[2] The
parish was perhaps the most dynamic element in this subculture.
Andrew Greeley has written that "institutional Catholicism in the
United States prospered as long as it did because it provided self-defi-
nition and social location for the immigrants, their children, and their
grandchildren; and it did so precisely through the institution of the
neighborhood parish."[3] It certainly commanded the allegiance of mil-
lions of Catholics. Without the parish, it is doubtful whether Catholic
culture could have survived in America.[4]

The parish proved to be a very versatile and flexible community-
generating institution. It broke impersonal, industrial cities into intimate neighborhoods. Networks of territorial parishes ensured that
Catholics could repeat their community experience and still be economically and geographically mobile. Abandoning an immigrant
neighborhood did not mean abandoning a Catholic way of life.

Unlike Protestantism with its focus on the individual, Catholicism
had traditionally emphasized the importance of the community. To
partake of the sacraments, which were crucial to salvation, Catholics
needed a priest and a parish. Devotionalism, with its emphasis on
examination of one's sins within a community setting, further encouraged the diminution of the individual and the elevation of community.
Forgiveness depended upon repentance and doing one's duty toward
family and friends. This form of Catholicism combined with Irish
gregariousness created a personality that was inextricably entwined
with the parish community. A former parishioner of St. Sabina's
recalled the humbleness of the people. He said "there was no big deal"
when it came to sharing and helping one another.[5]

The Irish were also very loyal to the parish because it played such an important role in helping them rise above their humble and often degraded beginnings in America. The nineteenth-century Irish-American community battled poverty, alcoholism, broken families, and crime. The parish provided institutional strength to this struggling community. It protected, championed, disciplined, and forgave its members. The parish did not, of course, completely eradicate these problems, but it provided support for faltering individuals. Perhaps no other institution was as responsible for the ultimate success of Irish America.

Anti-Catholicism contributed to Catholic dependency on parishes. However, this adherence to the parish community was also encouraged by devotional Catholicism, the parish school, and a philosophy that stressed separation from the American mainstream to protect the faithful from Protestant and secular influences. Yet this desire for separation was not wholly defensive. By the mid–twentieth century Catholics felt confident that they could have a salutary effect on American society.

As much as Catholics might have wanted to insulate themselves from the rest of American society in their parish communities, Chicago demographics as well as the fluid nature of American society made this impossible. Catholics for a time had been able to avoid compromising their sense of parish community. Their chain of territorial parishes had enabled Catholics to escape congested, industrial neighborhoods. Moving from one parish neighborhood to the next assured Catholics of a similar cultural environment. They could easily disregard white Protestants, who in turn wanted little to do with them. The Great Migration of African Americans, however, challenged Catholic isolation in a way it never had been before. The worldview they had developed out of their own historical experiences unfortunately made them psychologically unprepared to deal with broader social issues that encroached on their community. These Catholics thought of religion in personal terms— something practiced within their own community. Their religion helped ensure their personal survival in a difficult world and secured salvation in the next.

St. Sabina's liberal clergy and laity tried to broaden their parishioner's religious and community vision. Parishioners were brought to accept blacks individually since their religious instruction instilled in them obedience to the clergy and Christian behavior. But parish Catholicism, with its emphasis on devotionalism, had not demanded a broader social conscience. When Chicago's black belt inched its way through South Side neighborhoods, many Catholics had a difficult time seeing this incursion as anything but a threat to a way of life on which they depended. The parish was their defense against a threatening society. These Catholics were unwilling to see the situation in terms of abstract social justice. If their community was disrupted, so was the parish upon which they were so spiritually and psychologically dependent. St. Sabina parishioners could only approach race relations within the context of a parish mentality. For example, when N. Hagerty was told by a sister that a white dress was needed for a May crowning at Holy Angels—a black parish, she volunteered her wedding dress. Mrs. Hagerty shared the general view of blacks held by most parishioners, yet, when asked by a "moral" authority to provide a dress, she gave the most personal dress a woman could own.[6]

Racism certainly was an important factor in the inability of St. Sabina's to achieve permanent integration. The notion that the two races could not live together was unquestioningly accepted in many white Catholic parishes. It gelled with their tendency to exclude those who seemed to pose a threat to their own peculiar way of life. It was a difficult idea to dispel. Although St. Sabina's initially tried to accept blacks, a fatal gunshot across from the parish complex destroyed these years of uneasy experimentation with racial coexistence. The "evils" of the world had intruded upon their "sacred ground." Community residents quickly moved away, hoping that perhaps another parish farther south and west could re-create a world they had lost.

The demise of communities that resisted integration was generally cheered by liberals in the 1960s and 1970s. They had their own set of biases against kinship, nationality, religion, and ethnic bonds. They condemned these "tribal" loyalties as relics of an ignorant, backward past that must give way to progress and the abstract notion of the universal brotherhood of humanity.[7] In 1963, when Chicago was experiencing the strain of racial conflict, *Time* magazine referred to this area as "Chicago's Seamy South Side."[8] More recently, the term "white ethnic," used to describe the diverse people of the Southwest and Northwest sides, has become a pejorative term and a stereotype suggesting narrow-minded and bigoted people.[9]

Traditionally, most Americans have believed that the survival of this country depends upon the fusing of its diverse peoples. While a worthy goal, this expectation has turned a blind eye to the painful and disruptive process integration creates for those caught in the middle of the meltdown. While seriously flawed by exclusionist beliefs, communities such as Catholic parishes had many advantages. They were able to support families in raising children, providing the children with a value system as well as a variety of supervised activities to shelter them from social problems that parents today often face alone. Parish communities gave men and women beauty and tradition in their ordinary lives. Although their shortcomings should not be overlooked, neither should their strengths be too quickly dismissed.

The experience of Catholic parish life also raises the question of whether true cultural pluralism is a real option for American society. Catholics made some adaptations to America to protect their way of life. The moral climate of the 1960s was against them, as well as American political values, which protect the rights of the individual over the community. Ironically, at the same time, multiculturalism was becoming the "enlightened" social ethos that was to end the past repression of assimilation to mainstream culture, particularly for non-Europeans. Many Catholic communities still try to retain their unique subculture, but its character, like that of other minority communities, is less and less of their own design. A truly distinct subculture may prove impossible to maintain.

The transition from a white neighborhood and parish to a heavily black neighborhood and parish is a major theme in twentieth-century urban and religious history. The experience of St. Sabina's in Chicago's southwest neighborhood of Auburn-Gresham can provide insight into this aspect of American history. St. Sabina's was an Irish-American community with a strong sense of parish tradition. The purpose of this case study is to shed light on the character, values, and mores of the parish community, as well as the beliefs that shaped their attitudes toward their fellow Americans. This is St. Sabina's story.

1

The Making of the Irish Parish Community: A Historical Background

Chicago's South Side Irish have played a prominent role in the city's history. In the neighborhood of Bridgeport they established a political base and network that launched one of the strongest political machines in the country and gave Chicago several of its mayors. Another South Side establishment and tradition is the Chicago White Sox formed by Charles Comiskey, son of an Irish immigrant and city council alderman. In 1910 Comiskey laid a green cornerstone for his new ball park at 35th and Shields in the midst of an Irish neighborhood.

The South Side Irish community has been immortalized in the literary works of humorist Finley Peter Dunne and novelist James T. Farrell. Both writers were concerned with the Irish and their relationship to Chicago's ethnic and racial communities. Competition over jobs and neighborhoods was a major theme in their work. Dunne introduced Mr. Dooley, his philosopher-bartender, to Chicago in 1893 in weekly Irish dialectal pieces for the *Chicago Evening Post*. Mr. Dooley's mythical saloon on Archer Avenue served the Bridgeport Irish. The barkeeper freely dispensed his wit and wisdom on community happenings and Chicago issues. By 1894, Mr. Dooley had become the pride of Chicago. Gradually, Dunne expanded the scope of Mr. Dooley's philosophizing to national issues, which earned him a place in national publications and made Mr. Dooley a national phenomenon.[1]

Martin Dooley's most poignant colloquies were on the Bridgeport Irish, whom he depicted with "objective realism and sympathetic understanding."[2] What Dunne found inspiring about this Irish community was that, in the midst of an ugly and depressing section of industrial Chicago, their social intercourse was "philosophic, gentle, kindly, shrewd, and witty." In addition, their parochial attachment to neighborhood and Church presented an interesting contrast to their fierce interest in worldly affairs.[3]

Dunne himself was a product of the Chicago Irish-Catholic world. The men of his family chose between two careers: either they went down to the riverfront to become ships carpenters or they went to the seminary and became priests. The Dunne family home was in St. Patrick's parish at Adams and Desplaines Streets just west of the downtown business district. St. Patrick's still remains a landmark to the Chicago Irish, yet, during Dunne's formative years, its middle-class Irish character was gradually eroded by its close proximity to Chicago's business district. This theme of neighborhood transformation was prominent in Mr. Dooley's observations of the Bridgeport Irish.[4]

James T. Farrell saw himself as a writer of the city in the tradition of Theodore Dreiser, James Joyce, and Emile Zola. Some have called him one of the greatest realists in American letters. He was also influenced by the intellectually vital period of America's Progressive Era, during which so much hope was pinned on the rational reform of society and the melting of ethnic groups into one people. The writings of John Dewey, George Herbert Mead, and Thorstein Veblen were very influential in shaping his views of the city. Farrell's literary work documents the evolution of Irish Catholics in urban America from the turn of the twentieth century to the end of the 1930s. His most noted novels are the Studs Lonigan trilogy and the Danny O'Neill pentalogy. These novels depict the "spatial, temporal, cultural, and emotional dimensions" of Chicago's South Side Irish community.[5]

For Farrell the cultural diversity of Chicago and its promise of a common democratic community was a potentially liberating force which could lift the Irish from their ethnic and religious insularity. However, most of his characters refused to break out of their parochial world. Farrell portrayed the Irish sympathetically in their struggle with the disrupting effects of immigration and their poverty. He appreciated the spiritual needs met by parish Catholicism, yet he was impatient with and condemning of its narrow-minded quest for middle-class respectability at the expense of a more authentic humanity and empathy for others.[6] The works of Dunne and Farrell provide a literary examination of Chicago's South Side Irish-American community and provide many of the themes for this historical investigation.

The Irish began their "exile" to the United States in large numbers in the 1820s. Ireland's population had been increasing. Young men and women who had no hope of attaining their own farms saw no reason to put off acquiring the few comforts available to them, namely, marriage and family. Only a small plot of land was necessary to cultivate enough potatoes to feed a growing family, and a family could be sustained on a diet of primarily potatoes and milk. There was little alternative industry in Ireland to relieve the overburdened agricultural sector. Therefore, emigration became the one choice left for those who did not want to sink further into misery and poverty. At the same time, the United States was embarking on an era of tremendous economic and geographic expansion and needed immigrant workers.

The Irish were first drawn to the South Side of Chicago in 1836, when work began on the Illinois and Michigan Canal, an endeavor to connect Lake Michigan with the Mississippi River. They had gained experience on the Erie Canal and followed what seemed to be their "national occupation" westward when the new canal project began. Once the project was completed in 1848, many Irish made their home at the canal's terminus just outside the city in Bridgeport.[7] For many decades this was the premier Irish community in the Midwest.[8]

In the 1840s and 1850s, just as Chicago was making its bid for economic pre-eminence in the Midwest as the region's transportation center, the Great Famine struck Ireland. Many famine refugees escaped to Chicago, where they could find jobs. By 1850 the Irish made up 20 percent of the city's population, which for a time made them the largest ethnic group.[9] Employment opportunities in this prairie boom-town opened up just when the Irish desperately needed the work. The employment they qualified for was primarily unskilled work in the industrial sectors of the South Side. After the completion of the I & M Canal, obnoxious industries near the expanding downtown commercial district moved to the South Branch of the River and the Canal area. Slaughterhouses found the waterways useful for the processing of livestock. Cattle driven up from the south and west were more easily corralled there. The coming of the railroads made Bridgeport and the South Side destined for further industrialization. In the 1860s a large steel mill began operation at Archer and Ashland Avenues. Brickyards and breweries added to the productivity of the area. On Christmas Day 1865 the Union Stock Yards opened through the joint effort of meat-packing companies and railroad lines. The Yards would become the principal industrial employer in the area.[10]

Almost from the beginning of their settlement in the Chicago area, the Irish plunged into the political arena. By the close of the Civil War the Irish were the dominant ethnic group in Chicago politics. Irish aldermen were a significant block in the city council and influenced the Democratic party as ward committeemen. Their ability to speak English and their knowledge of Anglo-Saxon political institutions were special skills they used to gain political clout. The arrival of other immigrants eclipsed Irish numbers in the city, but this did not hamper Irish power. Many newcomers were Catholic, which helped make Chicago the largest diocese in Roman Catholicism. Building on this common religious bond, Irish politicians enhanced their position by acting as power-brokers among the various national groups.[11]

The desire for economic gain was a crucial factor in the Irish-American quest for political power. Poor and unskilled, the Irish had few career opportunities that could provide them with a more comfortable and secure life. Politics brought city patronage jobs and other economic benefits. Irish politicians granted city franchises and contracts to companies willing to pay kickbacks. They enriched themselves and secured jobs for the Irish with companies doing business with the city. Because the nineteenth century was the age of rugged individualism, national and local governments did not believe that they had an obligation to care for the welfare of their citizens regardless of their situation. Irish politicians filled this void for their impoverished constituents with aid such as food and coal baskets, albeit in exchange for votes.[12]

Corrupt "boodle" alderman penetrated the workings of the entire city. The Irish worked on streetcar lines, on the construction of sidewalks and sewers, and on the installation of gas, electric, and telephone lines. Since Chicago was one of the fastest growing cities in the country, the demand for city workers increased. More police officers and firemen were needed to monitor the rambunctious city. Irish political connections allowed them to solidify control over both city departments. By 1900 48 percent of the Irish were engaged in city service occupations such as law enforcement and fire fighting. In 1890 six times more policemen were Irish than the next largest ethnic group. Although the city's labor force was only 14 percent Irish, 58 percent of gasworks employees in Chicago were either first or second generation Irish.[13]

Irish economic mobility came about in part from their political clout, which they were able to wield at a time when Chicago was undergoing rapid expansion. By the 1870s a small but significant Irish middle class began to appear. By 1920 their improved economic situation gave most Irish the option to leave behind inner city industrial areas for better apartments and houses in Chicago's newer neighborhoods south and west.[14]

Politics provided the Irish with power and jobs. It also reinforced ethnic cohesiveness. Nationalist causes also brought unity to the Irish in Chicago by providing social occasions and the lure of a job or the enhancement of a political career. In his influential study of Irish-American nationalism, Thomas Brown argues that besides an intense hatred of Britain, the driving motive behind this crusade for Ireland's freedom was a deep-seated sense of inferiority and a longing of the Irish for respectability. In Ireland, the British had shown little regard for the native Irish and their way of life. Many Irish emigrants blamed British misrule for their exile. Once in America, the Irish found the same Anglo disdain for their religion, culture, and poverty. Irish Americans thought that if Ireland were a free, self-determining nation, the condition of the Irish would be elevated not only in Ireland but in America as well.[15]

While the motivations behind Irish nationalism were fairly universal in America, the nature of the movement varied from city to city and region to region. Chicago Irish nationalism was different from that in the East, especially in New York and New England, in that it never exhibited the bitter conflict between advocates of constitutional methods and of physical force. In the East, bishops and clergy generally followed the standard Church position that revolutionary movements were contrary to the Catholic teachings of a just war and that the secret oaths members were obliged to take also violated primary loyalties to God and country. The eastern Irish community was divided on this issue. Some nationalists became even greater advocates of physical force, while others followed the dictates of the clergy and supported constitutional means to achieve Ireland's freedom.[16]

In Chicago, however, Archbishop Patrick A. Feehan sided with the "liberal" elements in the Church that thought it best not to antagonize Catholics who were essentially loyal church members but who were attracted to nationalist organizations. Feehan himself was one with his diocese in his nationalist feelings toward Britain and was reluctant to make an issue out of which nationalist organization one of his charges belonged to. The Chicago Irish community, then, never experienced the pressure to polarize their nationalist aspirations, although as time went on constitutional methods became dominant. From the days of the Fenian Brotherhood of the 1860s through those of the Clan-na-Gael, Chicago had a vital nationalist movement. The first organization of the Clan-na-Gael was established in Bridgeport in 1869. The Irish in this section of town also supported the Ancient Order of Hibernians, the Hibernian Rifles, and the Irish Land League. They were also enthusiastic devotees of picnics sponsored by the United Irish Societies of Chicago. These picnics did not pass the notice of Mr. Dooley who commented, "if Ireland could be freed be a picnic, it'd not on'y be free, but an impire." Nationalism was a vital part of the Chicago Irish community until the end of the Irish Civil War in 1923 when at least most of Ireland won its independence.[17]

Many issues and causes bonded the nineteenth-century Chicago Irish community. Historians have concluded, however, that "in spite of their intense interest in things Gaelic, the Irish failed to build lasting monuments that manifested their nationalism—their churches sufficed."[18]

Why was religion the glue of the Irish community? The answer requires a look back into Ireland's history. Catholicism has been a major component to Irish national identity and sense of social cohesion since the Reformation in England in the sixteenth century. In previous centuries the English colonized Ireland and gradually expropriated the land while adopting Irish culture. Anglo presence in Ireland was somewhat obscured by their cultural assimilation. When England converted to Protestantism, however, religion became an obvious mark of difference between colonizer and colony. The Irish refused to acquiesce to further cultural annihilation, and lines of resistance were drawn. In the seventeenth century Irish Catholics tried to take advantage of English political turmoil during the years of the English Civil War and Glorious Revolution. Their rebellions, however, were put down and the Irish paid a heavy price for them. Anti-Catholic legislation passed through Parliament from the reigns of William and Mary to George II. Bishops and members of religious orders were banished from the country. Secular priests from the continent were expected to register, pay a fee, and take an oath of loyalty. Catholics were excluded from political participation in Parliament and any aspect of the legal profession. They could not vote. They could not establish schools or send their children out of the country for education. Laws also sought to reduce Catholic property holding.[19]

This anti-Catholic legislation also applied to Britain and British North America, although its application was harshest in Ireland. British penal laws were not only out of step with eighteenth-century Enlightenment ideals of religious toleration, but were also more oppressive than any laws Protestants suffered in Catholic countries. These penal laws, however, failed to wipe out Catholicism and make the country Protestant. What they did do was terrorize, humiliate, and pacify the Irish people. The lines between Protestant and Catholic were more rigidly drawn between the Anglo-Irish Protestant minority who owned 90 percent of the land and controlled Ireland's political and legal system and the impoverished Catholic majority. Irish Catholic peasants were the most impoverished in Europe. They were illiterate, and, though nominally Catholic, their lack of access to religious instruction left them ignorant of the basic tenets of their religion.[20]

By the end of the eighteenth century rising feelings of Irish nationalism combined with Enlightenment ideals of the universal brotherhood of humanity led to brief overtures of toleration toward the Catholic community. Many penal laws that inhibited the practice of Catholicism were lifted. Maynooth Catholic Seminary was founded in 1795, and the young priests who emerged from this seminary were much more politically and socially radicalized than those who furtively entered Ireland in the eighteenth century after a continental education.[21]

This new vanguard of priests was recruited out of the small Catholic middle class or the somewhat prosperous farming class. Having no aristocratic pretensions and coming from politically disadvantaged social groups, Irish clergymen in the nineteenth century were one with their people in their bitter resentment of the Anglo-Irish Protestant ascendancy. Daniel O'Connell, a Catholic lawyer who emerged in the first half of the nineteenth century as Ireland's political leader, was able to capitalize on this union of spirit between priests and people to build a movement for Catholic emancipation. This movement culminated in the Catholic Relief Act of 1829, which allowed Catholic political rights; voting rights, however, rested on high property qualifications.[22]

The close political bond between the clergy and the Irish people further accentuated the connection between Irish national identity and Catholicism. However, this tie did not automatically make the Irish people the devout practicing Catholics the clergy wanted them to be. In the first half of the nineteenth century Irish priests battled "pagan" social customs and ill-informed religious ideas that had been perpetrated during the penal law period.[23]

In the absence of a coherent theological explanation of the workings of the universe, Irish peasants had resorted to supernatural practices to exert influence over nature and other situations beyond their control. Fairy doctors used white magic to treat sick people and animals. Holy wells or magic springs were sought out for their healing benefits and became associated with certain saints. Worshippers made pilgrimages to these sites as an act of devotion and penance. The practice of waking the dead was also a central feature of Irish rural life that disturbed the clergy. The general purpose was to pray for the soul of the deceased and give consolation to the family. However, wakes also had a very social and even festive aspect to them. Those who came to pay their respects to the dead also looked forward to drinking, dancing, singing, story-telling, and game playing.[24]

Among the most notorious forms of entertainment from the clergy's perspective were games that were obviously symbolic sexual dances or mimes. From an anthropological point of view these waking practices may have reflected both a primitive desire to appease the newly deceased, who may still dwell among the living, and the profound need of the human spirit to reassert its vitality in the face of death. These were among many popular social and religious customs that clashed with this new breed of Maynooth-trained clergy who hoped to elevate the beliefs and behavior of the Irish people. They met with limited results. To a certain extent people respected the hierarchical authority of the Church since Ireland had an authoritarian and deferential culture that had been established by the Anglo-Irish Protestant elite. Priests naturally assumed a prominent place in the social order. Without their influence rural Ireland most probably would have been a more violent society with fewer sexual restraints and much more steeped in popular magic and customs. However, the Church was limited in its ability to effect much change. Its constituents were too impoverished to support enough clergy or build enough churches to spread Catholic influences throughout Irish society.[25]

By the mid-nineteenth century, however, the church gained more influence, when Ireland underwent a "devotional revolution." This religious transformation was spearheaded by Paul Cardinal Cullen, who headed the Catholic Church in Ireland from 1849 to 1878. At the hierarchical level Cullen improved the administration of the Church and created a much more disciplined clergy. These changes occurred at a time when the Irish people were becoming more receptive to spiritual direction. In the 1830s and 1840s Father Theobold Mathew led a temperance crusade to rid Ireland of the curse of alcohol, and Daniel O'Connell continued to politically mobilize the Irish people for repeal of Ireland's union with Great Britain. Both made use of mass meetings to drum up support. The excitement these gatherings generated turned them into a type of spiritual and psychological revival.[26]

The Great Famine of the late 1840s also had a profound effect on the religious state of the Irish people. Many interpreted the disaster as God's punishment for sin. This made them more receptive to the teachings of the Church. The poor were the worst hit by the famine. With their death and emigration, the population of Ireland was reduced by at least two million. Therefore, the number of priests per person achieved a more favorable ratio, and the least "churched" elements of Irish society were gone.[27]

All of these changes made the Irish people eager for spiritual instruction; Cullen and his newly recruited and rehabilitated army of priests and nuns eagerly responded to this need. To create a standard religious community experience, religious leaders encouraged not only more frequent church attendance and receiving of the sacraments, but also a host of devotional practices, such as the rosary, novenas, forty-hours devotion, benediction, and pilgrimages.[28]

Lastly, Catholic devotionalism in Ireland was strengthened by the continued erosion of traditional Irish culture. Ireland in this century became more Anglicized. National schools indoctrinated Irish children with British culture and English became the language of modernization. Irish ways began to wane. Catholicism, which the Irish had used to distinguish themselves from Anglo-Protestants since the sixteenth century, was more dearly clung to as their Irish cultural heritage. In the process of this "devotional revolution" the Irish were transformed into one of the most devout Catholic ethnic groups in the Christian world.[29]

The Catholic Church in Ireland consolidated its position of authority in the latter half of the nineteenth century and into the twentieth century. The strong religious adherence of the Irish people coupled with the fact that the Church was not identified with the old feudal aristocratic order gave the Church a position of power and influence it did not enjoy in many continental European countries. The Church

instead supported the democratic constitutional process for nationalistic aims. By siding with the Irish people in their political, economic, and
social aspirations, but yet disciplining their actions into legitimate political channels, the clergy reinforced its authority among the Irish people.[30]

These changes in the Catholic Church in Ireland would profoundly
influence the Catholic Church in America. Over the course of the
nineteenth century Irish immigrants to the United States were increasingly better versed in the teachings of Catholicism and much
more conscientious about their spiritual duties. The nationalistic dimension to their Catholic identity did not diminish with their passage
across the Atlantic.

Unfortunately for poor Irish-Catholic immigrants, nineteenth-century America was also a very Anglo-Protestant society. Americans
exhibited much of the same prejudice that British Protestants har-
bored toward Irish Catholics in the United Kingdom. American Anglo-
Protestants deemed Catholicism incompatible with the democratic and
Enlightenment institutions and the values of the new republic. To
them Catholicism was authoritarian, antidemocratic, and steeped in
mysterious rites that bordered on hocus-pocus. The older, small,
Catholic American population of English and French stock had made
every effort to allay Anglo-Protestant fears of Catholic conspiracies to
destroy the republic for the pope. They instead emphasized their rich,
learned, and dignified cultural heritage, and for the most part did not
challenge anti-Catholic laws or customs.

However, the massive influx of Irish Catholics along with German
Catholics transformed the American Catholic Church into an immigrant and working-class church. Their "offensive" religion combined
with their foreignness and, in the case of the Irish, their extreme
poverty provoked hostile reactions in American nativists, who wanted
the country to be a preserve for Anglo-Protestants. Unlike earlier
Church leaders in America, the rising new breed of Irish and German
leadership had little patience with Protestant expectations that they
accept second-class status. They instead established a new tradition
of aggressive defense of their flock and turned the Church here into
"the most militant Catholic organization in the English-speaking
world."[31]

An example of how the parish became a bulwark against nativism
can be seen in Kathleen Gavigan's study of parishes in Philadelphia.
Between 1834 and 1849 Philadelphia was plagued by periodic outbursts of native American riots. Immigration, industrialization, and
strained municipal resources tried social relations in the City of
Brotherly Love. The worst riot in terms of lives lost and property
damaged occurred in 1844 and was primarily directed at the newly
arrived poor Irish. Bishop Francis Kenrick beseeched his followers to

stay away from the violence, remain home, and forgive their enemies. Most Irish Catholics heeded his advice and became more hesitant in their relations with the rest of the city's population. From this point on Catholics retreated into their parish communities and built separate social, educational, and sometimes even financial institutions. Most important in shaping this small world was the parish school, which, besides providing religious instruction, helped ensure Catholic marriages and vocations. This parochial world was an effective means of dealing with the fears and insecurities of a minority culture in a hostile environment.[32]

Over time Catholic churches in Philadelphia became the religious, social, and political hub of the Irish community. Irish identification with their parish was so strong that Philadelphians referred to their parishes rather than their street addresses or city neighborhoods to explain were they lived. This close bond among people, parish, and neighborhood was in reaction to nativism.[33]

Nativism, however, was not solely responsible for shaping parish communities in the nineteenth century. In her study of an Irish Catholic parish in Pittsburgh, Patricia Good also found that the Irish used the parish to create a self-contained and aloof ethnic community. She sees the parish as a positive method of adapting to urban America rather than just a response to nativism. For displaced subsistence farmers from Ireland, the parish became an effective arena in which to form friendships and find mates among people who shared the same attitudes, values, and beliefs. It provided them with a sense of identity and helped them overcome feelings of anonymity in urban, industrial America. The close emotional and psychological ties they had with the parish were matched by their desire to reside as close as possible to the church. In the parish they could find a supportive environment for their family. Patricia Good found remarkable numbers of intact families within the mid-nineteenth century Irish community, which was supposed to have been plagued by unstable households. While the parish did, of course, protect the Irish from ridicule and discrimination, it also isolated them from other ethnic groups and from mainstream American society. On one hand, the parish retarded Irish assimilation, yet, on the other hand, it also facilitated assimilation. By promoting family stability, education, and even economic mobility, the parish was a model for successful adaptation to a new world environment.[34]

Other factors were also at work to make the parish central in the lives of American Catholics. The Roman Catholic Church in the nineteenth century was aggressively promoting changes in worship. After the Reformation, the Roman Church sought to revitalize Catholicism and strengthen the bonds of the Catholic community. Medieval contemplation centered on monasteries was de-emphasized and a more active spiritual life centered on the parish was encouraged. In the nineteenth century the parish's role was seen as vitally important in protecting the faithful in an increasingly rational and secular age.[35]

The Church on the continent had also been more identified with the ancien régime and, therefore, was under attack by modernizing forces and advocates. To preserve its authority as the true avenue to salvation, the Church promoted a more popular form of religious expression that gave a human face to religion. Romantic images from the Middle Ages of saints, the Blessed Virgin, and Jesus provided images for contemplation and inspiration. Processions, pilgrimages, and veneration of relics became features of public displays of faith. The hallmark of this devotional revolution was the parish mission. Specially trained orders of clergy, such as the Jesuits and Redemptorists, traveled from parish to parish to preach a religion of the heart and to encourage personal conversion experiences.[36]

By the 1850s this type of devotional practice was carried across the Atlantic by these religious orders to the American Church. The religious climate in America was ripe for this form of spiritual experience. American Protestantism had helped make evangelical revivals the most popular religious movement in the nineteenth century. The shortage of priests and scattered settlements of Catholics across the developing North and Midwest created a need for itinerant preachers. The revival or parish mission became the central feature of Catholic life.[37]

Like Protestant revivals, Catholic missions emphasized personal experiences of conversion and achieving salvation through obedience to a demanding moral code, which forbade excessive drinking, dancing, and gambling, and encouraged hard work, frugality, and self-reliance. What made Catholic revivals unique was that they depended upon priests, who were the only ones allowed to preach the gospel and the only ones who could solemnize the close of a meeting by administering the sacraments, particularly penance and communion. Revival priests reaffirmed the prominence of the local pastor by telling mission attenders that they now had to follow the dictates of the local clergy. The revival reinforced the parish as the basic building block of the Catholic community.[38]

Because they followed a form of religion that emphasized the individual's personal relationship with God as the means to obtain reward in the hereafter, Catholics tended to view this world as fraught with moral danger. "Religion of the heart" down-played reason as a way of understanding God's universe. Extending oneself beyond the confines of the parish and engaging in crusades for social justice were not the hallmarks of American Catholicism.[39]

Their lack of attentiveness to and involvement in the social issues of the day has subjected Catholics to the criticism of Catholic and non-Catholic intellectuals and leaders. However, in their study of the rise and fall of religious denominations in America, Roger Finke and Rodney Stark found that the religions that have been the most successful in attracting members have been those that have focused on the sacred, satisfied the "otherworldly" needs of their adherents, and made serious emotional, material, and social demands on them. In the nineteenth century Congregationalists and Episcopalians lessened their demands on their followers and diluted traditional teachings. They, therefore, failed to keep pace with the rapid growth of Methodists and Catholics. Catholicism increased in numbers, of course, through immigration. However, their devotion to the Church was not as automatic as usually thought. The Church had to turn polyglot immigrants into practicing parishioners. Devotionalism and the parish mission were successful antidotes to Protestant and secular challenges, but, most important, they satisfied the deeper spiritual needs of nineteenth-century immigrant Catholics. Although American Catholicism was not as attuned to the secular needs of society as some would wish, its style of worship gave Catholics strength and self-confidence in a hostile milieu. This form of worship survived into the twentieth century.[40]

The Catholic hierarchy's efforts to Romanize and standardize popular devotions tightened the bonds between the laity and the institutional Church. Nativism aided their efforts by convincing Catholics of their marginal status in American life. The faithful were thus more willing to turn to the Church for guidance and reassurance. Therefore, they were more accepting of this form of worship that the hierarchy was promoting.[41]

In an increasingly pluralistic American society with tense denominational relationships, devotionalism provided Catholics with a distinctively different form of religious practice. They did not need to "sell out" to the Protestant culture of America. Where Protestants had individual Bible reading in the home, gospel hymns, prayer groups, revival meetings, and mission societies, Catholics had popular devotions to the Sacred Heart, Mary, and other saints; parish missions and societies; papal infallibility; and the Mass; all of which centered on the parish church. The different cultural experiences that these religious expressions fostered created starkly separate communities where there were clear-cut boundaries between Protestants and Catholics. There would be no confusing a Protestant with a Catholic—each knew where he belonged.[42]

Unlike Protestants, however, Catholics could not assert their religion as part and parcel of American character and tradition—at least not in the nineteenth century. Therefore, they began "celebrating their distinctiveness in private."[43] That private sphere was centered on their parishes.

The ethnic parish was another important component of the vigor of American Catholicism. As Catholic ethnic groups poured into the United States over the course of the nineteenth century and into the twentieth, the Catholic hierarchy faced the dilemma of how to hold together such a culturally diverse group of people, who had only their religion in common. Pushing common devotions was one answer. But the most immediate solution was to allow each group to form their own national parishes. This preserved the unity of the Church, but allowed local autonomy at the parish level. Each ethnic group could fashion its own spiritual and community life to fit its particular customs.

From Boston, to New York, to Philadelphia, to Pittsburgh, and across the Midwest, Irish Americans centered their community on the parish.[44] The Chicago Irish were no exception in their attachment to the parish. Irish clergy, who moved into leadership positions in the American Church, realized the important role the parish could play in the Irish community. Their chief concern was simply to provide the people with a pastor and a place to worship. As a familiar institution as well as a tie to Ireland, the parish formed a bridge between America and the Old Country and provided a supportive base for immigrants trying to cope with American life.[45]

The Catholic hierarchy in Chicago was dominated by the Irish, although they were politic enough to include representatives from other ethnic groups, particularly the Germans and Poles, in leadership positions. They worked to further enhance parish life. Bishops willingly assisted newly arrived immigrants in building churches and provided them with clergymen, regardless of their inability initially to meet these financial obligations. The first Catholic churches established in Chicago were Old St. Mary's in 1833 and Finley Peter Dunne's parish of St. Patrick's in 1846. Both were English-speaking parishes and served a large number of Irish.[46]

Initially parishes were organized geographically. The centrally located church served all who lived within its boundaries. Once national parishes were built to accommodate the non–English-speaking immigrants, the territorial base of the parish was modified. National parishes were formed within many territorial parishes. Although anyone could attend the territorial parish, each group remained loyal to its national church. Since they were the largest English-speaking Catholic group in Chicago, the Irish never formed national parishes, but once the territorial parishes lost their other ethnic constituents, territorial parishes became a type of Celtic national parish.[47]

These "national" parishes of the Irish helped to preserve the Irish community. The Irish were not forced to live solely with their own kind since they knew English. Irish settlements were scattered around the city, although they tended to be concentrated in South Side industrial areas. This lack of group cohesiveness could have led to the loss of an identifiable Irish community. The absence of other ethnic groups in territorial parishes allowed the Irish to create and maintain ethnic communities of their own around these churches. This inheritance of territorial parishes proved to be a treasure trove. By 1902 the Irish dominated 63 of Chicago's 132 Catholic parishes. These parishes formed the backbone of the Irish community.[48]

Parishes were not just religious centers for the Chicago Irish. Many Irish politicians used territorial parishes as an organizational base and network. In political terms territorial parishes had an advantage over national parishes. In ethnically diverse areas such as Bridgeport and Back of the Yards, Irish politicians, operating out of their geographically defined parishes, were able to unify antagonistic Central and Eastern Europeans from the national parishes within their boundaries. Many politicians came from the territorial parishes of St. Bridget's, Nativity of Our Lord, All Saints, and St. David's in Bridgeport. In Back of the Yards, Visitation parish served as powerbroker. Holy Family parish's boundaries coincidentally corresponded with those of the old nineteenth ward. The Irish took advantage of the fact that there were ten national parishes in their midst. Through divide and conquer tactics, the Irish were able to control the political life of the ward for many years despite the reformist efforts of settlement house workers such as Jane Addams and the gradual diminishment of the Irish population.[49]

Political careers were only a by-product of Irish parishes. Their primary purpose was to minister to the religious and social needs of the Irish. The clergy, rather than the politicians, were the community leaders here. It was the priests and the nuns who made the Catholic Church an intimate part of the ordinary lives of the Irish. One noteworthy example was Rev. Denis Dunne, who was vicar general of the diocese and rector at St. Patrick's Church from 1854 to 1868. Among his many ministerial works, Dunne helped form a chapter of the St. Vincent De Paul Society to aid destitute parishioners. St. Patrick's Society was so admired that many Irish parishes throughout the city adopted it. Dunne also took a great interest in the needs of the children. St. Patrick's supported a grammar school, and Dunne organized an industrial school for boys in Bridgeport. During the Civil War Dunne organized the 90th Illinois Regiment to prove the loyalty of Irish Catholics to their adoptive homeland. Dunne's work brought him the respect of both Catholics and Protestants in Chicago.[50]

Of all Irish parishes in nineteenth-century Chicago, Holy Family parish, established in 1857 by Arnold Damen, S.J., was the largest and most reknowned Irish parish. In 1881, twenty thousand Irish laborers, who worked in the lumber and railroad yards, and their families counted themselves members. Because it was a Jesuit parish, education was crucial to its mission. Under Damen's leadership Holy Family built an imposing Gothic church, three parochial schools, a convent academy, and St. Ignatius College, the nucleus of Loyola University. The Illinois Catholic Order of Foresters, a mutual aid fraternity, first began operations in this parish in 1883. It provided assistance to members in need and benefits to widows and orphans and eventually expanded to parishes throughout the city.[51] Holy Family parish has been described as "the single great Irish workingman's parish" because of all the services Father Damen and other priests and women religious performed.[52]

Holy Family Church was a model for devotionalism in Chicago and throughout the Midwest. Since they were Jesuits, Father Damen and several of his assistants became prominent mission preachers. Soon after he founded the parish, Damen wasted no time in starting devotional practices such as the Archconfraternity of the Immaculate Heart of Mary. The interior of the Gothic church was designed to encourage a devotional frame of mind in those who entered the structure. It had a fifty-two foot main altar decorated with angels surrounding the tabernacle that housed the divine presence of Jesus in the consecrated hosts. The church also had two side altars, one to give homage to the Virign Mary and the other to acknowledge the provider and protector of the Holy Family, St. Joseph. On the walls surrounding the congregation were the stations of the cross, which provided images of Jesus' path to his crucifixion. Other devotional symbols, such as votive candles, stained glass, and dim lights, "contributed to the creation of a distinctively Catholic interior."[53] The overall effect was to confirm for Catholics that Jesus dwelt within these walls and that the church was a sacred place. This interior style became fairly standard in Catholic churches.

St. Gabriel's Church, according to one of its parishioners, "became a haven and heaven for the Irish." It was established in 1880 at 45th and Lowe in Canaryville, which is just south of Bridgeport. Its pastor, Rev. Maurice J. Dorney, was called "the busiest priest in Chicago." His parishioners turned to him when they needed work, and businessmen looked to him to avert walkouts and strikes in the stockyards. His efforts won him the title "King of the Yards." Dorney was also known for his controversial sermons. Saloons were one of his obsessions. In 1888, he decided on a plan to restrict drinking establishments to nonresidential streets. Not all of his parishioners were fond of the idea and passed around a petition supporting the free establishment of saloons. On the next Sunday Dorney read the names and addresses of the sixty-four signatories. "He added caustic remarks to the names as he read them, 'bringing out some hard hits at the social status of some of those who had signed.' " Dorney's reasons for his position were based on his concept of the neighborhood being an extension of the parish. During the parish's "men's mission week" Dorney was successful at closing the local saloons during the evening. Faced with the united pressure of the St. Gabriel community, the liquor merchants caved in. Gambler Jim O'Leary, who had a tavern at 41st and Halsted, said, " 'We always do whatever Father Dorney wants us to do down here . . . I'll be glad to do it.' "54

St. Gabriel's is an excellent example of the intimacy created between neighborhood and parish. Like many other Irish Catholics, parishioners of St. Gabriel's simply referred to the church to describe where they lived. " 'For years the neighborhood and the parish were one,' " recalled a parishioner. " 'To refer to one was to refer to the other.' "55

Dorney was also a staunch believer in education and encouraged parents to send their children to school. Dorney himself earned a law degree when he was fifty. When he died, the flags over the International Amphitheater and most of the big plants in the stockyards flew at half mast. The stockyards suspended business for five minutes the day of his funeral.56

St. John's parish at 18th and Clark Streets was remembered as " 'a neighborhood of hard-working men and women.' " It buttressed Chicago's industrial belt and its poorest neighborhoods. Its heavily Irish population gave it the name "Kerry patch" after the county in Ireland. Father John Waldron, like many other Irish priests, used his superior willpower to protect and direct his parishioners. One of his most noted achievements was to keep the railroads of the Lake Shore & Michigan Southern and the Rock Island from infringing on his parish. Waldron also made every effort to keep his charges on the straight and narrow. His pride was the parish school. Waldron also took it upon himself to supervise their extracurricular hours. One parishioner recalled: " 'He always wore his cane, a heavy one, when out walking, and one of his stunts was to be about at night between nine and ten o'clock—that was a late hour then—and to walk into any crowds [of boys] he'd see on the corner and begin with his cane. That sent them all scooting for home.' "57

St. John's heyday as an Irish parish, however, did not last more than twenty years. Chicago's industries and poor pushed the increasingly prosperous Irish further south and west. The pride of its old-time parishioners was its legacy to other parishes. " 'There are many large parishes in this city in the territory immediately to the south, flourishing parishes . . . to practically all of these St. John's made large contributions of devout families and individuals.' "58

St. Bridget's parish was founded in 1850 with help from St. Patrick's and took on responsibility for the industrial school started by Father Dunne. The school cared for orphaned boys and those who needed correction. When a permanent church building was finally completed in 1862, Father Joseph M. Cartan, the pastor for over thirty years, let the Irish-controlled union from the stockyards use the old frame structure as a strike headquarters. St. Bridget's helped beget All Saints and Nativity of Our Lord parishes when Irish families moved beyond St. Bridget's.[59] Since Bridgeport had such a large Catholic population, failure to attend mass on Sundays risked one's reputation in the community.[60]

Visitation parish, established in 1886 at Garfield Boulevard and Peoria Street just south of the Union stockyards, enjoyed a distinctive reputation among the Irish. It was both a working-class parish, in which " 'some of the laborers never saw their children from Sunday to Sunday' " and a middle-class parish, in which some enjoyed a prestigious address on the stately boulevard. Visitation had the largest parish complex in the Archdiocese, with a grade school, a high school, and a social center. It also ranked among the largest parishes with nearly 15,000 members. In the 1920s Father Timothy O'Shea sought to provide opportunities for the physical and social needs of his parishioners. He transformed the basement of the grade school into a recreation center and the auditorium into a gymnasium.[61] These changes were so popular that "the community center has become the 'heart and hinge' of parish social life. As the Holy Eucharist is termed 'the social sacrament' so one may compare the community center to a shrine wherein the love of neighbor is sacramentalized (made holy) by a happy mingling of people after the example of the Blessed Christ."[62]

While most priests did not cut as high a profile as Fathers Damen, Dorney, Dunne, or Waldron, they were as concerned with both the material and spiritual welfare of their parishioners. They immersed themselves in the ubiquitous christenings, weddings, and funerals that provided joyous social occasions as well as religious observances for their flock.[63] Their parishes were places of faith, hope, and encouragement to the Irish who lived and worked in the slums and stinking neighborhoods of Chicago.[64]

In addition to being territorially defined, Irish parishes differed from national parishes in their purpose. National parishes separated themselves not only from mainstream America but also from other Catholics. They wanted to teach and preserve the languages and customs that they traditionally used to commune with God and each other. They were a complete world in themselves, with an array of social, ethnic, cultural, political, and recreational activities. Polish clergymen at one point speculated about beginning their own diocese.

They felt their large numbers and special cultural needs, which the Irish, German and Anglo-American hierarchy slighted, made it necessary for them to have their own bishops and institutional life.[65] The Irish, on the other hand, were quite content with the existing system. After all, they ran it. As was true for the Pittsburgh Irish, the Chicago Irish attachment to their parishes did not preclude some desire for acculturation. The community and family stability they derived from it, as well as the education they received, made economic mobility more possible. Because religion and nationality were so blurred for the Irish, preserving the faith preserved their sense of identity.[66]

Catholic religious instruction has been traditionally regarded as an integral part of parish life. Through the nineteenth century the Catholic hierarchy in the United States encouraged pastors to build Catholic schools. By 1884, the issue of parochial schools had become so important to the Catholic community that a formal declaration was made by the bishops at the Third Plenary Council in Baltimore requesting that each Catholic church support a parochial school. The parish school was so critical to the community that a " 'pastor without a parochial school was likened to a general without an army.' "[67] Chicago Catholics responded to this call by building the largest parochial school system in the world. By 1890, sixty-two of the eighty-one parishes in the diocese had schools. The parish school movement got its impetus from the conflict between public school supporters and Catholics over the Protestant orientation of the schools. Until 1875, all public school students were required to read from the King James Bible, and standard textbooks taught by Protestant teachers often made disparaging comments about the Catholic faith. Illinois lawmakers had also passed a bill in 1889 that required public elementary schools to teach in the English language, which did not sit well with ethnic groups.[68]

After the turn of the century the Irish began to move out of inner-city, industrial neighborhoods. Economic mobility, however, did not end their need or desire for parish-centered communities. New parishes continued the customs, traditions, and the shared experiences of the Irish and, in many ways, continued their "ghetto" experience. Leaving these old neighborhoods, though, presented a crisis among many Irish who feared a loss of their national identity. Archbishop James Quigley encouraged the work of the Ancient Order of Hibernians and the Irish History Society of South Chicago. He said, " ' . . . if the Irish-American is not to degenerate into a creature without distinction and individuality, he must know the history of his people.' " By 1909, Irish history was part of the curriculum of twenty-six territorial parishes. Quigley and his predecessor, Archbishop Patrick Feehan, had also set into motion a policy that would ensure that an Irish tone was set in these outlying territorial parishes by recruiting priests from Ireland and encouraging vocations in Irish parishes.[69]

Zeal for parish building was also carried into middle-class neighborhoods by the Irish in part due to nativist hostility. Nativist antipathy toward the Irish was provoked by the growth of Irish political power in the city and by the expansion of parochial schools and controversy over public funding for them. For the most part the Catholic hierarchy publicly ignored outbursts of anti-Catholicism; nonetheless, the Catholic community was profoundly affected by it for generations and it perpetuated a "ghetto" mentality.[70] A St. Gabriel parishioner wrote: "Our parish is God's and ours. We may differ among ourselves, we may quarrel among ourselves, we may even fight among ourselves. That's our affair. But let one outsider say a word against anyone of us, we show a united front."[71]

Irish-Catholic sensitivity was not just based on verbal assaults. Historian Ellen Skerrett has argued that "the majority of Irish-American parishes organized after 1890 were shaped more by Protestant-Catholic conflict than by ethnic rivalries."[72] American nativists at times took direct action to keep Catholics out of their middle-class communities. For example, in 1880, Holy Angels parish was established at 605 E. Oakwood for Irish residents who had moved to the area. Fear of anti-Catholic sentiment, however, forced the parish to purchase nearly all of its property through third parties.[73]

Instead of being cowed by nativist attacks, Catholics directly countered these charges with examples of their positive contributions to Chicago and America. Catholics even turned the construction of churches into demonstrations of Catholic power. Dedications became major causes for celebration in the Catholic community. People turned out by the thousands to watch the ceremonies and parades and hear speeches. Although these new Catholic churches and schools did not directly assuage all fears, some Protestants reluctantly admitted that they made the Catholic community more responsible and improved and stabilized neighborhoods.[74]

Like the Philadelphia Irish, Chicago Catholics began to respond to the question "Where are you from?" with the name of a parish instead of a street address. The intimacy between neighborhood and parish created a unique experience in urban living. William McCready has argued that the Irish parish "is one of the most creative ways to cope with an urban environment." He claims the Irish favor a personal means of conducting affairs, which they brought from the old country— whether it be politics or religion—and that they tend to be highly involved in local happenings. The parish satisfied this atavistic tendency. As many parish-bred men and women like to point out, living in a large city such as Chicago was not alienating or intimidating.

Big-city living, focused around parishes, was actually more of a small-town affair.[75]

By the twentieth century the Chicago Irish had created a well-organized community based on a parish system. Since their beginning days at the canal terminus in Bridgeport and the founding of St. Bridget's parish in 1848, the Irish had gradually expanded their network of parishes through the working-class neighborhoods of Bridgeport, Canaryville, and Back of the Yards, and into the middle-class neighborhoods of Englewood, Hyde Park, South Shore, and Beverly Hills. The desire for better housing, open spaces, and a respectable position in the larger community were the primary motives for the Irish southward migration. The parish provided stability for the Irish, but it was always a very fluid place. As people moved from one parish to another, they could remain within a familiar structure. The system of territorial parishes, therefore, did not inhibit geographic mobility for the Irish as national parishes did for other ethnic groups.

In the 1890s, even Martin J. Dooley, Finley Peter Dunne's creation, began commenting on the movement of the Irish population in Bridgeport. By this time many children of Famine immigrants, those "born away from home" according to Mr. Dooley, were in a position to move beyond their working-class roots into better neighborhoods. At the same time, more recent immigrants from other parts of Europe began to move into Bridgeport. Mr. Dooley lamented, " 'There was a time when Archey Road was purely Irish. But the Huns, turned back from the Adriatic and the stockyards and overrunning Archey Road, have nearly exhausted the original population—not driven them out as they drove out less vigorous races, with thick clubs and short spears, but edged them out with the biting weapons of modern civilization—overworked and under-eaten them into more languid surroundings remote from the tanks of the gashouse and the blast furnace of the rolling mill.' "[76]

The surest sign of " 'Change an' decay' " for Mr. Dooley was the appointment of a " 'Polacker on th' r-red bridge.' " Bridge-tending was a patronage job traditionally held by an Irishman, and this particular bridge was gateway to the South Side, where the Irish staked out their turf.[77]

Besides being pushed from their old neighborhoods by ethnic succession, the Irish, Mr. Dooley also noted, were hounded by a strong need for the approval of mainstream American society.[78] Many of his characters, particularly the young, were anxious to acquire middle-class values and mores. Educated children became ashamed of their working-class parents. Mr. Dooley noted that they ridiculed the "Come All Yous" ballads of Irish taverns and suggested that they acquire a taste for the piano pieces of "Choochooski."[79]

James T. Farrell was particularly sensitive to this theme. His Washington Park novels of Studs Lonigan and Danny O'Neill tell the story of the Irish pursuit of the middle-class dream. This quest demanded a migratory lifestyle of frequent moves from one apartment to another to reflect the family's improved economic status. The parish, though, remained central in the lives of Farrell's fictional characters. Their Irish identity, Farrell felt, was sacrificed in the process.[80]

For the Chicago Irish the flight from old neighborhoods was also prompted by the influx of blacks to the South Side after World War I. War jobs attracted thousands of Southern blacks anxious to leave behind Jim Crow laws and a depressed agricultural economy. Many traveled to the Land of Lincoln on the Illinois Central railroad, whose depot deposited them on the South Side. White flight and racial hatred haunted Farrell's novels. Both his principal fictional families, the O'Neills and the Flahertys, kept moving southward to stay ahead of the creeping black belt.[81]

It was from this historical setting that St. Sabina's emerged as a vital Irish-American parish in the twentieth century. The parish community of St. Sabina's was at once the product of Irish America's search for community, identity, and respectability. It was also the outgrowth of the city of Chicago's rapidly expanding South Side, whose industries demanded the labor of a culturally and racially diverse population. The parish represented both continuity and change. The Irish who founded St. Sabina's sought a middle-class lifestyle, but within the context of the parish communities in which they grew up. The cultural and racial diversity of the South Side was a reality of the world of work, whereas the solidarity and security of the parish community was a reality of the neighborhood. The Irish of St. Sabina's, like thousands of Catholics in other communities across urban America, sought to be part of the larger city while remaining within the security of a smaller, more homogeneous community. The story of St. Sabina's struggle to reconcile the tension between the demands of faith, community, and polity is one episode in a poignant and painful chapter in Irish-American history. It is at once the story of a unique community and an all too familiar incident in urban development. It is the story of one parish, and the lesson of many.

2

St. Sabina: A Parish
Founded on a Prairie

St. Sabina's began " 'on a prairie, with a few families and lots of mud,' " recalled the founding pastor, Rev. Thomas Egan.[1] On July 3, 1916, Egan, then assistant at St. Mary's in Evanston, received orders from Chicago's new Archbishop, George W. Mundelein, to establish the parish in the southwest community of Auburn-Gresham.[2] Like many parishes established in America, St. Sabina's had a humble beginning. Egan said his first mass on July 9th in a storefront at 7915 S. Ashland Avenue "on a borrowed table in a rented room" for two hundred parishioners.[3] The altar made its way by horse and wagon along unpaved roads from St. Leo's Church just to the east at 78th and Emerald Avenue. Old-time residents recalled losing their rubbers in the mud going to the first services.[4] With such a modest beginning, few would have predicted that St. Sabina's would become one of the largest parishes in Chicago and a "beehive of activity" on the Southwest Side.

The low, flat, swampy land of Auburn-Gresham was located in the southeast section of the Town of Lake, which was incorporated into Chicago in 1889. Its first settlers were German and Dutch truck farmers. When the Chicago, Western Indiana, and Pacific lines, along with the Rock Island, were laid in the mid-nineteenth century, Irish railroad workers came to the area.[5] By 1885 the Catholic population had grown enough to warrant the establishment of St. Leo the Great parish. The Columbian Exposition in 1893 encouraged further development of the South Side through the extension and improvement of city services to the area. In 1890 the horsecar line along Vincennes Avenue was extended to 79th Street and then along 79th to Halsted Street. This improvement in transportation truly began the development of eastern Auburn-Gresham.[6] The population grew, and between 1913 and 1918, the city extended the streetcar lines on Halsted to 119th Street and the cars on Racine and Ashland Avenues to 87th Street. The 79th Street car ran from Lake Michigan to Western Avenue. With the city more accessible, the western section of Auburn-Gresham became more appealing to prospective homesteaders. Catholics who settled on this western fringe were forced to travel long distances to attend Sunday mass at St. Leo's. It became clear to the Archdiocese that more parishes were needed to serve the expanding population.[7]

When Mundelein assumed command of the Chicago Archdiocese in 1916, he devised a plan to put an end to the haphazard and poorly managed process of parish establishment and church construction. To improve financial accountability and responsibility as well as to increase his control over the Archdiocese, Mundelein put all decisions for building construction in the chancery office. This office then worked with a Board of Consultors, composed of prominent pastors. Sensitive to the ethnic issues involved in parish formation, Mundelein gave the board a "balanced ticket." Of the five to six consultors, three were "unofficial" ethnic seats. They were generally given to Polish, German, and Bohemian delegates, with the latter representing the other Eastern European groups. These consultors tried to plan in a more rational manner where and when new parishes would be established to avoid the premature commitment of funds before there was adequate support for a new building venture. They consulted the records of city utilities to identify growing areas in need of a church.[8]

While St. Sabina's was formed only five months after Mundelein's arrival in Chicago, it seems to have been established according to this type of procedure rather than as a result of a formal petition of Catholics in the area. All obvious indicators for population growth, such as the expansion of city services and real estate development, were evident. The distances an increasing number of St. Leo's parishioners had to travel to attend services also confirmed the need for new parishes in the area. At the same time he organized St. Sabina's, Mundelein also called for the establishment of St. Justin Martyr at 71st and Honore Street and St. Dorothy's at 78th and Vernon Avenue.[9]

Mundelein's new method put to an end for good the trustee system that thrived in the nineteenth century. This system had thwarted clerical authority on parish ownership, government, and the hiring and firing of pastors. In Europe, parish government was firmly placed in the hands of the clergy. In the United States, however, the democratic spirit of the young republic proved hard to resist. The Church adopted the trustee system, which meant that the laity controlled the parish government and selection of pastors. Church leaders had even advocated the use of English instead of Latin in Catholic services in the late eighteenth century. Clearly the early Catholic American church was ahead of its counterpart in Europe in experimenting with a democratically structured church.[10]

When the Irish came to America, the trustee system was widely accepted throughout the country. While certainly willing to participate in this freer arrangement, the Irish were more used to deferring to the clergy on church affairs. Their involvement in parish organization was usually limited to petitioning bishops for priests, unlike the Germans, who bought land, built churches, and recruited priests themselves. Since the English-speaking Irish participated in politics, labor organizations, and other associations that were beyond the control of the church hierarchy, it was less of an issue for them to acquiesce to the clergy on parish issues than it was for other ethnic groups, who were more confined to their parishes.[11]

As the Church became more institutionalized with the arrival of more immigrants and as more clergy became available, clerical control over parish government increased. Priests began initiating and organizing parishes. "Brick and mortar" pastors became the most highly regarded priests because they built parish complexes of church, rectory, school, and convent. By the end of the nineteenth and into the twentieth century pastors were also staying on longer in their parishes, which added to their prestige and authority. The pastors' increased authority eclipsed lay dominance.[12]

Opposition by bishops and priests, however, dealt trusteeism its final blow. Conflict over church property ownership and the appointing and dismissing of clergy were constant sources of tension between the hierarchy and the people. Here is where Irish dominance in the hierarchy shaped the American Church. By the turn of the century English-speaking parishes were more firmly under the direction of the clergy, and deference by the laity was the norm. National parishes stayed with lay initiative and control a bit longer.[13]

In Chicago, Archbishop James Quigley, who presided over the Archdiocese from 1903 to 1915, tried to make parish formation more orderly. With large numbers of immigrants pouring into the city and older ethnic groups moving to the city's periphery, Quigley set a goal to have a parish for every square mile. He did not, however, hinder the formation of national parishes.[14] Mundelein clearly was taking the Church into a new era of organization, of which St. Sabina's was a part.

Through the efforts of real estate developers and because of its accessibility to transportation, Auburn-Gresham became an attractive area for families looking to escape older and more crowded sections of the city.[15] St. Sabina's early parishioners were generally the offspring of the Irish who had settled in working-class neighborhoods in Bridgeport, Canaryville, and Back of the Yards. As Table 1 indicates, many were baptized in the Irish parishes of St. Gabriel's, Nativity of Our Lord, All Saints, St. Bridget's, St. David's, and St. Rose of Lima. These parishes were founded in the nineteenth century, usually through the initiative of the laity. Visitation parish also gave many of its progeny to St. Sabina. Positioned on Garfield Boulevard and Peoria, the parish straddled working-class Back of the Yards and middle-class Englewood and reflected within its borders the economic mobility of the Irish.

Table 1. Top Twenty-five Churches of Baptism of Persons Married at
St. Sabina's, 1916-1941.

Parish	Nationality	Date Est.	No. Baptized	%
Visitation	Irish	1886	140	0
St. Gabriel	Irish	1880	121	8
Nativity of Our Lord	Irish	1868	85	6
Ireland	- - -	- - -	85	6
St. Brendan	Irish	1904	79	5
St. Leo	Irish	1885	65	4
St. Cecilia	Irish	1885	65	4
All Saints	Irish	1875	51	3
St. Anne	Irish	1865	40	3
St. Rose of Lima	Irish	1881	35	2
St. Basil	Irish-German	1904	34	2
St. Bridget	Irish	1850	33	2
St. Augustine	German	1879	28	2
St. Anthony of Padua	German	1873	25	2
St. George	German	1892	24	2
St. Martin	German	1886	24	2
St. John the Baptist	French	1892	24	2
St. David	Irish	1905	21	1
St. Bernard	Irish	1887	18	1
Sacred Heart	German	1894	17	1
St. Elizabeth	Irish	1881	14	1
St. Patrick	Irish	1846	12	1
St. John	Irish	1859	12	1
Holy Angels	Irish	1880	12	1
St. Agnes	Irish	1878	10	1
TOTAL			1,074	73
TOTAL MARRIAGES			1,464	

Sources: St. Sabina Marriage Records. For the history and nationality of these parishes
see Rev. Msgr. Harry Koenig, S.T.D., ed., *The History of the Parishes of the Archdiocese*
(Chicago: New World, 1980).

Note: Since Roman Catholics practice infant baptism, those baptized in these parishes
would have been recently born, establishing them as American-born Irish.

Some Sabina parishioners came from churches more solidly within
Englewood, such as St. Bernard's and St. Brendan's. Some of St.
Brendan's parishioners automatically became members of St. Sabi-
na's when its southern section was portioned off to form the new
parish. St. Leo's also relinquished part of its western territory to St.
Sabina's.[16]

Economic factors helped the Chicago Irish perpetuate and maintain their own community and ethnic identity. Ethnic groups seldom

retain the exact characteristics they had when they arrived in America. The development and persistence of ethnicity depends to a great extent upon the economic and structural conditions of the city in which they live and on their relationship to other groups. Rather than maintaining constant character traits or forsaking them altogether, immigrant groups can change and evolve ethnic identities that differ from those they arrived with but are not those of the host society.[17]

St. Sabina's was able to reformulate an Irish character through several favorable circumstances. Transportation improvements on the South Side in the beginning of the century opened up convenient, new housing developments. The ability of large numbers of Irish to move to this new neighborhood in the 1920s enabled them to become the dominant group in the parish. In addition to their religious experience, they also shared similar and related occupations. This provided them with common ground, which promoted group solidarity.

Many Irish police officers, firemen, and other city workers were attracted to the area by the accessibility to the streetcars and trains they needed to get to their jobs.[18] Many Irish had also moved into the teaching profession. In 1920 Mundelein claimed that 70 percent of teachers in the public schools were Catholic, the majority of them Irish.[19] Many South Side Irish also worked in industrial jobs, particularly in the Central Manufacturing District, one of America's earliest industrial parks, and the Union Stockyards, which was the largest employer in the city in 1919.[20] By the time St. Sabina's was formed many Irish had relinquished their difficult manual jobs, which required few skills, to newer immigrants and had taken jobs in the offices of the meatpacking companies or had secured more skilled positions. On August 5, 1922, the *Chicago Daily News* observed that "hundreds of people employed in the stockyards have bought homes in the Auburn Park district within the last three years. The great bulk of traffic of the region is along Halsted Street to the yards."[21] Tables 2 and 3 show the industries Auburn-Gresham residents were employed in and the occupations of residents within St. Sabina's boundaries.

T. O'Rourke's family moved to the area in 1915 because of his father's job. St. Sabina's was only a mile away from the streetcar barn on 69th and Ashland where his father worked as a driver. O'Rourke recalled that a large number of people in the parish worked in the offices of the stockyards in junior management and that many were railroad people who worked out of nearby roundhouses.[22]

Yet while St. Sabina's represented a step up the economic ladder for many new residents, it was a step made possible only by sacrifice by the entire family.[23] "I think that everybody . . . moved there with a sacrifice," noted J. Kill. "They didn't have a lot. It [the parish] was made up of . . . small people—streetcarmen, policemen, firemen, city work-

Table 2. Occupational Profile of Gainful Workers from Ten Years of Age in Auburn-Gresham, 1930

Industry Group	Male	Female
Construction		
Building industry	2,236	70
Independent hand trades	39	74
Other trade industries	458	98
Mineral Extraction		
Clay, glass, and stone industries	121	16
Chemical and allied industries	306	104
Light Manufacturing		
Textile industries	19	25
Electrical machinery and supply	269	64
Lumber and furniture industry	143	26
Shoe factory	11	2
Heavy Manufacturing		
Auto factories	164	27
Blast furnace and steel mills	258	45
Rubber factory	24	7
Other iron and steel industries	107	27
Other manufacturing industries	637	169
Professional		
Banking and brokerage	609	300
Insurance and real estate	559	261
Other professional and semiprofessional	676	871
Printing		
Printing, publishing, engraving	518	160
Public Service		
Postal service	210	12
Construction and street maintenance	90	1
Meat Industry		
Slaughter and packinghouses	909	203
Other food and allied industries	173	53
Service		
Laundries, cleaning and pressing shops	178	48
Domestic and personal services	334	410
Recreation and amusement	133	77
Garages, greasing stations	122	5
Auto repair shops	172	7
Transportation		
Steam railroads	1,490	238
Street railroads	710	25
Other transportation and communication	344	30

cont'd

Table 2, continued

Industry Group	Male	Female
Utilities		
Telegraph and telephone	325	605
Wholesale-Retail		
Bakeries	164	17
Clothing industries	111	86
Other	3,026	1,015
TOTAL	18,562	5,669

Source: Carrie Mae Barlow, "Auburn-Gresham: A Survey of a Local Community" (Ph.D. diss., University of Chicago, 1934), 45.

ers, who in those days didn't get much in the way of pay—people with big families."[24]

Although many parishioners were primarily employed in technically blue collar occupations and the lower rungs of the middle class, they generally considered themselves middle class. The newness of the area, good homes, and being removed from industrial neighborhoods no doubt contributed to their optimism. For many, Auburn-Gresham was worlds away from their grim industrial origins. In August 1922 the *Chicago Daily News* described Auburn-Gresham as an ideal picture of rural beauty and calm.[25] J. Kill recalled, "St. Sabina's was really out in the sticks. . . . Moving there was like going to the country."[26] "It was a new developing area," M. Dunne recalled. "[My parents] were looking for a less crowded area. They had lived in a four-room apartment on 58th and Peoria and it was too small for two children and parents."[27]

H. O'Connor's family was attracted to the neighborhood because "it was a brand new neighborhood. . . . At that time it was very attractive. . . . From our back porch you could see the hill at 87th. There was nothing in-between."[28] For many, an important feature in the new housing development was indoor plumbing. E. Clair said, "I doubt if there was more than one or two places [in the old neighborhood] that had the facilities indoors, and that's what young people at that time were trying to get away from."[29]

"You could play ball any place," T. O'Rourke recalled of his childhood experience in St. Sabina's founding years. "There were all kinds of prairies. West of Ashland, there were all these open fields . . . with beautiful flowers. People would go walking out there. . . . I had a collie. I'd take him out there to exercise him. They used to have bonfires in the prairies and you would roast potatoes and marshmallows."[30]

To most people the word "prairie" conjures up the image of the endless, treeless sea of grass that greeted the first settlers of the Midwest. However, "prairie" has been passed on into the urban lexicon

Table 3. Occupations of St. Sabina Parishioners and Persons with
Irish Surnames within the Parish Boundaries, 1916-1927

Occupation	Male	%
High white collar	16	9
Low white collar	51	27
Blue Collar Skilled	43	23
Blue Collar Semiskilled	64	34
Unskilled	16	8
TOTAL	190	

Sources: Names derived from St. Sabina Marriage Records and Chicago City Directories;
occupational categories based on those devised by Stephen Thernstrom in *The Other
Bostonians: Poverty and Progress in the American Metropolis, 1880-1970* (Cambridge:
Harvard Univ. Press, 1973), Appendix B: On the Socio-Economic Ranking of Occupations.

of Chicago as any open, grass field, even just an undeveloped, grass-
covered city lot. Its continued use by St. Sabina parishioners suggests
an affinity with the pioneering spirit of settling a new area.

Between 1920 and 1930 the population of Auburn-Gresham nearly
tripled, from 19,558 to 57,381.[31] St. Sabina's membership grew just as
rapidly. By 1930 it had 1,600 families and 6,900 "souls," and by 1936
it reached 2,100 families and 7,500 "souls."[32] Throughout the decade
the prairies gave up their grass and flowers to support brick bungalows
and two- and three-flats. These building styles were well-suited to
Irish-American needs and values.

The bungalow was typically a one-story urban house with perhaps
some small bedrooms in an attic-like second floor. It was designed to
appeal to an aspiring middle class that needed an inexpensive, efficient
single-family home. Its popularity in Chicago coincided with the Catholic migration out of the inner-city industrial neighborhoods. Many
designers of these homes were influenced by the 'simple-life' philosophy of the Arts and Crafts architectural school and, to a degree, by the
Prairie School of architecture, which strove to create an environment
conducive to a happy, harmonious family life. The bungalow's kitchen
was equipped with the latest in modern conveniences, and was advertised to appeal to the modern housewife who wanted a clean and
efficient workplace that the new domestic science associated with the
"good life."[33]

Flat apartments, which generally occupied one whole floor in a
building, were also designed with the same aim as the bungalow—to
nurture middle-class domestic life.[34] T. O'Rourke confirmed the appeal
of flat buildings for many people. He said, "Many of my friends were

tenants all the time. . . . [They] didn't want the responsibility of taking care of a yard and firing up the furnace. Other Irish did that so they could better themselves." Flats were particularly attractive to fire fighters, police officers, and streetcar drivers. Their odd shifts allowed them to be home during the day to fire up the furnace and take care of the yard. Joking about the willingness of the Irish to live as tenants, T. O'Rourke observed, "The Slavic people wanted their own homes, but for the Irish, it was more important to get the cemetery lot."[35]

The varied choice of housing in Auburn-Gresham—single-family bungalows, flat buildings, and some apartment complexes—gave the Irish residents the choice between owning a home, owning rental property, or simply renting. The housing stock reflected the varied values and economic well-being of an emerging lower–middle class.

During the prosperous years of the 1920s construction boomed in the Sabina's area. The neighborhood began to lose its rural feel as more and more "prairie" lots were given over to construction. Children regretted the loss of these play lots and the streets began to take on a more congested appearance. Of course the new construction provided new recreational activities. "We had one great big place to play with all this construction," one boy recalled. "We played in the buildings. . . . They mixed all the concrete and plaster right on the job so we had sand hills to play king of the hill and roll in and dig in."[36]

The Irish predominated in St. Sabina's. Through a combination of economics, geography, transportation, and timing, St. Sabina parishioners were provided with a solid base to reestablish a strong ethnic character. Auburn-Gresham had an Irish stock population of 21 percent, most situated in St. Leo's and St. Sabina's.[37] Based on the figures in Table 1, the parish was comprised of 60 percent American-born Irish. Although St. Sabina's was primarily composed of American-born Irish, Irish immigrants added a colorful dimension to the neighborhood. "They used to say that you could stand on 79th Street when the women were out shopping and hear the brogue of every county in Ireland," T. O'Rourke related. His thoughts on why the area was Irish were: "There was no place else to move and the Irish were moving. I think that's it. See, the Irish have always been moving. They're always going out, out, out. And I think that was the place to go. . . . They thought they were doing very well to come out there. I think it was *the* place to move."[38]

St. Sabina's did have other ethnic groups in it. After 1916, Mundelein limited the establishment of new national parishes. He believed that perpetuating national enclaves worked against the best interests of ethnic groups. Although he, himself, had grown up in a German national parish on the Lower East Side of New York, Mundelein was convinced that Americanization should be the ultimate goal of Catholic immigrants.[39] It must be remembered that he headed the Archdiocese

during World War I and through the 1920s when there was considerable pressure to be 100 percent American. Early German-American
support for the Central Powers and Irish-American insistence on an
independent Ireland at the Paris Peace Conference were convincing
reasons to fear the divisiveness of hyphenated, Catholic Americans.
Fear of foreigners still plagued American society in the 1920s.
Immigration restriction laws reduced considerably the influx of
southern and eastern Europeans, who seemed too foreign and unmeltable.

After 1916, when ethnic groups began moving beyond old immi-
grant communities, they were forced either to travel long distances
back to their national churches or to sign-up in the territorial parishes.
Like many other new territorial parishes, St. Sabina's had its share of
Germans. Most were American born. By the twentieth century many
Germans were moving up the economic ladder just slightly ahead of
the Irish.[40] Their ethnic stronghold, however, was on the North and
Northwest sides and, therefore, they did not overwhelm South Side
Irish communities.[41] The South Side Germans who settled in St.
Sabina's came from the same neighborhoods as the Irish, but from the
national parishes of St. Augustine's, St. George's, St. Martin's, Sacred
Heart, and St. Anthony of Padua (Table 1). At a distant third were
parishioners of French descent from St. John the Baptist, and behind
them were a scattering of other nationalities, such as Italians, Poles,
and Bohemians.[42] An old-time parishioner commented, "There were
always French there and a few Italians. . . . I know of one Polish
family." But by and large the Sabina's community was conspicuous by
the absence of eastern and southern European immigrants.[43]

The presence of these other nationalities, however, did not stop the
Irish from forming this parish in their own image and extending Irish
domination of the territorial parish. "They often said that the parish
assumed the nationality of the pastor," T. O'Rourke recalled.[44] The first
three pastors of St. Sabina's, whose services spanned the years from
1916 to 1971, and many of the assistant pastors, were Irish or of Irish
descent. St. Sabina's identity as an Irish parish no doubt profited from
the clerical leadership of sons from the Emerald Isle. They, however,
were aided by their "take charge" Irish flock. T. O'Rourke said with a
twinkle in his blue Irish eyes, that the Irish acted like "they kind of
owned the place . . . and other people seemed to fall in line."[45] Another
former parishioner, J. Hagerty, also confirmed this Irish proclivity for
"taking over." She said, "They have a certain quality, a kind of spiritual
imperialism within themselves. They can't be undercut . . . and they'll
find a way somehow to dominate in any situation."[46]

Since they had virtually controlled the English-speaking parishes
in ethnic neighborhoods, it perhaps only seemed natural that their way

was the norm and all others were to follow. Their larger numbers in the parish no doubt also added to their advantage. However, when in the minority, the Irish had no qualms about setting up their own organizations in national parishes. Our Lady of Sorrows, which was an Italian parish, hosted a chapter of the Ancient Order of Hibernians, a Ladies' Auxiliary of the Knights of Father Mathew—an Irish temperance group, and the Daughters of Isabella, which was the women's branch of the Knights of Columbus. St. John the Baptist, a French parish, supported a branch of the American Association for the Recognition of the Irish Republic. Based on a random sampling of parishes from 1895 to 1925, there were never any other ethnic groups who had infiltrated territorial parishes with their own organizations.[47] Even the Illinois Catholic Order of Foresters, which originated in Holy Family parish in 1883, became the chief beneficiary society in the Archdiocese.[48] The St. Vincent De Paul Society, a lay charitable group that was founded in France and came to the United States through St. Louis in 1845, became the chief philanthropic organization in the Archdiocese. It began in Chicago in St. Patrick's parish and was also an Irish-dominated society.[49] In the Church hierarchy and in the neighborhood parishes the Irish exerted their influence and pressured others to conform to their style of Catholicism and parish life.

Italian Americans generally were reluctant to establish their own national parishes, but they were not necessarily anxious to join the parishes of other nationalities. Nor did they send their children to parochial schools in large numbers.[50] J. Hagerty provided an example of the Irish spirit dominating an Italian family in St. Sabina's. Her father, she said, was a devoted churchgoer who frequented the missions. "He was always gathering other characters in the neighborhood to go with him." One day he decided to persuade an Italian man to join him. While the Italians were willingly baptized, married, and buried in the Church, she related, they were not so consistent with everyday devotions. Her father, however, was eventually able to get them to become "pretty good church members." Her mother, she recalled, "had a fit" when she learned the children of the Italian family were going to the public school. She went to work on them and eventually persuaded the mother of the evils of godless education. The girls went to St. Sabina grade school and then on to Mercy High School.[51] T. O'Rourke thought that because of the more relaxed attitude of the Italians toward the church and their reluctance to establish their own cemeteries, orphanages, and churches, they were content to "move in on the Irish . . . and use the Irish cemeteries . . . and were satisfied to go along."[52]

J. Hagerty said of other ethnic groups, "They just went along because there wasn't any thought of changing the way the Irish were doing things. They were in charge."[53] B. DesChatelets, who was of French descent, agreed that "I always say that I'm Irish by association if nothing else."[54]

There is very little evidence to suggest that the German Americans made much effort to impose a German character on the parish. One historian has called the Irish and Germans "the two great protagonists of early Catholic Chicago." With each generation, however, they found themselves more and more drawn to each other, cooperating in several political causes. In the 1870s the Irish and Germans joined forces against the Sunday Closing Laws, and in 1889 they came together again to oppose the Edwards Law, which threatened parochial schools. In 1904 they had formed a musical and literary society that met on St. Patrick's Day. As German nationalism began to wane in the beginning of the twentieth century, the Germans and the Irish found more common ground.[55]

When war broke out in 1914, German nationalism once again emerged to support Germany and the Central Powers. Historian Melvin G. Holli argues that no ethnic group was so quickly stripped of their ethnicity as were German Americans during the war years.[56] German immigrants had been very highly regarded in the nineteenth century because of their many economic and cultural contributions to this country. Yet, by the end of World War I, they became America's most hated group. Once the United States had become committed to the Allied cause in 1917, German Americans were caught in a bind. Their boasts of the superiority of German Kultur, which included authoritarianism and militarism, were an affront to the democratic cause of the United States; they were torn, too by the prospect of fighting their fatherland. Because of their perceived disloyalty to their host country, German Americans were subjected to a zealous Americanization campaign. At the vanguard of this movement were the Slavic nationalities. They deeply resented the Germans, who historically thought themselves racially superior to the neighboring Slavs.[57] By the war's end German-American ethnic, linguistic, and cultural institutions were irreparably damaged. Many German national parishes had forsaken the teaching of their language in their schools and began using English for their services. By 1920 many German Americans stopped claiming German as their nationality. What few remnants of Germanness remained were swept away at the onset of World War II.[58]

Through these trying years, German Americans found the Irish and their parishes more accommodating to them than Slavic-American neighborhoods. The Irish had no special affection for John Bull either and voiced support for the Central Powers. In August 1914 there was some talk between the two groups of forming an American Gaelic-

Germanic alliance, and they held German-Irish picnics at which England was routinely denounced.[59]

Irish Americans, however, had a different agenda than German Americans when war broke out. In 1914, when the British refused to enact a law passed by Parliament that would grant Home Rule and a degree of independence for Ireland, many Irish felt betrayed by English duplicity in its dealings with the Irish. Irish Americans thought Britain's war aims of protecting the sovereignty of small nations and saving democracy from German autocracy a farce. To them the conflict was nothing more than a contest between militaristic empires. A German victory, though, might release Ireland from John Bull's clutches. Initially, many Irish and Irish Americans supported the Central Powers. However, when the United States entered the war on the side of the Allied countries in 1917, few Irish Americans had personal conflicts with fighting Germany and most were anxious to prove their loyalty to their adopted land. They put aside their Irish nationalism to support the red, white, and blue and marched to the tunes of George M. Cohan.[60] The Irish embrace of American patriotism, however, did not extend to repudiating their ties with German Americans. The Germans, though, became "silent partners" in their marriage with the Irish and their parishes.

The relationship of the Irish with other ethnic groups was an important factor in ensuring St. Sabina's Irish identity. Other ethnic groups, which had come to Chicago later than the Irish, were not in a position to take up residence in large numbers in a middle-class neighborhood such as Auburn-Gresham when St. Sabina's was established. German Americans were the only ethnic group that could have challenged Irish hegemony in the parish. However, German-American nationalism was at an all-time low point when they settled in St. Sabina's. Irish Americans, then, were free to set the standard for the parish.

While the war eradicated German-American nationalism, Irish Americans, on the other hand, had no qualms about reasserting their Irishness after the war. After the Armistice on November 11, 1918 Irish-American nationalist activities were re-ignited. They were more committed to the revolutionary movement than to the discredited constitutional method of achieving independence for Ireland. Many Irish in St. Sabina's were not immune to the excitement in Ireland over the Anglo-Irish War. When, in the December 1918 British general election, Sinn Fein triumphed over the Irish Parliamentary party and, instead of taking their seats at Westminster, proclaimed an independent Irish Parliament in Dublin, the Chicago Irish responded by holding mass meetings and collecting funds for Sinn Fein. Edward F. Dunne, former governor of Illinois and mayor of Chicago, participated in the American Commission on Irish Independence that went to Paris to plead the Irish cause before the peace conference. Although unsuccessful in Paris, Dunne helped launch a bond-certificate campaign for the new Irish state. After two years of bitter fighting, the Anglo-Irish Treaty, signed in December 1921, granted the twenty-six southern counties dominion status. With the Free State secured, the flurry of nationalist activities in Chicago, as elsewhere, abated, although some Chicago Irish would continue support for the anti-treaty Irish force that wanted an independent republic rather than dominion status.[61]

The St. Sabina Irish were equally strong advocates of Irish independence. In January 1920 the pastor, Father Egan, appeared as a guest speaker for the Friends of Irish Freedom at St. Anne's Church hall. He, himself, had recently traveled through Ireland "where he made a thorough study of existing conditions" and tried to clarify misleading and inaccurate accounts of the Anglo-Irish War.[62] Following this speaking engagement, St. Sabina's formed its own branch of the Friends of Irish Freedom and appointed a committee to assist the Irish bond drive.[63] By February 13, 1920 they were holding what was described as "an enthusiastic meeting of the St. Sabina branch of the Friends of Irish Freedom in Auburn Park Hall." Irish music, oratory, and dancing were featured along with solicitation of subscriptions for the Irish loan.[64]

The St. Sabina branch also sponsored a slide lecture on the "Rebellion in Ireland" given by Rev. Hugh P. Smyth of Evanston on March 16. The Rev. Smyth had also visited Ireland for ten weeks and brought back a series of pictures of the subject.[65] It was advertised in *The New World* as an " 'Exclusive Showing': A most vivid and moving picture of the most discussed subject in the world."[66] The Rev. Smith's talk was "to settle conclusively the exact nature of the means being used for and against the advancement of the Irish cause."[67]

T. O'Rourke, whose parents were from the Old Country, recalled that during those years his "mother couldn't wait to get the *Tribune* in the morning. . . . She'd read it and then call somebody else who got the old *Examiner* and see what they were saying about it [the Irish cause]. If the old *Examiner* was more favorable to the Irish, she'd think that maybe we should change papers." He also remembered the bond sales. His mother and father would purchase them at the nearby undertaking establishment. Many of the Dominican Sisters in the parish school were also pro-Irish according to O'Rourke. When Mary MacSwiney, the sister of Terence MacSwiney the Irish hunger-striker, came to Chicago for a speaking engagement, many of the nuns went to see her. O'Rourke recalled that on the next day his teacher wore a badge urging the support of MacSwiney.[68]

Irish history had been a part of the curriculum in the early years of St. Sabina school.[69] Irish history courses had been nonexistent in the English-speaking, territorial parishes that the Irish dominated in the nineteenth century. By 1904 the Ancient Order of Hibernians lobbied to have them introduced in Irish schools. These courses, though, tended to emphasize Catholic aspects of Irish history, particularly the early medieval Celtic Renaissance, rather than modern Irish history. These courses did little to develop a sense of historical continuity for the diasporic Irish, particularly for those beyond the first generation. American-born Irish might have been able to build a stronger sense of identity if they had had a better understanding of the forces that brought them to the United States and Chicago than they had of their misty Celtic past.[70] By the mid-1920s St. Sabina's dropped Irish history from its curriculum. However, its early offering of Irish history indicates a quest for some sort of Irish identity.

Religion and a Catholic identity, however, were the more important components to the identity of St. Sabina parishioners. They were keenly aware of the strength and support they derived from the parish. Although they talked of their Irish nationality, it was the parish that would forge a more vital identity for Irish Americans and would create a new ethnicity.

3

"I'm from Sabina's," 1916 to 1941

" 'Chicago has the best Catholics,' " Rev. Cornelius Hagerty, a Holy Cross priest from the University of Notre Dame, used to quip on his visits to his family in St. Sabina parish. " 'They'll even wave to you from the back of a paddy wagon.' "[1] On another occasion he remarked to Father Egan, " 'I have heard that in country districts in Ireland a priest can hear confession all afternoon and never encounter a mortal sin.' " The native of County Tipperary defended his parishioners saying, " 'A priest can hear confession right in Sabina's Church in the midst of all the wickedness of Chicago, and find many people who live innocent, holy lives without coming close to mortal sin.' "[2] Relaxed and secure in post–World War I America, Catholics could now begin to laugh at themselves. Yet the Catholic community of the local parish remained a central and sheltering feature in their lives.

From its inception St. Sabina's reflected the coming of age of the Catholic Church in America and the Irish in Chicago. By the 1920s the Catholic population in the United States had grown to an estimated twenty million. With restrictions placed on immigration during this decade, the Catholic Church in America was able to move beyond its immigrant identity and mission. Its energies could now be directed toward the reorganization and consolidation of its internal affairs and it could begin the process of redefining its religious, social, and cultural place in the United States.

During this period of self-analysis, Catholic intellectuals strove to demonstrate the compatibility of American and Catholic traditions. Compared to mainstream intellectuals suffering from post-war disillusionment, Catholic thinkers began to see Catholicism, with its humanistic and "totality" view of man, as the true inheritor and champion of the American values and ideals of optimism, progress, democracy, and man's reasoning powers. Catholic isolation in the previous century proved to be a blessing in disguise, for now American Catholicism remained untainted by the moral miasma afflicting the new age. Catholicism would be the savior of America.[3]

At this juncture Catholic bishops sought to make Catholicism a force to be reckoned with in American society and confidently asserted themselves into local and national politics. They reorganized and centralized church administration and solidified their episcopal authority and control over the clergy and laity. They built on a grand scale more churches, schools, hospitals, and convents to boldly proclaim Catholic presence in American cities. These new-style bishops also assumed an aristocratic or "triumphal" style of leadership as a way to demonstrate the stateliness and grandeur of Roman Catholicism.[4]

Cardinal Mundelein became a leader of this new breed of bishops. He modernized the business administration of the Chicago Archdiocese, expanded its physical plant, and provided ostentatious displays of Catholic ritual. In 1926 he hosted the International Eucharistic Congress, which held an open-air mass in Soldier Field for 150,000 faithful. He cultivated a close relationship with Franklin D. Roosevelt during the New Deal years. During his reign, Mundelein was considered to be the most liberal and influential bishop in the American Catholic hierarchy. His high profile and grand leadership injected self-confidence and pride in Catholics in Chicago and across the country.[5]

In bringing Catholicism into the forefront of American society, Mundelein and his ecclesiastical colleagues were supported by a growing American-born, Catholic middle class. By the 1920s these children and grandchildren of immigrants, led by the Irish and Germans, began migrating out of central city and ethnic neighborhoods into new middle-class communities. In Chicago this near mass movement prompted many real estate developers to advertise for the first time in the diocesan paper, *The New World*.[6] These American Catholics looked to their leaders to carve out a new and respected identity that suited their new economic status.[7]

St. Sabina's first parishioners were among this new generation of American-born Catholics who left working-class ethnic communities for greener pastures. They exuded the growing confidence of Catholic Americans yet carefully nurtured their identity in a parish community setting. St. Sabina's experience provides a window into the character of American Catholicism and Irish America at the parish level during this optimistic era.

To start a new parish was no small undertaking, but the early members of St. Sabina's enthusiastically embraced the challenge. Father Egan wasted no time in acquiring property at 78th and Throop Street for a parish complex. On December 8, 1916, the Feast of the Immaculate Conception, ground was broken to begin the construction of Sabina's first permanent parish structure, a combination school and church. According to the archdiocesan requirements, the school received top priority. A severe winter, however, delayed the blessing of the cornerstone until May 13, 1917. On September 10, 1917 St. Sabina parochial school opened. It was staffed by the Sisters of the Third Order of St. Dominic of Sinsinawa, Wisconsin. In October the first mass was said in the auditorium. By May of the following year Archbishop Mundelein was called to officiate at the dedication of the building. In 1922 two more floors were added to the school to accommodate the growing number of pupils and the third floor was used as a temporary rectory. In 1924 a new convent was built at 1207 W. 78th Street for the sisters, who previously lived at St. Brendan's convent and then in a house at 79th and Elizabeth. In 1925 the foundation was laid for a permanent church and its basement was completed and used for services. By 1928 all of the $540,000 debt for these buildings was paid.[8]

The main source of revenue came from Sunday and holy day collections, with a considerable share coming from pew collections at the entrance of the church. The pew money at St. Sabina's was actually a seat collection—parishioners were expected to drop a nickel in a box upon entering the church. Pew rental, on the other hand, which was somewhat common in the nineteenth century, allowed families to rent and occupy specific pews, usually at the front of the church. Only the wealthier members of the congregation could afford rented seats. Poor Catholics often felt that this practice was undemocratic.[9] Many of the churches St. Sabina parishioners came from had a pew rental system. From 1900 to 1920, however, many parishes began to adopt seat money instead. The amount of revenue collected for seat money compared to pew rental varied from parish to parish. Because of this some moved more eagerly toward the more equitable arrangement, while others relied on rentals.[10]

As Table 4 shows, during St. Sabina's early years seat money equaled the basket collection. Toward the end of the 1920s seat money, while increasing as the parish did, began to fall more and more behind the general collection. By 1953 it was discontinued. The shift from pew rental to seat money can perhaps be seen as an egalitarian move, whereas the discontinuance of seat money implied that such a practice was no longer necessary for a prosperous parish; not expecting people to make a donation upon entering church was perhaps more decorous for an aspiring middle class.

Carnivals were an important source of income for the building fund. They were held annually from 1916 to 1928. They proved to be very lucrative operations. In one year the festival grossed $26,700.[11] M. Dunne recalled, "The carnivals were outstanding. . . . People worked very hard for those. That was one of the big sources of revenue for the building fund. . . . An awful lot of people did pitch in to provide the wherewithal for them to do the building and maintain it."[12]

Table 4. St. Sabina Revenue Collections, 1916-1960

Year	Seat Money	Sunday and Holy Day	Carnival/Bazaar
1916	873	600	2,055
1920	6727	6,169	15,000
1924	11,906	11,234	26,770
1928	19,766	51,884	- - -
1932	17,772	43,722	- - -
1936	20,428	45,185	11,234
1940	19,689	42,248	14,327
1944	22,283	58,919	- - -
1948	28,589	77,879	- - -
1952	25,009	105,807	- - -
1956	- - -	179,178	- - -
1960	- - -	239,842	- - -

Source: St. Sabina Annual Reports.

Like parades in the nineteenth century, carnivals in this period were bold announcements to the neighborhood and the city of Catholic power and presence. St. Sabina's week-long event was opened by a parade featuring 186 vehicles and floats. Capacity crowds packed the sixteen booths and concession stands. Each night of the carnival, according to *The New World*, "surpassed the preceding in successful achievement."[13]

The parade and carnival even seemed to interest local Protestants. T. O'Rourke told of how some reacted to all this fanfare. "Next door to us . . . there was an Erikson . . . and to open a carnival, they'd have a parade. Well, we didn't have a car in those days. But Erikson would drive us in his touring car with the top down and he'd be yelling 'St. Sabina always on the top!' in his Swedish accent. He got a big kick out of it. . . . They couldn't beat us so they joined us."[14]

Parishioners took great pride in the attention their social events received in the neighborhood. In the early years of the parish, St. Sabina's Social Club held Friday night parties sponsored by a different street in the parish each week. In April 1920, after the Lenten season, *The New Word* reported: "The Friday night parties are again being held with their usual success. The number and value of the favors each street secures has attracted many outsiders and has given these parties an enviable reputation."[15] Catholics dominated the social scene in Auburn-Gresham and seemed to think their way of life was the most desirable. T. O'Rourke claimed, "We thought we had everything!"[16]

Local Protestants, though, did not seem particularly threatened by

Catholics. Some even sent their children to St. Sabina school before the local public school was completed. T. O'Rourke said that "Cook School [public] was portable . . . and some fathers and mothers wouldn't send their children to the portables . . . so some non-Catholics went to St. Sabina's."[17]

However, Protestant aversion to Catholicism still subtly influenced Catholic attachment to the parish, but not in the same way it shaped parish building in the 1880s and 1890s. St. Sabina's was established in a new real estate development that had previously been farmland. There was no well-established Anglo-Protestant community in this area as there had been in Englewood. Table 5 provides a breakdown of Auburn-Gresham by religious affiliation.

The five Catholic parishes comprised 25,800 members or 44 percent of the population of Auburn-Gresham, which was 58,546.[18] Although numerically a minority in the area, Catholics were the largest single religious group in the neighborhood. The number of churches that could definitely be identified as Anglo-Protestant congregations was quite small. The Protestant congregations mostly represented non-Anglo immigrants. Church of Peace, which was the largest Protestant assembly, was Swedish Lutheran. In addition, most non-Catholics who settled in St. Sabina's boundaries came from working-class districts that had large numbers of Catholics. Many would not have had the same immediate historical experience of opposition to their presence in a middle-class neighborhood as the Irish who settled in Englewood in the previous century. T. O'Rourke claimed part of the reason Catholics were accepted in the area without opposition was because "they came so fast."[19]

Although not a majority in Auburn-Gresham, this large Catholic "block" made them seem to be larger than they were. "The area was heavily Catholic," claimed J. Hagerty. "When we moved there, the only Protestant lived next door to us. There weren't too many of them. . . . There were only a few Jews, who were the storekeepers along 79th Street."[20]

After the Irish and the Germans, the Swedes composed the next largest immigrant group in the area.[21] St. Sabina residents remembered them for their labor in building the homes in the area. "They use to say the Swedish people had built the houses and the Irish bought them," related M. Dunne.[22] "There were a lot of Swedish people in the neighborhood," said T. O'Rourke. "Of course, they weren't Catholics. They weren't in the parish."[23] Residents of St. Sabina's reported friendly relations with the Lutheran Swedes. J. Hagerty said, "I came in the house one day and I said to my mother, 'These boys say they're Lutheran. What is a Lutheran?' And she said, 'Oh, that only means that they go to a different church than we do.' But she said they were

Table 5. Churches in Auburn-Gresham, 1934.

Name	Date Organized	Membership
Catholic		
St. Leo	1886	8,600 persons
St. Sabina	1916	7,000 persons
Little Flower	1925	5,000 persons
St. Ethelreda	1926	1,600 persons
St. Kilian	1905	3,600 persons
TOTAL		25,800 persons
Lutheran		
Trinity Evangelical Lutheran	1934	330 persons
German Lutheran	1887	400 persons
Faith Evang. Luthern	1914	450 persons
Mt. Zion Lutheran	1914	318 persons
St. Matthew Lutheran	1911	NA
Church of Peace	1886	1,400 families
TOTAL		1,498 persons
		1,400 families
Methodist		
Gresham Methodist	1882	350 persons
Calvary methodist Episcopal	1915	1,000 persons
Swedish Methodist	1914	350 persons
TOTAL		1,700 persons
Episcopal		
Bethany Methodist Episcopal	1927	75 persons
Annunciation	1886	218 persons
TOTAL		293 persons
Other		
Brainerd Community	1893	230 persons
Seventh Presbyterian	1884	350 persons
Foster Park Baptist	1928	450 persons
Hope Reformed	NA	NA
TOTAL		1,030 persons

Sources: Carrie Mae Barlow, "Auburn-Gresham: A Survey of a Local Community" (Ph.D. diss., University of Chicago, 1934), 28; Parish Annual Reports, 1934, Archdiocese of Chicago Archives.

Note: Roman Catholic parishes count all baptized persons, which would include infants. Protestant congregations generally count adults.

nice boys and I could play with them. . . . We got along fine."[24] Others reported the same congenial relations and an absence of tension. "Although we lived at 79th and Aberdeen," said H. O'Connor, "80th and Aberdeen was Swedish turf. Quite a few Swedish people lived on our block. There was never animosity or anything between the Swedish people and the Irish."[25]

Although there seemed to be an absence of ethnic or religious hostility, residents of Auburn-Gresham still segregated themselves to a certain degree. There was a tendency of different religious and nationality groups to cluster together in certain sectors of the neighborhood. The census tract areas of 903 and 908 (See Map 2), which St. Leo's and St. Sabina's were in, had the highest concentration of immigrants from the Irish Free State. The highest proportion of Swedes were found in areas 904, 907, and 906 and the lowest in 908 and 909. Germans were greatest in 909 and 910, near many of their churches, and least in 905 and 908.[26]

Like their nineteenth-century counterparts, the Irish in St. Sabina's liked to live close to the church.[27] The nearer to the church one lived, the fewer Protestant people they claimed they knew. J. Kill facetiously said, "We lived directly across from the main church so that on Sunday, we didn't have to go to church. We just opened our windows and heard mass. . . . It [the neighborhood] was so Catholic that on our block, on Throop Street, there were no Protestants. I do not honestly know a Protestant from the area. That's how Catholic it was."[28] M. Dunne could not recall any Protestants on her block.[29] T. O'Rourke, who lived three blocks west of St. Sabina's, reported that his street was approximately 90 percent Catholic.[30]

Because of their greater numbers and the separate institutional life of church and school, the Catholics in the neighborhood, for the most part, did not associate with others not in their circle. The simple fact that the children in the neighborhood attended different schools largely determined who their playmates were. J. Hagerty stated that, "You just were separate. You didn't go to the public school and your associations with Protestant families were kind of just civil and strange. But they were good neighbors."[31] J. Kill commented, "You did grow up with the idea that mixed marriages were supposed to be bad. Therefore, you just stayed with Catholics and associated with Catholics. . . . Protestants were like 'over there.' "[32]

While there was institutional and psychological separation, the relationship between Protestants and Catholics was a bit more complex. Table 6 on marriages shows that only 11.7 percent of Catholics entering matrimony between 1921 and 1940 married non-Catholics. St. Sabina's mixed marriage rate was similar to that of other territorial parishes. From a random sample of territorial parishes, Catholics in

Table 6. Marriages in St. Sabina Parish, 1921-1940.

Year	Number within Faith	Number outside Faith	Total Marriages	% Marrying outside Faith
1921	26	7	33	21
1925	92	12	104	12
1929	90	18	108	17
1933	94	7	101	07
1937	106	20	126	16
1940	208	17	225	8
TOTAL	616	81	697	12

Source: St. Sabina Annual Reports.

Table 7. Marriages in Territorial Parishes, 1900-1930.

Year	Number within Faith	Number outside Faith	Total Marriages	% Marrying outside Faith
1900	512	52	564	9
1905	770	69	839	8
1910	830	102	932	11
1915	910	96	1,006	10
1920	878	101	979	10
1925	710	85	795	11
1930	544	80	624	13
TOTAL	5,154	585	5,739	10

Sources: Annual Reports from random sample of territorial parishes.

1900 were marrying non-Catholics approximately at a rate of nine percent (Table 7). By 1920 it was ten percent, and by 1930 the mixed marriage rate was 12.8 percent. While these percentages are not insignificant and show some increase, Chicago's Catholic community was primarily a self-contained system.

Although they did not come into direct conflict with Protestant nativists, hostility and resentment toward themselves still haunted Catholics in the parish. "There were a lot of tentacles of [discrimination] that reached everywhere," J. Hagerty recalled. "A lot of people in the parish used to say that you had to be a Mason to get ahead [in some businesses] and they were accusing the Swift people at the stockyards of being Masons. You couldn't get promoted unless you were a Mason. [My brother-in-law] ran into that at the Edison Company."[33] W. Hogan remembered signs along Ashland Avenue where the meatpacking companies displayed help wanted signs that read "Men Wanted, No Irish and Catholics Need Apply."[34]

The 1920s were especially difficult for Protestant-Catholic relations in Chicago and across the country. The United States was now an urban society with the majority of its citizens living in cities and towns. Since immigrants, especially Catholics and Jews, concentrated in northern urban areas, the growing dominance of their strongholds in American life threatened traditional rural Protestant America. The Ku Klux Klan had revitalized its attacks not only against blacks in the South, but also on the Catholic Church. This revival of anti-Catholic sentiment played a prominent role in the presidential campaign of the Irish-American Democratic candidate, Al Smith, in 1928. These events had an important impact on American Catholicism.

Although traditionally associated with Southern white supremacy, after World War I the Ku Klux Klan emerged as a national movement to champion 'Americanism' and preserve Protestant Christian values. The new Ku Klux Klan was more in keeping with the nativist tradition of the Know Nothing Party of the 1850s and the American Protective Association of the 1890s. Its enemies were Catholicism, integration, Judaism, immigration, and internationalism.[35] Between 1920 and 1926 the Klan accumulated over two million members, one-third of whom came from the Midwest. Thirteen of the country's fifty largest cities were in this region. Many of them teemed with immigrant groups, which made Anglo residents with nativist sentiments easy prey for Klan recruiters.[36]

Chicago seemed an unlikely place for the Klan to make much headway considering its large ethnic population. Chicagoans who fit the description of adult, white, native-born, Protestant male made up only 15 percent of the city's population in 1923. Yet there were as many as 40,000 to 80,000 Klansmen in the city. The first chapters to organize in Illinois were on the South Side of Chicago in Englewood, Woodlawn, and Kenwood. The city itself hosted more than twenty neighborhood Klan chapters. Klan recruits were generally low-level, white-collar workers, small businessmen, and semi-skilled laborers. It was this class that feared the increasing competition of the emerging Catholic middle class and the growing black belt.[37] Those who had not yet reconciled themselves to Chicago's diversity turned to the Klan.

The Ku Klux Klan's rise in Chicago was more an indication of an insecure and defensive Anglo-Protestant community on the retreat in the city.[38] The Catholic numbers in Chicago had grown dramatically in the beginning of the twentieth century to an estimated 40 percent of the total city population. Through their numbers and their movement into the middle class, Catholics were now able to challenge

Protestant hegemony in the city.[39] Numbers and aggressive leadership made Roman Catholicism the most visible and, to a large extent, the most dominant religious tradition in post–World War I Chicago.[40]

When the Klan decided to infiltrate Chicago, they failed to reckon with determined Catholic opposition. In 1922 Catholic priests and laymen formed the American Unity League (AUL) to destroy the Klan in the city and across the nation. Their weapon was a weekly newspaper called *Tolerance*. The strength of the Klan had depended on maintaining the secrecy of its members. Through various means, *Tolerance* obtained the names and business addresses of Klansmen and published them. As new names were exposed week after week, fear spread throughout the Chicago order and sapped its vitality. After 1924 Klan membership rapidly declined because of *Tolerance's* exposés. In the process of vanquishing its enemies, however, *Tolerance* was subjected to numerous lawsuits filed against it for libel. By mid-1924 the AUL was bankrupt and ceased to publish its paper. However, it had done its job and by 1928 the Ku Klux Klan was defunct in the city.[41]

Former St. Sabina parishioners recalled the Ku Klux Klan campaign in Chicago and the paper, *Tolerance*. T. O'Rourke remembered it being sold outside the church. "I remember one Sunday it came out and whose name was listed there but William Wrigley, the chewing gum family. He was a member. Well, we boycotted Wrigley Gum from then on. People were all excited about it. He had his factory at 35th and Ashland. It was upsetting for the people who worked there."[42]

William Wrigley, Jr., however, publicly denied that he belonged to the Klan and filed a $50,000 lawsuit against the AUL, and offered the same amount of money to any charitable organization that could prove he had signed an application with the Ku Klux Klan. Within a month a Klansmen came forward and admitted that Wrigley's application to the Klan was a forgery.[43] The interest of St. Sabina parishioners in *Tolerance* and the Klan's activities and the distress they felt by the appearance of Wrigley's name in the paper, show that they were still sensitive to and defensive about the status of their religion in American society.

Once the Klan was defeated another blow struck Catholics across the nation. In 1928 the Democratic nominee, Alfred E. Smith, lost the race for the presidency by a large margin to Herbert Hoover. Smith's Catholicism, along with other controversial issues he supported, offended Anglo Americans who feared the immigrant hordes in the dirty, corrupt cities of the North that made up the Democratic candidate's constituency. Catholics across the nation were stunned and hurt by the anti-Catholic insults hurled at Smith.

St. Sabina parishioners were no exception (Table 8). Smith carried

Table 8. Election Returns in St. Sabina Precincts, 1928

	Al Smith	%	Herbert Hoover	%	Total
18th Ward Precincts					
33	263	59	183	41	449
34	288	56	219	43	512
35	265	52	239	47	505
TOTAL PRECINCTS	816	56	641	44	1,457
TOTAL WARD	18,358	53	16,330	47	34,688
19th Ward Precincts					
22	318	68	152	32	499
23	214	64	122	36	377
24	281	57	212	43	494
25	266	66	139	34	406
TOTAL PRECINCTS	1,079	63	625	37	1,704
TOTAL WARD	19,318	41	27,548	58	46,866

Source: Board of Elections, Presidential Election, Nov. 6, 1928, Chicago Municipal Reference Library.

63 percent of the votes in nineteenth ward precincts within St. Sabina parish. While it is difficult to precisely determine the percent of the Catholic population in these precincts, it seems likely that Smith captured at least 80 to 90 percent of the Catholic vote. Of the precincts of the parish that were in the eighteenth ward, Smith won by 56 percent. However, the thirty-fourth and the thirty-fifth precincts extended westward from St. Sabina's almost to Western Avenue. These precincts would have a sizable Swedish population, which may account for the lower returns compared to those in the more Irish precincts.[44]

The majority vote in favor of Smith in St. Sabina's precincts is even more significant when compared to the overall vote of other wards. Smith only carried 53 percent of the eighteenth ward, whereas he lost the nineteenth by a margin of 17 percent. The nineteenth ward included Beverly Hills and Morgan Park, exclusive Protestant neighborhoods. Clearly, voting patterns in the area, at least for Catholics, indicated heightened religious sentiments.[45]

T. O'Rourke recounted the feelings of the parish. "We were all for him and were all disappointed. . . . I was in my second year of high school [at Leo's, an Irish Christian Brothers' school]. The next day after the election I overslept and was late for school. My mother had to write a note. She said I was all tired out from the night before. So I gave it to the brother and he looked at it and said, 'Oh, I know how you people feel, and how we all feel.' So it was all right to be late." Smith's defeat left us feeling that "we couldn't be president; that we were just dealt out."[46] J. Hagerty recalled those years saying that people at St. Sabina's "were 100 percent for Al Smith . . . and were of course opposed to the bigotry . . . so you would certainly not be for Herbert Hoover. You'd be for Al Smith!"[47]

How did members of St. Sabina's deal with these outbursts of prejudice? J. Hagerty believed that the parish church and school played an important role in building self-confidence to withstand the subtle pressures of prejudice and discrimination. "You were brought up with the idea that you were as good as anybody else and these Protestant people were trying to control things and you were just not going to go along with it. . . . That was the mind set. . . . You always took that into the same context as Christ saying that you would be persecuted if you were in the Church."[48] W. Hogan recalled Catholics having the feeling that "we did not have full equality with Protestants. . . . We had not yet taken our place in the sun." He felt, though, that the fact that Catholics were as numerous on the South Side as in Chicago helped form a bulwark against hostility. "We were taught that our Catholicism was something to be guarded," and the parish provided a forum for their identity.[49]

T. O'Rourke confirmed the protective and supportive function of the parish. "I think they [Catholics] were on the defensive, and I think it brought them closer together. They were raised in a kind of enclave, maybe you should call it a ghetto, but we didn't feel persecuted in it. We thought we were on top of the world. But I think we did close ourselves in."[50]

St. Sabina parishioners were not alone in their attitudes about themselves and American society. In her study of Boston, Paula Kane found that middle-class Catholics developed what she has called an "insider/outsider" mentality to cope with their unsettled status in American society. On the one hand they depicted themselves as persecuted and marginalized citizens, yet on the other hand they saw themselves as superior to Protestant America. Catholicism empowered them with values that helped them more effectively battle secularism and materialism, yet at the same time they still espoused American political and economic values. This insider/outsider dichotomy was difficult, if not impossible, to reconcile.[51]

While Catholics were not threatened or mistreated in their immediate neighborhood, anti-Catholicism reinforced in them the need for a Catholic community. During these years Catholics continued to use their parish as their home base for support against the hostile attitudes of Anglo-Protestant America. Parishioners were defensive and recognized the need to turn to their parish for support. Within this community they found reinforcement for their faith, camaraderie, and mutual support.

The Chicago Irish, like other Catholics, resisted the ultimate expression of Yankee America—the Eighteenth Amendment, which sought to restrict America's drinking habits from 1919 to 1933. Protestants, particularly Evangelicals and Scandinavians, traditionally scorned drinking as an evil that led to only more moral lapses. These Prohibitionists sincerely believed that if the consumption of alcohol were curtailed, American life would soon reflect the Anglo-Protestant ideals of thrift, industry, and piety, and that the evils and corruption that hard-drinking immigrants brought to urban life would be destroyed.

Like other Catholics and some Protestant groups across the country and in Chicago, those who resided in the confines of St. Sabina's resented Prohibition. "They didn't like it," recalled T. O'Rourke. "They thought a right was being taken away from them." Prohibitionists "thought it was saving the country, but my people didn't like it. My father thought a working man had a right to have a drink if he wanted it. . . . So the saloons closed up, then the speakeasies came along. . . . Some of those were in houses in the area. My father had a place where he could go. It was a corner bungalow, an Irish family operated it and he could get something to drink. They sprang up in apartments, too, particularly on 79th Street up above the stores."[52]

The Irish not only considered alcohol social, but they also used it for medicinal purposes. Its unavailability proved frustrating. "They used whiskey as medicine," explained T. O'Rourke. According to neighborhood folklore, doctors who prescribed whiskey to their patients during the great flu epidemic of 1919 saved more lives than those who did not.[53]

Nor did the St. Sabina's community condemn those who sold alcoholic beverages. Before Prohibition Hickey's saloon at 79th and Racine was an important donor to the parish building fund. The publican was "a prominent member of the parish" in the eyes of his neighbors. Not only did the Eighteenth Amendment fail to change attitudes toward drink, but there is every indication that it increased interest in public drinking within the community. After repeal, saloons not only were quickly reestablished in the parish but their numbers increased. "There were all kinds of them after a while. I think there were probably too many."[54]

St. Sabina's experience makes it clear that these parishioners were not complete imitators of Protestant America. What they could use and adapt to American society, they kept, steering a middle course between the culture and expectations of Protestant America and what was important to them. While still aware of prejudice in the country and in certain sectors of the city, St. Sabina parishioners did not find it particularly disabling. Although still defensive, they were beginning to reflect a more self-assured Catholicism, but were still committed to a parish-centered community. The Catholic community in Auburn-Gresham in the post–World War I years was slowly opening itself to the wider society. Yet their strong numbers, their perceived marginal status in America, their continued separate institutional life, and attitudes toward fraternizing with and marrying people of other religions still helped maintain a Catholic community unto itself.

St. Sabina parishioners remained deeply attached to their parish even during the Depression. At the onset of the Great Depression in 1929, Father Egan found himself with only a finished basement for his main house of worship. Despite the financially adverse times, he decided to proceed with the completion of the upper main church. His plan also aimed to provide employment for building-trade workers of the parish and to take advantage of lower-priced materials. He specified to the contractors that parishioners be hired first, an informal Catholic affirmative action plan.[55] His decision proved to be a sound one. By June 18, 1933 Cardinal Mundelein officiated at the dedication of the English Gothic church of "the most complete and vigorous parish in his or any other diocese."[56] The main church, valued at $600,000, also erased its debts within a few years.[57]

Egan, now a monsignor, could not act independently on any of his building ventures. He proceeded with construction plans only with the approval of Mundelein's Board of Consultors.[58] However, the fact that he was able to erect so many buildings and have them all paid for in such a short amount of time indicates impressive leadership abilities and enthusiastic support from his parishioners. It also suggests that during this economically trying time, the parish as a whole continued to be financially healthy. Sunday and holy day collections were down only 8 percent, while pew collections increased by 1 percent. However, the total parish membership of 2,000 in 1935 had increased by 25 percent over the 1929 total of 1,600. While individual donations were down, it did not hurt parish finances, as is demonstrated by the full payment of its debt on the church. St. Sabina grade school also posted an increase in attendance. From 1930 to 1937 the parish set up a $1,000 scholarship fund out of general revenues.[59] Tuition was kept deliberately low, to just seventy-five cents.[60] M. Dunne said that during the Depression, "tuition was low . . . provision was always made for families who had a problem and were out of work or [had experienced] a death, so that if they wanted to go to the Catholic school, they made it possible for them to go."[61]

The continued fiscal strength of the parish during the Depression was due in large measure to the fact that many people in the parish remained employed. The Irish proclivity for city work and politically connected jobs worked in their favor during this troubling time. "I think it [the parish] did pretty well," T. O'Rourke recounted. "I'm sure some people suffered in the Depression . . . the building trades were hit very hard. . . . But again, there were a lot of people who had steady work because of their job . . . like the streetcarmen kept working. . . . In my father's case, streetcarmen didn't make a lot of money, but the salary came in all during the Depression and that made a big difference. . . . The firemen kept working, and the policemen." Police officers, fire fighters, and school teachers had problems collecting their salaries, though. The city's ability to tax was severely hampered by the economic crisis. It handled its payroll crisis with scrip, which was more or less an I.O.U. Scrip was later redeemable and was even accepted in lieu of cash in some stores.[62]

M. Dunne confirmed the steady work of parish city workers. She said, "My father was a school engineer, a city employee. . . . He was getting paid in scrip. . . . Very often he had to discount it in order to buy groceries."[63]

The Irish-American community's access to the pork barrel of the Kelly-Nash machine in city hall helped the unemployed hold things together during hard times. According to parishioners local politicians did a "terrific" job getting Sabina's workers jobs with the Works Progress Administration (WPA), which they jokingly referred to as "We Poke Along." "People who never were in politics, took political jobs when they lost out," T. O'Rourke recalled. "They were glad to get those political jobs. They had steady income. . . . [The parish] didn't have any soup kitchens set up."[64]

Actually Mayor Edward J. Kelly and the Chicago Democratic machine did not have access to or control over New Deal relief and public works money or jobs. Kelly became mayor in 1933 upon the death of Anton Cermak thanks to the help of Pat Nash, the Cook County Democratic Chairman. Together these two Irishmen built one of the nation's most powerful political machines. To capitalize on votes, they took advantage of the federal government's largesse by encouraging people to believe that they could get relief jobs. The New Deal, though, was instrumental in helping build the Kelly-Nash machine. Since the federal government took over the burden of providing relief and jobs, Chicago's coffers were not as strained. This allowed Kelly and Nash to use the city's resources for patronage and to deliver excellent police and fire protection along with other city services.[65]

These political connections and benefits reinforced the notion that sticking together could be a means of economic survival. The parish priest was often an important conduit between politicians and people.

These "feudal barons," generally through unspoken means, could make or break a political career. If streets or sidewalks were not repaired or garbage not picked up, they only had to let it be known that they were not happy with the local political representative. "Politicians had to make sure things ran well or they would have to answer to monsignor," recalled W. Hogan.[66]

What were the attitudes and feelings toward the parish and community that bound members together? E. Clair and T. O'Rourke thought that Irish clannishness fostered parish community building. "We kept together. I don't know if that was good or bad for us, but we did."[67]

The Church community was also considered an important support for family life. M. Dunne said, "They were young families and they were working for their own families as well as other young families coming up. . . . It was built and paid for by little hard-working people who sacrificed to contribute. . . . They were pretty much family oriented and their goals were to probably see that their children had a better life than they had."[68] St. Sabina's financial reports support her assertion. There were few large donations made to the parish. The major source of money was from the collections and entertainments.[69]

J. Hagerty provided another reason why the parish was an attraction. It was simply because of the lack of development in the area. She related, "I remember there weren't many places around the area. It was sort of a wasteland . . . so that it was a gathering place, the church was and the school, for people to congregate and that's how you got to know the neighbors."[70]

The experience of the Dunne family demonstrates the strong attachment a family could have to a parish. In 1925, St. Therese of the Infant Jesus (Little Flower) parish was established at 80th and Wood Street out of a portion of St. Sabina's western territory. The Dunne family unhappily found themselves automatically assigned to the new parish. "With the problems of the new parish and a change in schools—there was no church really—my father sold the three-flat at a loss and went back to St. Sabina's."[71]

Monsignor Egan, who was fondly referred to as "God's gift to the South Side,"[72] was another important factor in fostering community solidarity. "I think the pastor was greatly responsible for the cohesiveness," M. Dunne related. "He was a very fatherly kind of man with a soft little Irish brogue and he had wonderful foresight in planning those buildings. . . . He really built a beautiful set-up there. . . . He was a peacemaker. He had a way of drawing people together."[73] J. Hagerty confirmed Monsignor Egan's role in building community spirit. She said, "The fondest memories of a priest that you could have would be of the pastor, Father Egan. He was made to be a pastor. . . . He was

like everybody's grandfather to the kids in school. I remember him well
from the earliest days. Everybody respected him. He was an Irishman
by birth and he had a jovial attitude but he was a wise person, too. He
never sounded off at people. He was a very kind and loving person.
Everybody loved him, without exception, of every age group."[74]

Monsignor Egan's personality was the glue that bonded the community. People who considered moving from the neighborhood would
change their minds when faced with the prospect of disappointing him.
He also reached out to Protestant congregations in their neighborhood.
Egan formed a long-term friendship with the pastor of the local
Lutheran church. Informally they cooperated with one another to avoid
having Catholic carnivals or fund-raising efforts competing with Lutheran activities."[75]

The monsignor's subtle leadership worked best with money matters. The massive financial requirements of building a parish infra-
structure from scratch forced many a pastor to become, in the eyes of
their parishioners, "obsessed with money." Egan avoided the resent-
ments caused by incessant financial pleas from the pulpit by working
through indirect means. He brought several prominent men in the
parish into his confidence. At meetings of the Holy Name or other
societies there would always be several men present to propose and
second fund-raising activities. It became a standing joke in the Holy
Name society that every year they had to raise money to pay the debt
on the church's elegant rose window. Year after year the society's
officers raised money for the window only to be faced with the task
again next year. But in this incremental way the church was eventually
fully funded. Of course, Egan could take a subtle approach to fund-raising because the people of Sabina's were fully aware of their responsi-
bilities as members of a new parish. "We were taught from an early
age," one parishioner recalled, "to give what one could to the church."[76]

Parishioners also recalled how interested Monsignor Egan was
with the personal concerns of his flock. H. O'Connor related this story.
She had been married five years and had been waiting and praying for
a child. When she finally received the good news from the doctor, she
"stopped at the rectory and told Father Egan before I came home and
told my husband." Fifty years later she said, "I still pray for him."[77]

Monsignor Egan's death in 1942 saddened the entire community.
"I remember when Father Egan died, the night he died, getting on a
bike and riding up and down the streets, shouting the news like we
were newspaper carriers or Paul Revere," recalled J. Kill. "And the
church bells were tolling. When the church bells tolled, everybody came
out in front of their houses to find out what's wrong or what's going
on . . . and we yelled, 'Monsignor Egan died! Monsignor Egan died!' "[78]
"When he died," J. Hagerty said, "the entire plant of the church, the

school, the convent, the rectory, and the community center were paid for 100 percent. And those were working people. And he had to live through the Depression so it was a great tribute to him."[79]

St. Sabina parishioners also warmly embraced the assistant priests as part of their community. "The other priests were very friendly with everyone," said J. Hagerty. "There was enough opportunity for people to get to know them. . . . They were all the kind that people took to."[80] J. Kill said, "I would say the priests had a good image at Sabina's—well, they did all over."[81]

Father Ashendon, in particular, stood out in their memories for his involvement in parish activities. He was especially devoted to the young people of the parish and stories of his antics were a regular feature of St. Sabina's. On one occasion he flooded the prairie before the main church was built for an ice skating rink. He started the water running on a Saturday evening, went in to hear confessions, and completely forgot to turn it off. Sunday morning the whole block was coated with ice. "Everyone liked him. He and Monsignor Egan . . . got along like father and son."[82]

Nineteenth-century devotional practices created an intimate world for Catholics to inhabit, one which historian Ann Taves has called "the household of faith." Catholic members of this household received "supernatural relatives" into their community, home, and lives. This kinship network included God at the head of the family as father, Mary as the mother, Jesus as the big brother, and a host of other saints and angels who were like special aunts and uncles.[83] By the twentieth century these "relatives" had made themselves quite comfortable in the homes of the parish community. Their pictures and statues decorated the rooms of these homes providing reminders of their presence and watchful concern. Holy water fountains were often placed near doorways so people in the house could bless themselves with baptismal waters upon entering or leaving the house.

The clergy in the twentieth century could see the positive aspects of devotional worship in strengthening the institutional Church. It fostered loyalty to the Church and separated Catholics from Protestants. It also encouraged an "otherworldly" frame of mind to help Catholics resist the material world. The devotions the Church advocated also sought to weed out popular ethnic religious customs so as to standardize and unify a Roman Catholic form of worship. The Irish were eager followers of devotionalism not only for its spiritual benefits, but also because it fostered an alternative identity to the insidious infiltration of Anglo ways into their lives.[84]

St. Sabina parishioners were enthusiastic practitioners of devotionalism. It was no accident that the architectural style the parish selected for the church was English Gothic. In the early part of this century, the Boston firm of Maginnis and Walsh revived the Gothic style in church architecture in Massachusetts. From there it spread across the country. While the style was also popular with Protestants, Catholics felt they had a special claim to it since they had never repudiated the medieval Church like Protestantism had. The medieval church was the source of their devotional practices. The architects felt that the otherworldly qualities of Gothic art were an ideal counterpoise to the materialism and crassness of the industrial age that ethnics were forced to work in.[85]

The interior of St. Sabina's was like many other Catholic churches of the period. It had an imposing main altar with two sides altars, one dedicated to the Blessed Virgin and the other to St. Joseph. One could imaginatively participate in Jesus' crucifixion by following the images along the walls of the nave. Incoming light was filtered through the resplendent rose-shaped, stained-glass window in the rear of the church. As they had for the interior of Holy Family parish, the devotional images and special lighting in St. Sabina's definitely created a Catholic space.

St. Sabina parishioners were very attentive to communal religious practices and observances. The most important religious observations were the Mass (attendance at Sunday services was expected and at daily mass was strongly encouraged) and the sacraments of baptism, marriage, penance, and Communion. Other devotions such as Benedictions, processions, a Friday Mother of Sorrows novena (begun in 1937),[86] and a parish mission every two to three years were regular features of St. Sabina's liturgical year. According to many former residents, St. Sabina parishioners were not remiss in their obligations.

"People went to church," reported M. Dunne of the religious practices of the parish. "I think they made a very decided effort to do what the Church expected of them. They went to church. They belonged to the societies."[87] From his vantage point across the street J. Kill reported, "I honestly can say that I never knew anybody who didn't go to church. . . . Even during the week, the number of people who went was phenomenal. During Lent, it was almost like Sundays. The church was filled."[88]

"When I was young, churches would be crowded," recalled T. O'Rourke. "They'd be packed with people . . . and they'd be pushing them into pews, pushing them in. . . . And they'd stand in line for Confession. . . . You'd get in line and you might be there two hours, just standing." He further commented on the strictness of Catholicism at that time. "We followed a lot of rules and our fasting and abstinence was stricter. Fasting before going to communion—many things would happen between midnight and mass time in the morning, especially on First Communion. Some kids would break their fast and, of course, they wouldn't let them go to communion, even if they [only] drank water at six in the morning."[89]

J. Hagerty agreed that people in St. Sabina's were steadfast in their religious obligations. "They were very devoted to the church," she said. "My mother went to mass every morning and to the big devotions, like the First Fridays and . . . novenas. . . . My father always went to the missions." The reasons, she explained, for this exacting adherence to religious practices was early instruction. "You were taught from an early age that this religion thing was not automatic," she said. "You had to do something about it. And it was expected of you and you did it." Upon reflection she added that "the social conditions of the time had a lot to do with a person's . . . dependence on the Almighty. . . . During the Depression, everybody was down. Everybody was praying for jobs and for whatever you could do."[90]

Novenas were perhaps the best indication of the strength of devotionalism at Sabina's. Novenas were popular in the Middle Ages. In the nineteenth century the Church revived them by offering a plenary indulgence to those who fulfilled the devotion's requirements. A novena is nine successive days of prayer in honor of certain saints or the Blessed Virgin Mary. Usually novenas preceded Saints' feast days, but some churches, like Sabina's, held novenas once a week. The petitioner asked the honoree to intercede with God about their special intention. Novenas can be said in private or corporately.[91]

St. Sabina's Mother of Sorrows novenas were said corporately in the church seven times on Fridays. They were very well known and would attract worshippers from neighboring congregations. On the afternoons of a novena residents recalled seeing people getting off the streetcars on Halsted and walking in groups to the church. The novenas were so crowded that the parish would hire Andy Frain ushers to control the overflow. The pews were packed with men and women in their work clothes. A six o'clock novena would attract policemen and streetcar conductors straight from work. Boys in Little League baseball uniforms stood shoulder to shoulder saying "Hail Marys" for a victory in their game. An opportunity to ask a favor of God through the intercession of Mary was the principal appeal of the novena. The effect of silently making your personal request within the crowded congregation heightened community solidarity. The disappointments and loneliness of everyday life were addressed in a service that reduced individual isolation and which brought unhappiness and hope together. During World War II the Mother of Sorrows novena was a particularly poignant experience. She was considered to be the patroness of U.S. troops. Even Protestants were reported to have participated in the novenas.[92]

The emotionalism of the parish novena left an impression on young Jim Kill. "A novena was a funny thing. . . . It was almost some sort of a need in people to go and pray the same prayer over and over with other people. The music was very sentimental. . . . The closing hymn was 'Good Night Sweet Jesus.'" He admitted that "there was something in people at that time that they needed that novena and it fit. . . . This was their means of an outlet. You would pray with other people aloud and loudly."[93]

Novenas were not, however, necessarily somber occasions. J. Kill said, "On Fridays they had seven novenas with 8,500 people. It was fun for us as kids because we lived across the street. They used to block the street with horses because some people would wait two and three hours to get into church to go to the novenas, the church was that crowded. . . . You waited until you were able to get in. While it was blocked off, we used to play hockey out there on roller skates. We had an audience. People would be cheering for you. . . . We kind of entertained the people who were waiting to go to church."[94]

Other devotional activities were also popular. Since the Middle Ages the month of May has been associated with the Blessed Mother. Marion devotions generally emphasized her purity as the only human conceived immaculately without Original Sin. Mary has also been portrayed as the nurturing and protective mother. Special consideration of these qualities was set aside for May. "Marion devotions were very strong . . . in Catholic parishes and in Catholic family life," related W. Hogan.[95] Many churches decorated the Blessed Mother's side altar, and on Mothers' Day the statue of the Queen of the May was crowned with flowers. Parishioners of all ages participated in the devotions. School children were especially involved with them. "One of the big things in those early days were the May altars and the May processions," recalled M. Dunne. "A lot of children would, instead of buying candy on their way back to school in May, they'd be into Farrell's Florist buying, maybe with ten cents, one flower to take to school for the May altar."[96]

Altars were erected in each classroom. It became a matter of class pride to have each shrine as resplendent as possible. The highlight of the Marion devotion for the parish children was the May Crowning. Long lines of young girls in white dresses marched into the church singing the praises of the Queen of the Angels. Crowded pews were filled with proud family members and friends. Participation in a May Crowning was an important rite of passage that helped to prepare young school girls on the brink of puberty to become Catholic women.

In 1920, *The New World* wrote of St. Sabina's May devotions: "Last Sunday evening the procession and the crowning of the May Queen was held in the church. The long lines of little children marching and chanting the litany and praises of their Blessed Mother was a beautiful sight. The children have entered deeply into the May devotions; each room of the school had its little shrine to the Blessed Virgin."[97]

Devotional life permeated Catholic life. T. O'Rourke explained, "We'd never pass a church without tipping our hat. We were very careful. We wouldn't eat meat on Friday at all. That would be really terrible. On Holy Thursday, we'd visit churches. . . . We could walk to St. Leo's, and then we'd go down to Sacred Heart. That was a German parish. They'd be saying the prayers in German, and we thought that was very interesting. We'd go to St. Brendan's and then back to St. Sabina's. Sometimes we'd go out to St. Kilian's. . . . Then in later years when we had autos, we went by automobiles . . . and the Blessed Sacrament was exposed in all these churches and that's what we were honoring—the Blessed Sacrament." In addition to honoring the Blessed Sacrament, a first time visit to a church was believed to grant the visitor three wishes.[98]

Benediction of the Blessed Sacrament was a common feature of the Catholic liturgical year. Catholics believed that Jesus was present in the consecrated host which was displayed before the congregation in a monstrance for veneration. Benediction had been a popular devotion in the Middle Ages. It began with short evening devotions such as Vespers. In the nineteenth and twentieth centuries it became part of Forty Hours Devotion, which recalled the forty hours Jesus' body spent in the sepulcher after his crucifixion. The purpose of this devotion was to encourage worshippers to contemplate on the devoted love of Jesus in the face of hostility and indifference. By doing so they might draw inspiration from Jesus' self-sacrifice and share in his love and protection in the face of their enemies. This devotion rotated throughout the year from parish to parish. As T. O'Rourke's experience indicates, veneration of the Blessed Sacrament was a church-centered or corporate devotion.[99]

Closely associated with the Blessed Sacrament was the devotion to the Sacred Heart of Jesus. It became a ritualized devotion in the seventeenth century and was popularized in the United States after 1870. In this devotion Jesus was generally portrayed as suffering for his people, even when their hearts were hardened to his love. A crown of thorns and a bleeding heart were the images depicted for contemplation The patronage and protection of the Sacred Heart could help shield believers from the materialism and sensual indulgence of the age.[100]

There were many other types of devotions that were common practices among Catholics of the period, such as the rosary, wearing scapulars, and prayer books. The rosary was associated with Marion devotions from the Middle Ages, and it became an indulged devotion.

The rosary is a series of prayers that are counted off on a string of beads. By the end of the prayer session, the petitioner has said 150 Hail Marys, 15 Our Fathers, and has contemplated on 15 meditations on the life and passion of Jesus. The 150 prayers are modeled on the 150 psalms of David. The rosary could be said either individually or corporately. The rosary was a very common and widespread practice. Catholics were encouraged to say it daily. "The Living Rosary" was a popular way to include several people in the devotion. Fifteen people divided up the rosary. Each person was to recite one decade of the rosary a day. Even though he or she might only say a portion of the rosary, full benefit was extended to all.[101]

Prayer books were also common aids to devotional worship. Since the hierarchy was trying to standardize Catholic worship, devotions prescribed by prayer books were more indulged. Prayer books were often used in conjunction with the mass. Many included the vernacular translation of the Latin which the faithful would use to follow the mass. They also included devotions for mass which people turned to during communion. Since masses were so crowded and communion received in a kneeling position at the altar rail, "communion went on forever!" These devotions and the rosary gave people a time of quiet contemplation. Prayers for the dead and the souls in purgatory were fairly common in the prayer book.[102]

Many Catholics also wore scapulars as a symbol of devotion to the Blessed Virgin. Scapulars worn by the laity were scaled-down versions of those worn by monks. Two small pieces of woolen cloth held together by string were worn over the shoulders, with one piece of cloth in front of the chest and the other on the back.

St. Sabina parishioners lived their lives in rhythm with the liturgical calendar, which began with the advent season preceding the birth of Jesus at Christmas. The highlight of the Church calendar was, of course, Easter Sunday. It was preceded by forty days of fasting and devotions. The faithful would often abstain from alcohol, cigarettes, sweets, or other "weaknesses" and pleasures as an act of spiritual discipline. Fridays in Lent meant attending the Stations of the Cross. There would generally be three to four sessions and they were so crowded "there was no room to think!"[103] Friday required abstaining from meat. Holy days of obligation, such as the Feast of the Immaculate Conception, Ascension Thursday, All Souls Day, and The Assumption of Mary, dotted the calendar. On these days Catholics were expected to attend Mass. Other days of the week and months of the year had their particular devotions. It was not uncommon to find St. Sabina parishioners wearing a scapular, carrying a rosary in their pocket or a prayer book to mass, or tipping their hat when they passed a church. Few parishioners reported feeling that the pervasiveness of religion was suffocating. "There was religion," related M. Dunne. "But it wasn't made uncomfortable. It was a joyous kind of thing."[104]

This type of Catholicism gave people a great sense of security. God may be so transcendent that direct appeals to him were either too intimidating or beyond one's imagination, but a "human" intercessor was more approachable. "Mary played such a large role in people's lives," recalled W. Hogan, "because 'she is from us.' She was a model of complete love, dedication, and sacrifice to God . . . someone to pray for us . . . 'put in a good word for me.' " Marion devotions, he explained, were popular with both men and women. Sometimes people might also choose a particular saint as a personal "hero" for guidance and inspiration. Their major function was to serve as an aid—"to help me live my life as I *should* live it." [105]

Devotional Catholicism gave ordinary men and women a sense of purpose in their everyday lives. What they did daily mattered because this world was preparation for the next world. It also gave people a sense of belonging. They had "relatives" in heaven looking out for them, and a sense of unity and common belief with others. The Apostle's Creed was said every day and stated very clearly what one believed. Only the Tridentine Rite was used at mass. The mass was very ceremonial and ritualistic. There were no variations. It was a strict society where people had a definite sense of what was expected of them. "It sounds jejune or simplistic today," related W. Hogan, "but we had a sense of right and wrong, good and evil."[106]

Another important aspect of parish life in addition to devotional observances were the various parish associations. The bedrock organizations of St. Sabina's from the beginning were the Altar and Rosary Society for the women and the Holy Name Society for the men.[107] Both societies were confraternities, which meant that their intention was to promote public worship. The Altar and Rosary Society required its members to say fifteen mysteries of the rosary once a week. The Holy Name Society's purpose was to be a public manifestation of homage to Christ's name. Its members were required to receive Holy Communion together on the second Sunday of each month. In addition to their spiritual aims, the Holy Name and Altar and Rosary Societies had other practical goals: they aided the pastor in raising money for parish buildings and engaged in philanthropic activities—the Holy Name had a Big Brother program—and both societies included a good deal of socializing in many of their gatherings.

"The Altar and Rosary Society and Holy Name Society were very active," M. Dunne recalled. "The Holy Name Society was outstandingly active in the whole diocese. They were recognized in the whole Chicago area for their turn-outs on the Sundays for the Holy Name."[108] In June

1931, the Holy Name Society sent a thousand of its members to receive Holy Communion on the second Sunday of the month.[109] While the Altar and Rosary Society was not required by its definition to receive the Eucharistic together on Sundays, they imitated the Holy Name Society in this regard. This led to friendly competition at the communion rail. In October 1931 *The New World* reported: "The women of the parish received Holy Communion last Sunday and had over eight hundred in line. This showing was very gratifying to all concerned and proves that the women of St. Sabina's are trying to take the honors from the men. Since the organization of the parish the Holy Name Society has always set the standard of attendance at Communion leading all other societies by a large margin, but if we wish to keep this leadership we ask every man to talk to his neighbor and his friends and impress upon him that we want every man in the parish to be in line next Sunday."[110] The following month the men of the parish, not to be outdone, also sent eight hundred to the Communion rail. *The New World* reported: "Last Sunday St. Sabina men turned out with their usual demonstration of loyalty to their Society. With Scout troops 638 and 669 in the lead as they marched into church, the bystander might well remark, 'What's going on?' However, the well informed Southsider knows that this is just the usual monthly Communion Sunday in St. Sabina parish. Each of the nearly 800 Scouts and men felt that they had a duty to perform and were proud of their task."[111]

"The Holy Name . . . had social affairs and a regular business meeting and after that they'd play cards and they'd have beer," E. Clair related. "They enjoyed each other's company. . . . Nearly everybody belonged to it."[112] The Holy Name also sponsored athletic events, had a bowling and basketball league, had musical programs, "Ladies' Nights," and held dances.[113]

J. Hagerty recalled her mother's involvement with the Altar and Rosary Society and some of their activities. She said, "During the weeks that the carnival was on, you didn't see much of her at home. And they had bake sales . . . and there were bingo games and card games that they used to sponsor. And they were of course interested in the school. These women were more or less the mothers' club then because most everybody had kids in school."[114]

Besides the Altar and Rosary Society the women of the parish also had an organization called the Daughters of Isabella, a beneficiary society begun in 1920. Its membership reached 150.[115] It held neighborhood meetings and monthly socials. St. Sabina's also had a Social Club and a Booster Club. In addition, it sponsored a chapter of the Catholic Order of Foresters, a life insurance beneficiary society. The St. Vincent De Paul Society, a charitable society, formed a St. Sabina chapter, but was not activated until the Depression. There were several sodalities one could join, such as the Young Ladies' Sodality, the St. Agnes Sodality, a Young Peoples' Club, and the Sacred Heart Confraternity. St. Sabina's also briefly sponsored a Dramatic Club and Parents' Band Club. Through these organizations parishioners, then, had a continuous array of social activities to choose to attend within the parish. They would all have a priest assigned to them as a spiritual director. All seemed to be very successful.[116]

Although it was not a parish-based organization, many members of St. Sabina's belonged to the Auburn Park Knights of Columbus.[117] The KCs were such a popular organization with second and third generation Irish Catholics that the organization was jokingly referred to as the "Caseys." Forty-nine councils had been established in the city between 1886 and 1918 with 25,303 members. To counter the charges Protestants made that Catholics could not be true Americans, the KCs championed both American values and Catholicism. They did this by pledging loyalty to the Constitution and promising to be law-abiding citizens, while making no apologies for their religious practices. The KCs made the most out of the war efforts during World War I to prove their loyalty to the United States. While an Irish-infiltrated organization, the KCs were primarily interested in cultivating Catholic pride and identity.[118] Certainly Catholicism was more central and loomed as a larger issue in the lives of Irish Americans. The comments former parishioners of St. Sabina's made in regard to the Ku Klux Klan and Al Smith demonstrate the immediacy of the question of their faith in American society. The centrality of the parish in their lives also testifies to the prominence of Catholicism in their lives. J. Kill said being Irish was something you just took for granted "because everyone was Irish."[119]

St. Sabina parochial school played a crucial role in the community life of the parish. It was staffed by the Sinsinawa Dominican order, which was founded in America by Rev. Samuel Mazzuchelli in 1849 in Sinsinawa, Wisconsin. The core of the Dominicans' educational mission was religious instruction. Preserving an ethnic culture was not part of their calling.[120]

Parents sent their children to the parochial school for various reasons. T. O'Rourke explained, "People were very supportive of the nuns and priests. . . . I think they [parents] wanted to give you [a religious education]. I think they thought it was their responsibility that we got it. And they thought that the nuns were the ones to give it to us. . . . If the nuns said your daughter ought to take piano lessons, the daughter took piano lessons . . . and if they thought a boy should take violin lessons, he'd take violin lessons." They thought that the nuns, "would do the right thing . . . and they felt sure that they were fulfilling their obligations as parents when they had them in the Catholic school."[121]

"It was almost like it was the thing that was expected," J. Kill said of why people sent their children to the parish school. "There was no comparison made. It was like, you learned God in the Catholic school and you didn't learn God in the public school."[122] H. O'Connor said, "I never even considered sending them [her children] to the public school."[123]

Table 9 on school attendance demonstrates that St. Sabina grade school had almost the unanimous support of the parents in the parish. These figures bear out J. Kill's remark, "I didn't know anybody who went to public schools."[124] Although the figures on public school attendance appear to be estimates, they still reflect the low level of attendance of Catholic children in public schools, even during the Depression.

In addition to religious faith, discipline was a major attraction for parents of school-aged children. Catholic schools emphasized discipline, and Catholic families trusted the nuns to dispense corporal punishment safely and fairly. Because the parents respected the nuns as women with genuine vocations for teaching, they surrendered to them great authority. "In those days," J. Kill explained, "the child didn't go home and say 'The teacher hit me' because he would get hit again by the mother. . . . It was always that the teacher was right." Parents also appreciated the school uniforms, which made it easier to dress children in the mornings, evened out class differences, and restricted what seventh-and eighth-grade girls could do to make their wardrobe appealing to the boys. Discipline was an integral feature of the financial success of St. Sabina's school. The nuns' "perfect discipline," enabled them to educate much larger classes than teachers in modern schools. It was not unusual for there to be as many as fifty students in a classroom at Sabina's. "The nuns told you something," B. DesChatelets recalled, "and that was it—that was the way it was!"[125]

St. Sabina parishioners generally thought that they received a good education. J. Hagerty recalled of the nuns, "They were good teachers. They ran a fine school. You got a very good basic education."[126] J. Kill concurred. "When you went into class, you expected to learn. You really wanted to learn. . . . There was competition, but there was friendly competition, a kind of desire to excel. . . . We used to have . . . competitive scholarship examinations and everybody in the city in eighth grade could take the examination to any school and, then, if you won, you got free tuition. For our family, that was a lot. . . . One nun helped me and I got a scholarship. I got one to St. Rita [High School] and I won one to Quigley [Seminary]. . . . When I was ordained, I remember that nun came to my first mass."[127]

Table 9. Children Attending Grade School in St. Sabina Parish, 1917-1940

	Number at St. Sabina's			Number at Public Schools		
Year	Boys	Girls	Total	Boys	Girls	Total
1917	116	124	240			
1918	137	128	265	8	10	18
1919	200	189	389	5	7	12
1920	221	220	441	6	5	11
1921	249	251	500	5	8	13
1922	290	260	550	16	19	35
1923	290	310	600	- - -	- - -	30
1924	431	419	850	18	11	29
1925	512	464	976	- - -	- - -	- - -
1926	452	449	901	12	12	24
1927	530	485	1,015	24	16	40
1928	544	489	1,033	- - -	- - -	40
1929	602	533	1,135	- - -	- - -	100
1930	595	555	1,150	- - -	- - -	190*
1931	576	568	1,144	- - -	- - -	80
1932	592	548	1,140	- - -	- - -	80
1933	669	572	1,241	- - -	- - -	50
1934	664	568	1,232	- - -	- - -	50
1935	665	575	1,240	- - -	- - -	50
1936	651	569	1,220	- - -	- - -	50
1937	645	589	1,234	- - -	- - -	50
1938	642	588	1,230	- - -	- - -	45
1939	617	571	1,188	- - -	- - -	40
1940	593	584	1,177	- - -	- - -	60

Source: St. Sabina Annual Reports.

* Including high school

The educational level of the sisters in the school was, initially, not very high. Throughout the nineteenth century and even into the 1920s most Dominicans, like their other religious counterparts, were not well-educated or prepared to enter the classroom. Since religious instruction was their primary goal, secular subjects were often neglected. They did not have a college education and they received their teacher training on the job. However, at the turn of the century teaching orders began to address the shortcomings of their education as diocese and states began to demand teacher certification. Initially, convents and motherhouses offered lectures and summer institutes to prepare their sisters for certification. Female religious orders, how-

ever, were prevented from attaining higher education because most
Catholic universities refused to admit women. These institutions only
gradually began to admit women to summer programs. Some Sinsinawa Dominicans enrolled at the University of Wisconsin. Their course
work was usually done on a part-time basis so it often took nearly
twenty years for some to obtain a college education.[128]

Despite their struggle to educate themselves, the Dominicans at
St. Sabina's recognized the value parents placed on education and
did their best to provide a solid one for their students. Sister
Cecilian, who taught at St. Sabina's in the late 1920s and early
1930s, said children in the school won many scholarships in citywide
competitions.[129]

As part of their religious training, the children of the school
received instruction for their First Communion, Confession, and Confirmation—events that took place under the auspices of the clergy
in the church. After their First Communion children were inducted
into the parish's junior societies. The girls became members of the
Children of Mary and the boys were initiated into the junior Holy
Name. Graduation exercises were also held in the church and were
closed with Solemn Benediction of the Blessed Sacrament.[130] "Every
day we had religion in the class," recalled J. Hagerty. "We had cate-
chism and we used to have to recite that. . . . They would always have
the kids marching in the processions. There was a lot of religion."[131]
The major events of a child's early life were church-school related.
There was no escaping the moral authority of parents, nuns in the
school, and the priests in the church. They were all integrated and
mutually supportive.

The parish priests also played a prominent role in the lives of the
school children. J. Kill related that, as an altar boy, "you always used
to have to learn these long Latin prayers and . . . a lot of actions . . . so
the priests spent time every week with the boys and they got to know
the priests better and to heroize them. . . . You wanted to be like them.
In those days in grammar school, other than the White Sox and Father
Damien of the Lepers, parish priests were my heroes."[132]

Nuns and priests were part of the everyday lives of every girl and
boy educated in parochial schools and formed an integral part of their
parish experience. The authority of the nuns over their children was
not restricted to the confines of the parish school. Along with the
priests, they also exercised moral leadership throughout the community. If children were spotted doing something they should not have
been doing anywhere in the neighborhood, residents or local merchants
would often contact the pastor or the principal, who in turn made the
rounds of the classrooms, explaining how good Catholic children should
conduct themselves.[133]

The school educated the children in secular and religious subjects. Its primary goal was to reinforce Catholicism as a central feature of the children's lives. It also served as an important support for the family and integrated the children into world of the parish.

Since the area was largely Catholic, the territorially defined parish community was almost synonymous with the neighborhood. This created close ties with neighborhood institutions and people. "The one thing you always noticed about the South Side of Chicago," said J. Kill, "people always talked in terms of what parish do you belong to and not what street they are from. Nobody would say 'I live around so and so park,' or 'I'm a South Sider' even. They would just say, 'I'm from Sabina's' . . . because they were proud of it. Because it was something special to them." He described the relationship between the parish and the neighborhood: "Father Tom McMahon had an agreement with [Dressel's Bakery] that he got the stale buns for a penny or two the next day. We had a softball league in the summertime . . . and he'd come and give us all the buns. That was just kind of a friendship towards the parish. Everybody was always doing things for the parish."[134]

The small-town ambiance benefited children whether they thought so or not. It was the era of beat policemen, who were of course Irish. People knew them by name from chatting with them while they made their rounds. As a young boy W. Hogan recalled that "they would call your parents if you did something wrong."[135] There were other cheerier aspects of neighborliness for kids, however. Ice skating at Foster Park was popular. When the weather would hover between 32 and 34 degrees, kids were unsure of whether the ice was still frozen. One home that had a view of the park served as the local weather station. "There was a number that everybody knew they could call to see if the ice was frozen," related J. Kill. "The number had to get called two hundred times a day at that time, and never did you get a smart answer or a harsh answer or a quit bothering me. Never knew who the people were. . . . You would call and they would say, 'Yes, they're skating over there. Yeah, you can come up.' "[136]

There was a definite feeling among those who lived in the parish during the 1930s and 1940s that the parish was a community. Through parish activities people claimed, "We knew everybody." The sense that they knew everyone around them was one of the most enduring memories of the parish. Nostalgia, no doubt, in part accounts for these sentiments. It is well to remember, however, that this was also a time before television, air conditioning, and individual automobile ownership segregated people into private spaces. On summer evenings during the Depression most people sat on their front porches or strolled through the neighborhood. "Visiting" with neighbors was one of the delights of daily living.[137]

"The Irish liked that sociability," T. O'Rourke stated. "My mother would go around visiting with all these women . . . and they'd do it any time of the day or night. There was no formal invitation. . . . It was very important [to be a close family]. My mother and father didn't have any brothers or sisters in the parish, but they had very close friends, some of them were from . . . the same part of Ireland. They made a big deal of them. . . . There was always the children in the same grade or in the same confirmation class. It was a big event for the kids. . . . Baptism, of course, they'd have family parties, and I think the Irish kind of liked that."[138]

St. Sabina parish was supported by a diverse commercial strip. "79th Street was a busy thoroughfare," recalled one parishioner. "It had everything from the obstetrician to the mortician. They didn't have to go any further. . . . All the doctors were there. All kinds of specialty shops, women's clothing, men's clothing. . . . They knew the butchers and the grocers and all . . . and often they were members of the parish, too. . . . I think they got to know all of them. . . . It was a very social place."[139]

"I'd say probably 90 percent of the shopping that the family did was right along 79th Street," said B. DesChatelets. "Back then you lived along 79th Street. All of the stores you needed were there. And with St. Sabina's, this was especially true. . . . You didn't have to go far. We had a class reunion not too long ago and . . . we went down 79th Street and we went down Racine and named the stores that were there. That's how steady the stores were."[140]

J. Kill remembered the hospitality parishioners extended to each other. When the new church was dedicated "the crowd was such that it came all the way out the front doors, all the way across the street and overflowed into our house. . . . People came right through our house. I remember when we went to eat dinner, there were strangers there who were eating off our table that had been to mass. We just shared everything with them."[141]

While exceedingly toned-down from practices in pre-famine Ireland, observing the death of a parishioner was a community occasion. In the 1920s wakes were still held in the home of the deceased. The women would sit in the front room while the men often occupied other rooms or the doorstoops. Sandwiches and beer were served to visitors. By the 1930s funeral parlors became the scene of wakes. They were held over a three-day period. While there was no eating or drinking at the funeral home, visitors stayed two and three hours. Part of the attraction of staying so long was to visit with the parade of neighbors and friends, which often turned such gatherings into boisterous occasions. Every time a priest came in, which could be quite frequently, everyone dropped to their knees to say prayers for the dead. W. Hogan remembered thinking at his father's wake that he could not bear it "if one more priest came in" and he'd have to drop to his knees one more time. Funeral masses were often crowded with mourners "dressed to the 'T' in 'ceremonial' black.[142]

"It was nice to live in St. Sabina's," E. Clair said. "The people were cordial, cooperated with each other, above the normal standard. . . . I don't know why, but facts are facts."[143] "They were outgoing," concurred J. Hagerty of the Irish in St. Sabina's.[144] "I would say it was a unified parish," said M. Dunne. "For a neighbor in trouble or a neighbor with a problem, my mother would be right over there if there was something to be done."[145]

While St. Sabina's was a tight-knit community, tensions did exist. J. Kill regretfully remembered that "the only reason we moved out was the lady who lived next door to us was nuts . . . My mother had a son, a priest. . . . This woman had a son who was studying to be a priest and he was in an accident. One leg became shorter than the other. In those days, they wouldn't let you continue. So he tried a couple of seminaries. He finally went to the Trappists and died at the Trappists. Well, she was mad that we could have a son be a priest and she couldn't. So she did crazy things. For instance, you'd go out to clean your gutters and put up your ladder. She'd come out and say the bottom foot and a half of the ladder was on her property and take an ax and start to chop down the ladder while you were on top. . . . Anyone who came to our house was bad because we were the bad guys. So she would chase them with a broom and crazy things like that. Well, she was so annoying that we finally had to move out. . . . We would have lived there forever. My mother always wanted to go back until she died."[146]

The building of St. Sabina's from a store-front mission on a muddy prairie to a large and vibrant community in an English Gothic church created an enduring sense of camaraderie among the parishioners as well as with the clergy. Together they had built something that reflected their devotions to family, community, ethnicity, and religion. In the nation's second largest city, they had created a neighborhood with the feel of a small town. But Sabina's also had some of the narrowness that was part of small-town life. People were channeled into accepting the same values and doing the same things. Individual spiritual expression and free thinking were not encouraged. "It was a strict society," related W. Hogan.[147] By defining the parish community by geographic limits, involvement in larger issues or other neighborhoods was discouraged.[148]

The confining features of parish Catholicism are seldom mentioned in the memories of those who built St. Sabina's. More typical is J. Kill's claim that "it was one of those parishes that was like a gem. Everybody loved it. . . . I'm proud of having been a part of it."[149] "It was a kind part of our life," said E. Clair wistfully. "There are still a few people around to meet every once in a while, mostly at wakes."[150]

During this period between the World Wars, the parish continued to be the focal point of the Irish Catholic community on the South Side of Chicago. St. Sabina's was generally composed of people of common national origin bound together by the same religion, who continued to share similar work experiences. St. Sabina parishioners were devoted to their local church and zealously applied themselves to recreating a parish community they had known in their old neighborhoods. They were generous with both their money and their time to achieve this goal. This is evidenced by the financial health of the parish, even during the Depression. The devotional Catholicism that they followed further reinforced the centrality of the parish. In addition, they supported with large numbers a rich parish-centered organizational life of devotions, service, and sociability. The parish school, which educated nearly all the children, reinforced the bonds between children, parents, and the parish. Neither the prosperity of the 1920s nor the Great Depression of the 1930s interrupted parish community building. On the contrary, they both seemed to reinforce it. The modest wealth of parishioners ensured their ability to erect a church-school plant, and the decision to finish the main church despite economically adverse times rallied the people once again around a common goal. J. Kill best summarized the relationship Catholics had with the parish when he said, "The church was like . . . a part of your family."[151]

The "parish" had its cultural precedent in Ireland and was reinforced in the United States by immigrant needs and a hostile host society. Nativist outbursts in the 1920s reminded Catholics of their marginality in American life. However, after World War I American Catholics embarked upon a period of increasing confidence, and behaved in a manner that historian Ed Kantowicz has called "easy arrogance."[152] From the bishops' office down to the parish level, Catholics began to celebrate their own culture as American Catholics. As a familiar institution the parish was a natural expression of Catholic pride as well as a shelter. Besides being proud that the Catholic Church helped to make America a more pluralistic society, Chicago Irish Catholics could also look with a sense of pride and accomplishment to their arrival in city hall with the Kelly-Nash regime in 1933. By the end of this period Irish Catholics in the city had their man in the mayor's office and a Cardinal of national stature. Who of them could help but look eagerly to the future?

4

Ticket to Heaven: Community and Religion at St. Sabina's, 1940 to 1960

The pride and confidence that Catholic America acquired after the First World War remained unshaken by the Second and continued to grow in the next decades. The postwar economic boom and the GI Bill of Rights provided greater opportunities for white Catholics to move up the economic and social ladder. By the mid-1950s the Catholic Church in America was primarily middle class. Other ethnic groups were now joining the ever increasing Irish and German middle class. Their new economic position created a need to reshape Catholicism to reflect their higher status and greater sophistication. "A parish is not only a mass of people living together, but a group of human hearts united by collective woes and joys," wrote *The Seraph*, a parish publication, in the mid-1950s.[1] This generation of clergy, intellectuals, and laity not only sought to demonstrate the superiority and grandeur of Catholicism, but they also believed American society desperately needed the benefits of Catholic religion and culture in this troubled modern world. Catholicism, they believed, could save American society and the world.[2]

As for their relationship with Protestant America, the Great Depression and the war had helped alleviate some tensions between the religious groups through common suffering and a common cause. Mixing with other Christians in the military and the work force helped dispel mutual misconceptions.[3] Catholics enjoyed greater acceptance in American society than they ever had before. However, the ecumenical movement had not yet arrived. A theological cold war of hostility and suspicion remained. And Catholics *wanted* to be separate and distinct from their traditional foes. They preferred their own religious culture and hoped to instruct the rest of America on its merits.

Many thought Catholicism had the unique ability to combat "Communism [and] Worldliness and Secularism."[4] While American Catholics, like their fellow compatriots after World War II, feared and loathed Communism, many, like St. Sabina parishioners, saw Catholicism as the best champion of the anti-Communist cause. "Every thoughtful person realizes that American citizenship under the present system of government is a precious privilege. . . . Ours is rapidly becoming the one great country which, like the church, will be able to champion the cause of the individual."[5]

These "enemies" of the Church could be combated at the parish level. Communism was particularly feared because, according to the parish bulletin, a Communist was "not interested in morality. He esteems as good that which brings him material happiness and as evil that which stands in the way of his physical desires."[6] Parishioners, though, were still encouraged to take a Christian attitude toward their "wayward" brethren. "Love all people," wrote Father William J. Quinlan in *The Seraph*. "We tend to hate the A.P.A. [American Protective Association], the Communists and the like, but Christ died for all."[7] For a religious group that was accused of foreign allegiance to the pope in the nineteenth century and, therefore, ill-equipped to be a full-fledged member in a democratic American society, Catholics, who had never really doubted their ability to be good citizens, resolved this seeming dilemma by identifying as common the values of the Church and America. They thought that, if anything, Catholicism could edify American society.

Catholics even possessed unique weapons to fight Communism. In *The Seraph* St. Sabina parishioners were instructed that "daily Mass is the most powerful weapon we Catholics have. The Rosary, another very important means the Blessed Mother gave us to save the world must be said daily. When the world turns to Her, there will be everlasting peace. Do your part and help convert Russia."[8]

In Chicago, the flowering of Catholic religious pride coincided with political success. Almost a hundred years after they arrived in the city, the Irish finally got a firm grip on city hall when Edward J. Kelly succeeded Anton Cermak as mayor in 1933. They kept control through the Richard J. Daley reign which ended in 1976. Being an Irish Catholic in the city now had some prestige.[9]

Under the tutelage of Monsignor William Gorey, who became pastor in 1942 following Monsignor Egan's death, and that of Monsignor John McMahon, who assumed Sabina's pastorate in 1952 when Monsignor Gorey suddenly died of a heart attack, St. Sabina's parishioners retained much of their old-style, parish-centered Catholicism. This was fortified by new ideas of Catholicism's place in the United States. Although Catholics were confidently asserting the value of their religion in national life, this "new" thinking still encouraged an exclusive mentality toward others. Catholicism was to lead by example rather than to reach out beyond the community of faith.

The growing confidence of St. Sabina parishioners was encour-

Table 10. Occupations in St. Sabina Parish, 1957-1963

Occupation		%
High white collar	211	8
Low white collar	930	37
Blue collar skilled	642	25
Blue collar semiskilled	731	29
Unskilled	18	1
TOTAL	2,532	

Source: St. Sabina Parish Census.

aged by the economic prosperity that followed the Second World War. The population of Auburn-Gresham grew by 6 percent from 1940 to 1950, to a total of 60,978, which remained steady for the next decade.[10] Many of these new residents were upwardly mobile Catholics from older city neighborhoods. St. Sabina's family membership increased by 58 percent, growing from two thousand in 1935 to 3,478 by 1957.[11]

The postwar generation of St. Sabina's showed some occupational advances (Table 10). Whereas low white-collar workers had accounted for 27 percent of the workers in the founding population, they composed a full 37 percent of the workers in the postwar parish population. Skilled blue-collar workers, however, who had constituted 23 percent of workers in the founding population, accounted for only 25 percent of the postwar workers in the parish. Many parishioners continued to share similar job experiences, and the basic character of the parish did not change substantially.

The wealth of the parish rose considerably. Both the parish as a whole and individual families prospered during this time. From 1930 to 1960 the number of families in the parish increased by 46 percent. The Sunday and holy day collections, however, rose by 77 percent.[12]

Rather than allowing it to erode parish solidarity, prosperity was used to reinforce it. The parish was seen as a vehicle for mutual monetary support. In January 1953 St. Sabina's initiated a credit union. Its twelve-member board of directors, chosen by parishioners, presided over an operating budget of a quarter million dollars and 732 members.[13] Parishioners benefited from low-interest loans and free life insurance policies. The credit union also aimed to strengthen the parish. In 1952 *The Seraph* wrote of the credit union: "It will not only be a means of improving the financial situation of the individual, but it will be a common bond for strengthening the loyalty of all its members toward all parish activities."[14] The credit union also demonstrated Catholicism's compatibility with democratic organizations. According to *The Seraph*, it made "St. Sabina's more splendid in its achievements of putting democracy to work by reaching down and asking and receiving the help of everyone in various parish endeavors."[15]

Another indication of the upwardly mobile aspirations tied to parish life was the annual Marion Cotillion, which began in 1960. All girls from the parish who were graduating from high school and their families were invited. The event was held at the elegant South Shore Country Club, and the "Daughters of Mary" were presented to the bishop, escorted by a full-dress honor guard of the Knights of Columbus.[16] The event was quite successful, although some parishioners thought a debutante ball was a bit "hoity-toity."[17]

Parish-defined neighborhoods became standardized as Chicago's South Side expanded. Not only did Catholics refer to their neighborhoods by the Catholic church, but their high profile in this area of Chicago forced others to follow suit. For example, the local newspaper, the *Southtown Economist*, catered to this penchant by advertising property in its real estate section by parish. Captions read "St. Sabina Two-Flat" or "Little Flower Bungalow."

Even realtors recognized the importance of knowing what parish a home was in. T. O'Rourke related, "I knew a Jewish man . . . in real estate. To know what [a piece of property] was like . . . he would ask 'What parish is it in?'. . . . He said one of the first things that *he* had to determine when he moved from one neighborhood to another was what parish *he* was in. And everybody referred to the parishes even if they never went into the churches. So it was used to identify a section of the city."[18]

Even Protestants were impressed by the imposing aspect of the Catholic parishes. J. Nelligan was among the few graduates from St. Sabina grade school who attended the public high school, Calumet (referred to by Catholics as Our Lady of Calumet). He recalled the following incident. At an after-school function, one boy asked another where he was from. The young man said he was from St. Ethelreda's. He, however, made the mistake of saying it within earshot of his father, who was a Protestant minister. When his astonished father asked him why he said he was from a Catholic parish, the son replied, "If I gave them my address, no one would know what I was talking about."[19] It was not uncommon for others not affiliated with a Catholic parish to use them for residential identification. It was also an acknowledgment of Catholic dominance in the area.

For the younger generation, naming neighborhoods for parishes was as natural as breathing. "I was taught as a youngster growing up that the parish was an identity in itself," related G. Hendry. "In Sabina's . . . there were so many "refugees" . . . people from 'Vis' [Visitation] and Gabriel's who had identified with their parish so . . . it was

Table 11. Children Attending School in St. Sabina Parish, 1942-1960

Year	Number at St. Sabina's	Number at Public School	Year	Number at St. Sabina's	Number at Public School
1942	1,155	75	1952	1,075	71
1943	1,102	120	1953	1,103	55
1944	1,125	116	1954	1,090	60
1945	1,080	104	1955	1,083	58
1946	1,095	144	1956	1,083	46
1947	1,048	100	1957	1,033	65
1948	1,080	108	1958	1,027	62
1949	1,074	99	1959	1,024	68
1950	1,086	90	1960	1,015	46
1951	1,070	67			

Source: St. Sabina Annual Reports.

an absolute evolution of tradition and heritage. . . . It was not spoken, but since time immemorium this has happened."[20]

Catholics still remained institutionally separate from other religious groups. "Those days were the last vestiges of . . . the fortress mentality—'them against us,'" said G. Hendry. "You didn't know Protestants. . . . It was a self-protective Catholicity."[21] "All of my close friends were Catholic," recalled J. Nelligan. "As we got older, we probably did less with [Protestants] because I think their activities were probably with their churches."[22]

As Table 11 demonstrates, most children from St. Sabina attended the parish school, perpetuating the institutional segregation of young people in the neighborhood. As Table 12 shows, the rate of mixed marriages remained approximately the same as for the 1916 to 1941 era. Most Catholics were still marrying other Catholics.

The clergy also encouraged the separation of religious groups. In *The Seraph* Catholics were alerted to the activities of Protestant organizations. In 1959 under the caption "Good Reading," parishioners were encouraged to examine an article in *Our Sunday Visitor* regarding POAU, Protestants and Other Americans United for separation of church and state. "POAU is one of the largest anti-Catholic organizations in the United States," it warned. "You should be aware of the activities of this organization."[23]

On the local level, Catholic pastors in the area clashed with the Auburn Park YMCA. When the "Y" showed the films "Human Growth" and "Human Reproduction," Catholic pastors protested. The films did not conform to Catholic teachings on sexuality. The YMCA board slighted the pastors by refusing to even respond to their letter of

Table 12. Marriages at St. Sabina's, 1940-1959

Year	Number within Faith	Number outside Faith	Total Marriages	% Marrying outside Faith
1940	208	17	225	8
1941	158	31	189	16
1942	134	13	147	9
1943	92	11	103	11
1944	90	14	104	13
1945	94	13	107	12
1946	170	23	193	12
1947	220	16	236	7
1948	166	21	187	11
1949	138	16	154	10
TOTAL	1,472	175	1,647	11
1950	190	12	202	6
1951	210	9	219	4
1952	130	21	151	14
1953	190	18	208	9
1954	152	9	161	6
1955	168	13	181	7
1956	166	20	180	11
1957	162	9	171	5
1958	132	14	146	10
1959	156	9	165	5
TOTAL	1,656	134	1,790	7

Source: St. Sabina Annual Reports.

complaint. When the Y then embarked on a fund drive in the neighborhood, this affront was not forgotten. *The Seraph* wrote: "The announcement of this campaign reminded us of the unceremonious fashion in which the management of the local branch dumped into the wastebasket as unworthy of a reply the combined protests of all the Catholic pastors . . . when the sex films . . . were shown at the Auburn Park 'Y.' The contempt shown for the wishes of the twenty thousand Catholic families which comprise the parishes represented . . . must not be overlooked." St. Sabina parishioners were forbidden to contribute to the organization. "It is time to renew our warning that the YMCA is a Protestant Church organization and teaches the Protestant religion in its classes. Catholics . . . may not belong to it nor support it."[24]

Besides avoiding the Y, Catholics were also instructed to stay away from Protestant churches. *The Seraph* printed an excerpt from a pastoral letter from Samuel Cardinal Stritch with guidelines for their relationship with Protestants and attendance at their services. The Cardinal wrote of the Catholic Church: "She and she alone is the true Church of Jesus Christ. . . . ACCORDINGLY, IT IS UNDERSTOOD THAT THE FAITHFUL OF THE CATHOLIC CHURCH MAY NOT IN ANY CAPACITY ATTEND THE ASSEMBLIES OF COUNCILS OF NON-CATHOLICS SEEKING TO PROMOTE UNITY OF THE CHURCH. We ask you, however, to pray for our separated brothers and to beg God to give them the gift of Catholic faith."[25] So, Catholics and Protestants maintained their social and institutional separation in the neighborhoods in which they coexisted.

Devotionalism continued to be the chief means of energizing and purifying the individual and the soul against evil in the world. It still played a key role in enhancing the parish's central position in the community as well as shaping members' views of the world beyond its boundaries. The Mass was the most important devotional feature of the parish and of Catholicism. "In the Catholic Church," Father Tom McMahon instructed, "the important thing . . . is the consecration of the Mass. That's what brings people to the church. That's the focal point. They wouldn't come to hear just a sermon. That's why you have a thousand . . . in Catholic Churches for every mass."[26] "In our family," recalled J. Nelligan, "we went to mass even on Saturdays. . . . We went to mass every day during Lent."[27]

It is impossible to know the percentage of people who regularly attended mass. Yet from the number of services offered, it is quite clear that St. Sabina's priests accommodated the desire of most of their flock to frequently partake of the Eucharist. By 1957, St. Sabina's 3,478 families were served by eleven Sunday masses, seven in the upper church and four in the old basement hall. For three of these services, two masses were being said simultaneously. Six choirs sang for the different masses. That there were five masses each weekday demonstrates the support many St. Sabina parishioners gave to daily devotions. Mass attendees on holy days of obligation had ten masses to choose from; seven masses were held on first Fridays of the month for those who wanted to fulfill the nine consecutive monthly devotion.[28] Clearly, a large majority of parishioners adhered to the devotional expectations of their Church.

Since the Mass was so central to Catholic devotions it made the strongest impression on parishioners of all ages and sexes. They loved the beauty and grandeur it brought into their ordinary lives. "You felt the magnificence of the Church," G. Hendry reminisced. "The Mass in Latin . . . the Latin songs . . . Catholics bound themselves together by a universal language. It gave you the feeling that it was holy. That it was Catholic. It was one. . . . And the beauty of it . . . its quietude, the solemnity, the reverence. . . . That's one thing I can't forget."[29]

For the boys in the parish, serving mass provided many opportunities. "Being an altar boy tied you right into [parish devotions] because you were very active. The funerals you'd go to [to] get out of school. The weddings which would give you some spending money and you'd go to the candy store right after it."[30] "As an altar boy, we served mass a lot and went to the novenas," said J. Nelligan.[31] Novenas, though, were arduous for altar boys. "It was tedious as an altar boy to do that because you were holding the cross and it would kill you. The candle would be worse. The cross was heavy but you could set it down. The candle you had to hold up all the time."[32]

Other regular devotions included the veneration of the Blessed Sacrament on Friday afternoons. The Sorrowful Mother Novenas continued with five services each Friday. "During Lent [novenas] were the big thing, and my Dad would go quite a bit," G. Hendry recollected. "He would drag me along unwillingly."[33] First Saturdays of the month, which traditionally were associated with Marion devotions, were "Our Lady of Fatima Day." This observance was inspired by the apparition of the Blessed Mother in the Portuguese village of Fatima. The cult of Fatima received papal endorsement in 1942. In Sabina's Fatima's message of prayer and repentance was observed with a holy hour in the morning. One of the specific prayer requests was for the conversion of Russia. As the Cold War heated up in the late 1940s and 1950s, this devotion became part of anti-Communist furor. Before Vatican II Friday was, of course, a day of abstinence from meat. The dominance of Catholic culture in this area of Chicago and the need to find alternatives to tuna casserole prompted the *Southtown Economist* to solicit and print recipes for nonmeat meals. Prizes were often awarded for the most original dish.[34]

St. Sabina parishioners were encouraged to attend the various services. Monsignor McMahon wrote his flock in *The Seraph*: " Ponder often during the month on the justice of God and the evil of sin. Bear those daily crosses that come to us and never let an opportunity go by to attend daily Mass and to receive daily Communion, to say the rosary and do everything to make your soul as perfect as possible, as ready as can be to enter the beautiful presence of our Holy God."[35] He also encouraged them to go to confession frequently: "Like all the Sacraments, its primary purpose is to give us grace. Go to Confession often for the beauty treatment it gives the soul. It takes away sin and it strengthens the soul with new fresh grace. To gain all the plenary indulgences for ourselves and the Souls in Purgatory, we should go to Confession every two weeks."[36]

"In those days," Father McMahon related, "we emphasized that you're supposed to live a life of grace in favor of God. So keep yourself in a state of grace. Don't have any sin on your soul. You'd go to confession and get the absolution for the sin and an increase in sanctifying graces."[37]

"Part of living [in the parish] was going to confession every Saturday," J. Nelligan said. He, however, would often go to the next parish west. Besides receiving absolution, there were certain considerations to be made when receiving the sacrament, such as which priest to go to. "We used to go to Little Flower and Father Warmser— better known as 'Hail Mary' Warmser," he said. "The line for Father Warmser was as you walked in the door. And there might be one or two novices that didn't know any better that were waiting in the short lines. . . . You would . . . be out of confession before they were, even though there were twenty-five people ahead of you. . . . He use to say 'Come on, move it along.' "[38]

During this era, St. Sabina's also introduced Block Rosary groups. Parishioners were encouraged to take turns inviting men and women on their block to their homes one evening a week to say the rosary. An advertisement in *The Seraph* for the gathering proclaimed: "Praying together you will do the world a lot of good and you will become better neighbors. Add yours to the growing number of distinguished blocks in St. Sabina Parish with the Block Rosary."[39]

Another community devotion that began during this time was the Pilgrim Virgin. The devotion began in Portugal in 1946. Since most of the faithful could not make a pilgrimage to Fatima to pray to the Blessed Virgin, a statue of Our Lady of Fatima was fashioned to bring the benefits of the shrine to Catholics the world over. In 1954 Cardinal Stritch allowed the lay organization, the Ambassador of Mary, to promote the devotion in Chicago.[40]

St. Sabina parish was given the rare opportunity of hosting the Pilgrim Virgin perpetually. The statue was installed in the lower church for one week and then moved each week from one home to the next. Parishioners were required to register with an "ambassador" to have the statue and the devotion come to their home. Names and addresses were printed in *The Seraph* and nearby neighbors were encouraged to visit the host family.[41]

B. DesChatelets described the practice. "We had a Pilgrim Virgin that just went around St. Sabina parish. . . . It would go from one home to the other. . . . We'd go up to Sabina's, and meet on Saturday night. Then we'd go to whatever house it was at. We'd say the rosary. We'd pick it up and we'd carry it to the next house and say the rosary and leave it there for the week. . . . The people that had it in their house, every night at seven o'clock . . . would have all the neighbors come and say the rosary with them. There were a lot of people in the Pilgrim

Virgin."[42] *The Seraph* reported, "Our people in St. Sabina's are so devoted to Our Blessed Lady that many of them have had the Pilgrim Virgin visit their home with some most pleasing results. . . . Perhaps one of the most pleasing by-products is the spirit of neighborliness and helpfulness which has developed."[43]

Other community devotions, such as Forty Hours in the fall, Advent, Lenten observances, and May Crownings of the Blessed Virgin, marked the seasons for Catholics. Forty Hours devotion was "the high spot in the calendar of any parish."[44] It began with a solemn High Mass, and then the Blessed Sacrament was exposed for forty hours before a continuous succession of worshipers. It closed with another High Mass. The benefits of the practice were explained in *The Seraph*: " A plenary indulgence may be gained once a day by those who receive Confession and Communion either during the Forty Hours, a week before or a week after and recite the Our Father, Hail Mary, and Glory Be to the Father five times and an additional Our Father, Hail Mary and Glory Be to the Father for the intention of the Pope. A partial indulgence of fifteen years may be granted for each visit."[45]

The practice of parish missions, begun in the nineteenth century, continued to be a familiar feature of life in St. Sabina's. Their purpose was to revive flagging religious feelings and devotional practices. In 1954, twelve hundred to thirteen hundred women and girls attended their portion of the mission, and the men and boys were counted in the hundreds for theirs.[46]

St. Sabina parishioners were responsive to entreaties that they be diligent in their religious observances. Sunday services were crowded. They were so jammed that parishioners were scolded in *The Seraph* for failing to accept the ushers' direction for seating. "Each of us should accept the ushers' guidance to a seat and move all the way in so that no one will be denied an opportunity to worship God under the best available conditions."[47]

Devotionalism was a means to greater union with Christ. However, it could often lull devotees into thinking they were living a virtuous life simply by adhering to rules and going to devotions. This danger did not escape pastors who warned their parishioners not to become complacent in their spiritual lives. Monsignor Gorey, who succeeded Monsignor Egan after his death in 1942, had cautioned his flock: "Catholics are sometimes befuddled in the matter of their obligations and delude themselves into believing that they are living virtuously if they merely attend mass, novena, Holy Hour, a sodality meeting, use the missal and subscribe to a church publication. They forget that the two great commandments, which contain the whole law and the prophets are, Thou shalt love the Lord thy God, and Thou shalt love thy neighbor as thy self."[48]

Parishioners were also reprimanded for coming late to mass and leaving early. However, the priests were generally pleased with their charges. In January 1955 on the Feast of the Holy Family Monsignor McMahon praised families in the parish: "Despite the fact that our families are numerous (over 3,000 units), nevertheless, juvenile delinquency is a negligible factor in our midst. It is rare that a case is sent to us from the courts. . . . A parish that sends every year, at least five to ten young people to the religious life, that has so many Confessions and Communions among young people, that is teeming with activities that occupy their minds and bodies! Such a parish is not on the downgrade"![49]

The ubiquitous devotional activities in the parish had the profound effect of making religion something that had to be reckoned with and the parish a strong psychological force in the lives of individuals. "The solidness and the strictness of the faith [we practice]," said D. Foertsch, "has been my main sustenance for life with all the tragedies that have happened since."[50] "There was a big support system," agreed G. Hendry.[51] "I really got my religion at Sabina's," confided B. DesChatelets. "It was there. You went to church every Sunday. I don't know if it became habit. . . . I can't say that I was ever that wild about going . . . when I was younger. But, I guess I make up for it a little now."[52]

St. Sabina's organizational life of confraternities, sodalities, and social clubs expanded and enjoyed great support. They helped maintain the parish's position in the Catholic community. "If there was something worthwhile, Sabina's did have it," related D. Foertsch. "If you wanted an organization . . . the pastor would say, 'That's fine, go ahead' . . . and they'd give you a chaplain."[53]

The Holy Name Society of St. Sabina continued to be a vital organization in the parish and was one of the leading chapters in the Archdiocese. The Society proudly proclaimed in *The Seraph* that "St. Sabina has enjoyed an enviable reputation amongst other parishes in the archdiocese in almost all its undertakings. One of this parish's strongest pillars has been the Holy Name Society."[54]

In 1951 the men's confraternity claimed twelve hundred members on its rolls. On their Easter Communion mass, seven hundred men received the sacrament together. During the rest of the year the attendance at the Holy Name Communion masses averaged five hundred.[55]

The Society, however, was not always satisfied with this usual turnout. The spiritual director and officers continually admonished the men of the parish to do their duty, suggesting that "they don't realize they are throwing away an opportunity to gain a plenary indulgence every month, and many other partial indulgences. We can think of nothing more pertinent to a man's business than his salvation. It should be his first order of business. And the Holy Name Society could very easily be the means of saving his soul."[56]

In 1955 the Society began the practice of marching into church together for the Communion mass. Members arrived fifteen minutes before mass so they could "form for the march into Church behind the Holy Name banner." Besides gaining them an indulgence, marching together was "most edifying to others in attendance."[57] Some Sunday masses were reserved for fathers to receive Communion with their sons, with their daughters, and with their wives on Mothers' Day. Members were praised for their turn-outs on these occasions. "We always have an exceptional turn-out when we have a Father-Daughter Communion Sunday," *The Seraph* boasted.[58] Every January the Holy Name Society held a Communion Sunday Breakfast following the eight o'clock mass.[59]

The St. Sabina Holy Name Society worked for various parish concerns. They had a Youth Committee, a Sick and Vigil Committee which remembered ailing members in their prayers and provided transportation for those who could not get to the communion masses; a Literature Committee that recommended "good" Catholic books to the parish; and a Military Committee that encouraged parishioners to write to parish boys in the service and to remember them in their prayers. The Society also sent the servicemen rosaries along with a subscription to *The Seraph* to keep them abreast of parish news.[60] Every year the Society participated in a retreat at Mayslake in the western suburbs and "for several years St. Sabina has been the leading parish in attendance," averaging one hundred retreatants.[61]

The Holy Name Society reflected the philosophy that parish devotional and communal practices and organizations were major avenues to salvation for the individual, the preserver of the sanctity of the family, and even a means to save the country. World peace, they claimed, "depends largely on the power of family participation in Mass attendance, the family Rosary, and other holy endeavors."[62] On another occasion they wrote, "A good Holy Name man is a credit to his church, his community and the nation."[63]

The women's Altar and Rosary Society had even greater success than the Holy Name Society in membership and attendance at their meetings and functions. In June 1956 the women's society reported an enrollment of 1,525 and the officers expressed satisfaction at the turn-outs for their events.[64]

The organization's main purpose was to "Promote the Family Rosary, attend Daily Mass and receive communion more frequently."[65] "The biggest push was for the spiritual life of yourself and the family," stated M. Joyce. "And to do that meant emphasizing daily mass."[66] During Lent the women's confraternity established a Daily Mass Guild for the entire parish.[67] Even third graders joined, promising to attend the 8:30 A.M. mass.68 Daily mass was also promoted during the month of May "to show our devotion to the Immaculate Heart of Mary."[69]

In addition to its main purpose of public devotion and worship, the Altar and Rosary Society engaged in charitable work. It organized a St. Vincent Orphanage Sewing Unit and a Medical Mission group. "We had a bench where we worked for the Medical Missions. We sewed articles to send overseas to the missions."[70] Members also annually assisted the TB Mobile Unit of the Tuberculosis Institute X-ray Survey. In 1956 the TB Unit presented "an award to the Altar and Rosary for meritorious work."[71] The Society also hosted a monthly Sabina night at the local USO. They provided food and entertainment. In February 1956 "turkey dinners were served and thoroughly enjoyed by 500 servicemen. A fine representation from the parish helped to make the men feel at home."[72]

Members of the Altar and Rosary Society acted as ushers at the novenas and at the funerals of their departed members. "When we had a deceased parishioner, as blocks we used to go to the wake and say the rosary. . . . At one time I was promoter for the Altar and Rosary and on our block I used to call on twenty adult women. . . . We used to wear our badges . . . for a funeral . . . and we would all stand the guard of honor [for deceased members] on each side of the pews towards the back and follow after the casket."[73] Society members also staffed a parish religious goods store located in a room off from the lower church. Missals, bibles, rosaries, medals, books, pictures, and statues were for sale on Fridays.

Unlike the Holy Name Society, which was a centralized diocesan organization, the Altar and Rosary Society was strictly parochial. While Cardinal Mundelein was head of the Chicago Diocese, many Catholic women had written letters to *The New World* petitioning the Cardinal for their own centralized organization similar to the Holy Name Society. In February 1931 the Archdiocesan Council of Catholic Women (ACCW) was formed. It, however, never had a clearly defined purpose or function. Initially, Mundelein encouraged the women to engage in charitable work. His suggestion was coolly received from the women who were looking for a less traditional and a more challenging mission. Their spiritual director, Bishop Sheil, who was working to make Catholicism more "muscular," was not of any more help to the women in defining their organization's objectives. The ACCW was left to grope for its own reason for being.[74]

While all women's parish groups, such as the Altar and Rosary Society and the Mothers' Club, were automatically members in the

ACCW, St. Sabina's societies did not federate with the new organization until 1943.[75] When Samuel Cardinal Stritch succeeded Mundelein in 1942, he helped give the ACCW new direction. Among his first mandates to the Catholic women of his archdiocese was to engage them in the Decency Campaign. They were to survey literature in their local newsstands and magazine distributors and compare them to the list of acceptable reading material as established by the Catholic Episcopal Committee of the National Organization for Decent Literature (NODL). The NODL was founded by the U.S. Catholic bishops in 1938 to provide an instrument to protect young people from being exposed to morally, socially, and intellectually harmful publications, such as magazines and pocket-sized books. Objectionable materials glamorized crime, described how to commit criminal acts, advocated disrespect for lawful authority, exploited cruelty and violence, contained sexually offensive materials and pictures, carried advertising that promoted harmful products, used offensive language, or ridiculed any national, religious, or racial group.

Stritch warned: " 'It is not enough for Catholic women today to devote themselves to making their own families Catholic. They have to protect their families against certain influences which prevail in their communities and in society. The real test of our lay women's apostolate is going to be what is this organization doing to Christianize contemporary society."[76] He urged the women to approach "the retailers within their parish boundaries and secure their cooperation for the protection of the morality of youth."[77]

Throughout the 1950s St. Sabina's women worked to fulfill this mandate. "We were allocated different areas," said M. Joyce. "I went to 63rd and Halsted with another friend to go and appeal to the different places that sold magazines."[78] The women were able to persuade many shopowners to conform to the standards set by the NODL. In 1959 they had persuaded at least ten merchants, primarily drug store proprietors, to give them their complete cooperation.[79]

The willingness of women to join the crusade and their success demonstrates not only the confidence Catholics had in their ability to contribute, as Catholics, to American society, but also the imposing stature of the parish in the neighborhood. It also reveals their worldview. This world was a battleground between good and evil in which there were constant threats and dangers to one's soul. Personal moral problems required a response from the parish.[80]

Other organizations in the parish were the St. Vincent De Paul Society, which engaged in charitable work; Third Order of St. Dominic; Mother Most Pure Sodality for high-school girls, whose aim was both spiritual and social. Father Robert McClory was their chaplain and was amazed at their interest in the sodality. Before coming to St.

Sabina's he had been assigned to a parish in the exclusive North Shore suburb of Winnetka, where he had felt lucky to interest ten to twelve teenagers in a discussion group. He found the exact opposite situation in St. Sabina's. He said, "They had the high-school girls' sodality. [They] would have a communion mass and communion breakfast . . . once a month. And there would be 180 girls there. And you're stupefied! You'd say 'How did they get them? How did they get all these girls to come to mass and communion and come over and have talks?' . . . The girls organized this themselves! You didn't have to do anything."[81]

St. Sabina's also hosted the Sacred Heart League, also known as the Apostleship of Prayer.[82] Those joined together were to remember all members' intentions and "to channel through the League the prayers and spiritual activities of all members."[83] These intentions were sometimes tallied in *The Seraph*. For example, for the month of February in 1960, 260 acts of charity were performed along with fifty hours of silence. Four hundred twenty-five masses were heard, and one hundred "Ways of the Cross" were performed. Three hundred prayers for the sick, 250 for the dead, 125 for reconciliations, and 325 for families were said.[84]

Some boys of the parish were selected by Monsignor Gorey to join the St. Sabina Junior Conference of the St. Vincent De Paul Society which he began in 1943. He chose ten eighth-grade boys and "invited them to begin a serious study of the great virtue of Charity in its nature and its practical application to the poor."[85] These young men assisted the priest in visiting the aged and sick of the parish and ran errands for them. Every week two members visited a local hospital to distribute the *Sunday Visitor* and help patients to mass.[86]

The boys were also encouraged to visit the St. Joseph's Home for the Friendless and the Little Sisters of the Poor Home where they watched "the great heroes and heroines of the Church at work in the service of God's blessed unfortunate."[87] The Junior group looked after the orphanage in St. Sabina tradition. When the Junior Vincentians learned that St. Joseph's Home needed new flooring in the boys' dormitory, they staged "Memories," a variety program. "All local talent was assembled, arranged into acts, perfected, and then displayed in the production." The successful show not only covered the cost of new flooring but also paid for the repair, redecoration, and refurnishing of the entire dormitory. "Memories" became an annual production.[88] Those who attended also benefited. "By paying for your admission ticket to Memories, you may have bought your ticket to heaven because you performed a corporal work of Mercy."[89]

While the parochial school remained a cornerstone of parish life in post-war Chicago, a subtle shift in the parishioners' attitudes toward education occurred. As Table 11 demonstrates, the vast majority of parish children continued to attend St. Sabina school. St. Sabina's clergy emphasized religious reasons for parents to avoid sending their children to the public schools, since "the amount of time available to them for [religious] instruction is very limited and it is certainly not to be considered equal to Catholic school instruction."[90] Parents by no means eschewed this advice, but they were further motivated by the optimism of America's expanding economy and saw in the parish school a proven vehicle to boost their children into a more solid position in the growing middle class. "You're going to be better than me!" was the message parents gave to their children.[91] "Our parents stressed education," concurred J. Nelligan. [You were taught] "you had to work to achieve anything in this world. . . . I think most parents made the opportunity for [their children] to go to college."[92]

Tuition at St. Sabina was deliberately kept low so all could afford to send their children to the parish school. Even by the early 1960s tuition was only one dollar per month. This fee was the lowest charged by any Catholic school in the Archdiocese. The Archdiocesan Superintendent of Schools set the maximum tuition rate at sixty dollars per year per child or a hundred dollars per family. The median rate charged in the Archdiocese was thirty dollars per child and sixty per family. St. Sabina's school costs were supplemented by the parish treasury.[93] These rate were, of course, dependent on the vocations of the Dominican nuns who still staffed the school. The credit union provided low-interest loans to parents who could not afford to pay Catholic high-school tuition or to send their children on to college.[94]

The moral authority of the church continued to be reinforced in the classroom. Priests conducted religious instruction and often disciplined the children.[95] J. Nelligan recalled his school days during the war when he was sent to Monsignor Gorey. In a class full of Marys and Josephs, he often had a hard time finding his name in the corrected piles of papers. To make it easier for him to spot his work, and having a boy's romantic notions of war, he began putting swastikas at the top of his page. He was promptly sent to the pastor, who kindly suggested that there were more appropriate symbols for a Catholic school boy to use to distinguish his work from others.[96]

With the backing of the entire Roman Catholic Church, the moral superiority of the nuns and priests could be quite intimidating to young children. "It was monolithic," recalled G. Hendry. Authority "was coming from the on high down. . . . School was strict. We knew our place. . . . There may have been [some problem kids], but I didn't see many."[97]

The sisters were also aided by the Mothers' Club, which began in 1942 and generally enjoyed a 100 percent membership.[98] Mothers watched children during lunchtime and recess and provided an annual Christmas party and end of school picnic, among other social activities. They also conferred with the nuns on their children's progress and on how they could help them with their studies. Mothers were to encourage their children to read and to receive the sacraments regularly, and to make sure altar boys lived up to their duties.[99] This watchful and intimate atmosphere created some problems for the children. "You could hardly go any place and do anything wrong because you were known," complained G. Hendry. " 'Who is that boy? You better tell me who he is or I'll find out. I have ways!' "[100]

Devotional activities continued to help solidify in children's minds the bond between their parish and their school experiences. For example, "the third grade formed the Living Rosary for an assembly program. The girls wore white blouses and the boys wore white shirts. We sang a short song for each mystery of the Rosary."[101] With the aid of the Mothers' Club, the school children still staged the annual May Crowning of the Blessed Mother.[102] All school children were required to attend the nine o'clock Sunday mass. The service was designed for their active participation and the sermon was adapted for their level of understanding. Children were only allowed to go to mass with their parents with written permission.[103]

Unity and commonality among the pupils was also created in parish schools by wearing a distinctive uniform. "Everybody wore the same thing," J. Nelligan said. "You didn't buy too many clothes. You wore your school uniform." Uniforms disciplined children and helped instill pride in their school. J. Nelligan recalled being taught that "when you were outside walking around with the uniform, you represented your school and you ought to behave yourself."[104]

Like their counterparts throughout the city, the vast majority of children from St. Sabina's parochial school went on to Catholic high schools. This experience tended to reinforce parish values and maintain a fairly Catholic experience even within eclectic Chicago. Catholic high schools did not receive much attention in the Catholic community until the twentieth century. By the turn of the century Catholic educators, like their public school counterparts, were beginning to recognize the importance of secondary education in an increasingly economically complex world. In 1904 the National Catholic Education Association was formed to address the growing need for Catholic secondary education. However, they had difficulty agreeing on the purpose of high-school education—whether it should be college preparatory for the elite or whether it should serve those who needed further training but would not go on to college. How they were to be organized and under whose auspices they would be directed raised additional questions. The debate continued for a decade without much progress.[105]

George Mundelein gave the Catholic high-school movement the impetus it needed. By the mid-1920s the Archbishop devised a master plan for central high schools. They were strategically located so as to be easily accessible for all Catholics and were owned and operated by religious orders. By 1940, 53 percent of Catholics who graduated from parochial schools attended Catholic high schools, and by 1945 the number had reached 72 percent.[106]

St. Sabina graduates generally followed in this pattern. The girls attended Visitation, Longwood (Academy of Our Lady), and Mercy High Schools. The boys went to St. Rita and Leo High Schools.[107] Leo was technically a central high school, but it was owned by St. Leo parish and operated by the Irish Christian Brothers. As St. Sabina's neighbor, Leo High School was a virtual institutional extension of St. Sabina's grade school.

The clergy, the nuns, and the parents placed strong emphasis not only on grade-school and high-school education at St. Sabina's, but also on higher education. They wanted their children to participate in the postwar economic mobility that was increasingly dependent upon higher education. Education was seen by the incipient Irish middle class that had emerged since the First World War as a key to the American dream. Back then only one in five Americans attended college. However, one in four Irish Catholics did. During the Great Depression the number of Irish seeking higher education continued to rise. Outside of the east coast 43 percent went to college. By the mid-1970s Irish-Americans continued to enjoy educational levels above the national average.[108] They were the most highly educated Gentile group in the nation. They also had the highest income levels.[109] While statistics are unavailable for how many of St. Sabina graduates went on to college, oral testimony seems to indicate that St. Sabina parishioners were clearly attuned to the changing economy and the possibilities it offered their children for a better life.

Interest in learning was not confined to the school. In 1949 St. Sabina's created a parish library. "After taking good care of the teenagers with the community center, the needs of the adults were surveyed. . . . It seemed evident there was an adult group whose interests lay in informal Catholic literature. These people would welcome a parish library."[110] The library aimed to provide the latest books on Catholic subjects appropriate for Catholic readers. By 1957 St. Sabina's had seven hundred holdings and led other parish libraries in circulation with 350 card holders and 250 books circulated each month.[111] By 1959 the parish owned fifteen hundred publications, many financed by the pastor, Msgr. John A. McMahon, with parish funds.[112]

St. Sabina parishioners' reading was also automatically supplemented by the Archdiocesan newspaper, *The New World*. The parish

Table 13. Top Twenty-five Parishes of Baptism of Persons Married at
St. Sabina's, 1942-1951

Parish	Nationality	Number	% Total Marriages
St. Sabina	- - -	238	26
Visitation	Irish	83	9
St. Leo	Irish	76	8
Out of Town	- - -	70	8
St. Brendan	Irish	53	6
St. Basil	Irish-German	33	4
St. Gabriel	Irish	31	3
Nativity of Our Lord	Irish	19	2
St. Theodore	Irish	19	2
Sacred Heart	German	18	2
St. Bernard	Irish	17	2
St. Anne	Irish	16	2
St. Kilian	Irish-German	15	2
All Saints	Irish	15	2
St. Rita	Mixed	15	2
St. John the Baptist	French	14	2
St. George	German	13	1
St. Raphael	German	12	1
St. Augustine	German	12	1
St. Agnes	Irish	11	1
St. David	Irish	10	1
St. Anselm	Irish	10	1
St. Thomas Apostle	Irish*	9	1
Little Flower	Irish*	8	1
St. Justin Martyr	Irish	8	1
TOTAL MARRIAGES			908

Source: St. Sabina Marriage Records.

Note: The remaining parishes were primarily Irish as well. However other national parishes became increasingly represented over the years.

*Most likely contained other ethnic groups, but this is impossible to document.

was on the 100 percent plan. Every family recorded in the Sunday envelop book was provided with a subscription to the paper. The subscription costs were met from the parish treasury. An article in *The Seraph* explained why this method was used: "Every decent person views with abhorrence the degraded character of countless modern publications and the failure of the secular press to champion truth and virtue. . . . Our Holy Father and Our Cardinal Archbishop have repeatedly emphasized the importance of Catholic papers and Catholic literature in the fight against falsehood and sin."[113]

Table 14. Top Twenty-five Parishes of Baptism of Persons Married at
St. Sabina's, 1952 and 1955-1959

Parish	Nationality	Number	% Total Marriages
St. Sabina	- - -	141	26
Ireland	- - -	37	7
St. Leo	Irish	34	6
Visitation	Irish	23	4
Little Flower	Irish*	20	4
St. Rita	Mixed	18	3
Sacred Heart	German	17	3
Holy Cross	Irish	16	3
St. Brendan	Irish	15	3
Out of Town	- - -	15	3
St. Kilian	Irish-German	14	3
St. Bernard	Irish	13	2
St. Columbanus	Irish	13	2
St. Basil	Irish-German	10	2
St. Theodore	Irish	10	2
St. Gabriel	Irish	8	1
Nativity of Our Lord	Irish	8	1
St. Anne	Irish	8	1
Mercy Hospital	- - -	8	1
Santa Maria Incoronata	Italian	7	1
St. Margaret of Scotland	Irish-German	7	1
St. Dorothy	Mixed	7	1
St. Carthage	Irish	7	1
St. John the Baptist	French	6	1
St. Martin	German	6	1
TOTAL		468	86
TOTAL MARRIAGES		547	

Source: St. Sabina Marriage Records.

*Most likely contained other ethnic groups, but this is impossible to document.

The pastor also used *The Seraph*, with its "Pastors Page," to teach,
admonish, enlighten, or praise his flock. The "family" was frequently
discussed, and Catholicism and the parish were believed to be its chief
source of inspiration and protection. Msgr. John McMahon, who became pastor of St. Sabina's in 1952 following the death of Monsignor
Gorey, wrote, "We find, as other priests find in other parishes, that
there is very little delinquency among the children whose parents
cooperate in Church activities."[114] On another occasion he wrote, "I
think there would never be a greater blessing on our wonderful parish
than that which would come from a steady increase in the number of

Table 15. Parishes of Baptism of First Communicants in St. Sabina's, 1950-1959

Parish	Nationality	Number	% Communicants
St. Sabina	- - -	735	56
St. Leo	- - -	93	7
St. Columbanus	Irish	44	3
St. Bernard	Irish	37	3
St. Brendan	Irish	33	3
Sacred Heart	German	33	3
Little Flower	Irish*	32	2
Visitation	Irish	26	2
St. Carthage	Irish	24	2
Out of Town	- - -	19	1
St. Dorothy	Mixed	18	1
St. Rita	Mixed	16	1
St. Ethelreda	Irish	15	1
St. Kilian	Irish-German	15	1
St. Adrian	Mixed	15	1
Nativity of Our Lord	Irish	13	1
St. Justin Martyr	Irish	13	1
St. Theodore	Irish	13	1
Holy Name	Mixed	10	1
St. Margaret of Scotland	Irish-German	10	1
St. Gregory	German*	9	1
All Saints	Irish	9	1
St. Thomas the Apostle	Irish*	9	1
St. Clara	German	9	1
St. Cecilia	Irish	8	1
TOTAL		1,258	96
		1,313 Communicants	

Source: St. Sabina's First Communion Register.

*Most likely contained other ethnic groups, but this is impossible to document.

families reciting the rosary."[115] "The rosary," he said, "is the groundwork for Catholic Action and Catholic perfection."[116]

"It was a faith parish," Father Tom McMahon related. "It was a parish where people loved their families and they centered all their activities around the church. . . . And the church was the home for the family where they had their baptisms and their confirmations and first communions and weddings and funerals. It was the center of Catholic life."[117]

D. Foertsch confirmed this. "My wedding was there. All my kids were baptized there. Half of them were confirmed and half of them graduated from there. My dad was buried there. So a lot of the emotional things happened there."[118] H. O'Connor said, "I never moved out of Sabina's. . . . I graduated from there. Both of my daughters graduated from St. Sabina's. I was married there and they were married there."[119]

The longevity of Mrs. Foertsch's and Mrs. O'Connor's residences in St. Sabina's was not unique. Many people who grew up there as children stayed as adults. M. Dunne started grade school at St. Sabina's and did not leave until the late 1970s. T. O'Rourke also began school there in the early 1920s and remained there long enough to see his children graduate from St. Sabina's. Parish statistics bear out this residential stability. As shown in Tables 13 and 14, 26 percent of those married in St. Sabina's were baptized there as infants. The statistics in Table 15 show that 56 percent of first communicants at St. Sabina's were baptized there as infants. While not a majority, there was a solid core of long-term parishioners at St. Sabina's to give continuity to parish traditions. T. O'Rourke said, "St. Sabina . . . held the neighborhood [together]."[120]

For those who did move, other parishes could fulfill the same needs. "You could move west of Ashland or east of Morgan and be almost in the same identical situation," said G. Hendry.[121] "I haven't moved that far since I've been born," D. Foertsch remarked. "I've been in my own little ghetto because of the philosophy of Sabina's."[122]

The parish of St. Sabina's was a vital center of community life for Catholics in the two decades from the start of the Second World War. "It was a community. It was very good spirited," said Father McMahon. "I think because of the priests and the sisters and the school. Everything was centered around the parish."[123] St. Sabina's also sought to fill the recreational needs of its members, thereby placing another dimension to the community under its auspices. The parish was not only a place to pray and a place to learn but a recreational and social magnet for Catholics from across the South Side of Chicago.

5

The Saints Come Marching In: Irish and Catholic Identity

In March 1954 freezing temperatures and snow flurries worried officials who had spent the past year organizing the second annual South Side Irish parade. They feared the inclement weather would keep Chicago's southern contingent of Irish away from the festivities. The first parade was a charming neighborhood event with Girls Scouts, Little League ballplayers, and the like marching before family and friends. This year, however, parade organizers recruited not only police and fire units but also the marching bands from the Great Lakes Naval Base, the 5th Army, and Notre Dame University. They need not have been concerned. Nearly 100,000 spectators turned out to celebrate Irish pride. One witness said the arrival of the Notre Dame Fighting Irish football team and band was "like bringing the saints marching in!"[1] The success of the parade encouraged parade planners to recruit Ed Sullivan, the television show host, to lead the parade in 1955. Sullivan, whose parents were born in County Cork, Ireland, proclaimed that "it was the happiest day" of his life.[2]

The South Side Irish parade originated in St. Sabina's as an expression of the parish's continued Irish identity. Celtic pride was openly expressed in many mundane features of community life. Local stores stocked Irish products. The neighborhood record store claimed to have the most complete set of Irish music available in the city. Many parents sent their children to learn the intricacies of Irish step dancing, while teens gathered at the Shamrock Corner for the all-American hamburger.[3]

In many ways Irishness pervaded St. Sabina's and accounted for its distinctive character. Tables 13 and 14 demonstrate the continued Irish origins of St. Sabina parishioners. By looking at what parishes newlyweds were baptized in as infants, it is possible to identify their nationality. Most people in St. Sabina's still came from Irish parishes in the working-class districts that bordered the stockyards. Table 15 perhaps provides a more exact profile of the parishes new settlers to St. Sabina's came from by showing the churches of baptism of first communicants, who were seven years old when they received the sacrament. They clearly would be more recent arrivals in the neighborhood and a more exact indication of postwar mobility. They, too, were primarily from Irish or German parishes, although a larger percentage of these young people came from parishes located in middle-class areas and could no longer be classified as having a particular ethnic identity. Yet, even most of these middle-class parishes had a large number of Irish.

St. Sabina's Irish identity continued to bind the parish together. Although he did not necessarily think it was a fully conscious decision, J. Nelligan thought the Irish flavor of St. Sabina influenced people's decision to move there. He said, "Basically, people moved from Bridgeport to Canaryville to Sabina's. . . . You wouldn't move to St. John of God [a Polish parish at 52nd and Throop St.]. You would move to a neighborhood which was probably Irish."[4] G. Hendry's parents were from East St. Louis. His father had come to Chicago to work in the stockyards. Being of Irish extraction eased their transition to St. Sabina's and Chicago. He said, "When they moved there, the Irishness of [the parish] helped my mother. . . . There were people out [saying] 'Your name is Nelly Burns. . . . Well, we've got a lot of Irish here! Sabina's is full of them!' Right away she made a connection."[5]

Although the immigration restriction laws of 1923 and 1924 severely curtailed immigration, after World War II many Irish men and women found their way to America, Chicago, and St. Sabina parish. They contributed to the Irish flavor of the neighborhood. According to the 1960 census, 31 percent of the foreign born population of Auburn Park were Irish.[6] "Around World War II," T. O'Rourke recalled, "there were more foreign-born Irish than there were in the early days. There seemed to be a lot of native Irish coming over here and they settled in the parish in large numbers. They kept it Irish."[7]

Irish immigrants were quite visible in the community. "You'd see them walking down 79th Street in the dead of winter," related B. DesChatelets. "Colder than the hinter of hell, and they'd have a suit coat on and a sweater. . . . Everything they had on was wool from Ireland. . . . And the suit coat would be wide open and they would be walking along . . . and you could spot them a mile away."[8]

G. Hendry concurred with this observation. He said, "After the war to '55 a lot of Irish immigrants settled in the area. So I think the people saw that there was a need for bringing out their ethnicity."[9] T. O'Rourke thought World War II, in which he served in Europe, played a role in reviving interest in Ireland because it enabled him and others to visit the homeland of their parents and grandparents. "The first time I went to Ireland was in 1945 after VE day," he said. "So many fellows got to see Ireland and liked it."[10]

The St. Patrick's Day parade was perhaps the most demonstrative celebration of Irish identity. The wide-spread celebration of the Irish saint's feast day led *The Seraph* in 1952 to boast that "St. Patrick has become almost the patron saint of America, as well as Ireland, so well-known has he become."[11]

One day in 1953 Father Thomas J. McMahon, an assistant priest, and Jack Allen, a St. Sabina parishioner, got the inspiration to start the parade. Father McMahon said, "I was watching the one in New York on TV every year. . . . Allen was with me in the gym one day. . . . The two of us were talking about it. Why didn't we have one? . . . [so] we decided we would run a St. Patrick's Day parade."[12]

Initially the parade was loosely structured. "Anybody could get in it," related Father McMahon. "They could push a buggy or ride a bike or skip a rope or anything. . . . We got a few school bands in there."[13] "They got all the Little Leaguers out, all the Cub Scouts, all the Girl Scouts, all the Brownies, and they marched them in different areas of the parade. It was very child oriented. . . . They had tremendous support from parents," recalled G. Hendry.[14] The parade was held on the Sunday nearest St. Patrick's Day so Samuel Cardinal Stritch, prelate of Chicago since 1940, could offer benediction at St. Sabina's at the close of the parade.[15]

The parade proved to be a real attraction. Over ten thousand spectators turned out that first year to watch the four-mile-long parade. Among the fourteen floats in the parade was one dedicated to the founding pastor, Monsignor Egan, "an enthusiast of Irish music and culture." Parishioners were aboard singing Irish music accompanied by an organ.[16] B. DesChatelets, whose father was the parade marshal and one of its principal organizers, said of that first year, "In order to finance it, they went up and down 79th Street and got some donations from some of the businessmen. They were a little reluctant to give. . . . But the parade was a big thing. . . . The second year they really didn't even have to go around. The bar owners came and said, 'Here's money.' They couldn't believe how much business they had! People just packed the sidewalks all the way."[17]

The parade's success prompted its organizers to expand the parade to encompass the South Side, and they devised rules for a more sophisticated procession. "You had to be really organized," Father McMahon related. "You could not march in it unless you were with a marching unit . . . or you had to have a float."[18]

The 1954 parade had 1,300 marchers, twenty-three bands, and forty floats. Besides Notre Dame's 125 piece marching ensemble and the bands of the Great Lakes Naval Base and the 5th Army, there was a Chinese band and a German band, which "added an inter-racial touch." Army, Navy, and Marine units marched along with police officers and fire fighters, American Legionnaires, Veterans of Foreign

Wars, the Knights of Columbus, and Catholic War Veterans. The reviewing stand at 79th and Loomis held state, county, and city politicos, prominent industrialists, businessmen, and church dignitaries.[19]

Parade day was a real holiday. N. Farrell, a florist who decorated St. Sabina church, had the school's nuns up to the apartment above her store on 79th Street to view the parade.[20] Many other parishioners held parties in their homes after the parade.[21]

The success of the South Side parade inspired the West Side Irish to resume their parade. "There were some West Side Irish parades up until two years before we started ours," related Father McMahon. "They had disbanded because they were fighting like the Irish sometimes do. . . . We started our parade and it was so successful, they inaugurated theirs again. . . . We would have ours on Sunday, then on St. Patrick's Day they would have our floats in their parade on the West Side. . . . It got so big, once [Richard J.] Daley was mayor, he wanted it downtown. So that's the parade you see downtown every year."[22] By 1960 political pressure ended the South Side parade. The Irish were powerful enough to make what had been a community event a city tradition.

The St. Patrick's parade celebration was not just an Irish parade. It was integrally entwined with the Catholic identity of the parish. An article in *The Seraph* expressed the opinion that the St. Patrick's Day parade "is part of the Catholic Action program, therefore, worthy of our support."[23] On Trinity Sunday of the Catholic liturgical calendar, in another piece in *The Seraph,* the shamrock was used to explain the mystery of the Holy Trinity: "When we think of shamrocks, we think of St. Patrick too, not so much because both are Irish, but because St. Patrick used the little shamrock to explain to his Irish converts the most profound truth of our faith, the doctrine of the Blessed Trinity."[24]

It was still difficult for St. Sabina parishioners to separate an Irish identity from their religion. Their every-day activities revolved around the church, which kept the parish, rather than their more intangible Irishness, central in their lives and hearts. Since the school was staffed by an American religious order, its curriculum did not have an ethnic content. The main goal of the Dominicans was to keep religion the core subject.[25] Since there were other nationalities in the parish, some priests felt that stressing an Irish identity over a Catholic one was divisive, so they discouraged excessive ethnicity.[26] This outraged some of the Irish parishioners, however. On the day of the St. Patrick's Day parade, "we found out that the kids had to go to school," recalled T. O'Rourke. "Well, myself and some of the other fathers . . . couldn't understand it. And we bombarded [the rectory] with calls to find out what was going on. Some of us wrote letters. . . . And they told us at the time, 'Well, we have a lot of other nationalities here now.' That was their excuse. . . . But after that they'd always have St. Patrick's Day a holiday."[27]

Many forces had been at work in the previous decades in Chicago and the nation to break down ethnic neighborhoods and identity; these would all have an effect on St. Sabina's Irish character. Cardinal Mundelein's policy of no new national parishes channeled economically and geographically mobile ethnics into territorial parishes were they joined the Irish and the Germans. The postwar prosperity brought a greater amount of diverse nationalities into St. Sabina's as Tables 13 and 14 demonstrate. This led to an increasing emphasis on a Catholic identity over an ethnic one.

Because their Irish and Catholic identities blurred, Irish Americans themselves tended to cultivate and defend more vigorously their Catholicism, which gave them group cohesion, leadership, and a source of belief and values, which they defended against the animosity of American nativists. The territorial schools that the Irish controlled were primarily geared toward educating children for economic and social advancement while preserving their faith. The Irish history courses that were sometimes taught dwelt upon the misty Celtic past of the Land of Saints and Scholars, which provided little to cultivate a dynamic Irish-American identity. The Knights of Columbus, which was the favored fraternal organization of the Irish, was much more concerned with defending Catholicism than with encouraging Irishness. This left Irish Americans without fertile soil in which to cultivate an authentic Irish-American culture.[28] Yet this did not prevent many Chicago Irish from wishing that they had one and expressing it in any way they could.

There were other forces working against ethnic solidarity. One historian has argued that the Great Depression, Prohibition, and the growth of mass consumer society and popular culture broke down ethnic parochialism in Chicago. Prohibition politically rallied together many ethnic groups to try and repeal it. The economic crisis of the 1930s made it all but impossible for ethnic associations or even local political bosses to meet the pressing needs of their constituents. Workers had no choice but to look beyond their immediate ethnic organization for help. They turned to the Democratic party and the federal government for assistance in ways they never before would have dreamed. With the passage of the Wagner Act in 1935, workers from diverse walks of life enlisted in the unionization of the mass production plants in the country under the auspices of the Congress of Industrial Organizations (CIO). Increasing cultural unity made it possible for ethnics and blacks to join in common political and economic efforts. Radio, chain movie theaters, and chain stores homogenized American culture and broke down barriers that had previously separated groups. They became more conscious of sharing similar fates.[29] World War II also created a shared national experience and shared fears, at least for white Americans in the armed services, in war work, and in civilian defense.

The Chicago Democratic political machine also played an important role in building bridges and ending isolation between the city's ethnic and racial groups. Anton Cermak, a Czech and head of the Democratic party, was elected mayor in 1928 and joined Chicago's various ethnic groups, including the Irish, into a powerful political coalition. His death in Miami 1933 from a bullet intended for president-elect Franklin D. Roosevelt, ushered in the era of the Irish triumvirate of Ed Kelly, Martin H. Kennelly, and Richard J. Daley, who built upon this coalition. These three mayors ruled Chicago through a powerful machine from 1933 until 1976. While the Irish dominated the machine, other ethnics and blacks were given access to political plums. Chicago's Irish took pride in their political ascendancy but realized it depended upon sharing it with these other groups.[30]

Despite the attempts of many in the parish, Catholicism was superseding "Irishness" as the conscious self-image of the parish. "At Sabina's," said G. Hendry, "it was Catholicity. Nothing ethnic really. You were definitely Catholic. And Sabina's and the neighbors on each side, [St.] Leo and Little Flower, certainly reinforced that."[31] "I never thought about [my Irishness]," said D. Foertsch. "I don't know that it was that big a deal then, or maybe I was just too busy raising kids to notice. . . . There was never any reason to even bring it up because so many around us were."[32] Speculating on why their Irish identity was downplayed, G. Hendry said, "What was gone by my generation was ethnic discrimination. Because, heck, we owned the city! You couldn't be discriminated against."[33]

But by this time, many of those who were of Irish descent were third or fourth generation Irish-American. For many of these, Irish identity was something to boast about while listening to a Saturday afternoon broadcast of Notre Dame football or an excuse for a "spree" on March 17. Their connection with the culture of the Emerald Isle was tenuous at best. "You didn't see anyone saying 'I'm South Side Irish' back then," claimed G. Hendry.[34] Those Irish Americans who strove to retain their Irish identity were pejoratively referred to by some as "professional" Irish. The forces of assimilation made such jingoists seem like they were almost an anachronism. Catholicism, however, remained a vital part of their lives, and despite the forces for accommodation, Catholics still cultivated a separate Catholic world.

Perhaps the biggest and most memorable attraction at St. Sabina's was the community center. On November 5, 1937, Bishop Bernard

Sheil dedicated the new center at 78th and Racine.[35] The athletic Irishman was an appropriate choice for the dedication. Sheil had given up a Major League baseball contract to enter the priesthood where he pursued a wide-ranging interest in social issues. He played a behind-the-scenes role in forming the Back of the Yards Neighborhood Council, an early success of community organizer, Saul Alinsky. He also gave very prominent support to the CIO. Sheil is perhaps best remembered by Chicago Catholics for building the Catholic Youth Organization (CYO).[36]

In the competitive environment of America, the Catholic Church competed with Protestant and secular society on many levels. The most visible arenas were, of course, churches and schools. However, there were other menaces to the integrity of the Catholic community, such as "Protestant" settlement houses, the YMCA as well as the lure of popular culture. The CYO, therefore, provided a Catholic alternative to these "questionable" attractions by creating social services and athletic programs.[37]

St. Sabina parishioners liked to believe that Father Ashenden, who served at St. Sabina's from 1919 to 1926, was the founder of the organization. His shocking death on February 11, 1931, in an automobile accident robbed him, many parishioners believed, of the honor of being recognized as the founder of the CYO. This belief was not without some foundation. Father Ashenden had been involved in some of the early activities of the CYO and was a leading figure in the Catholic Boy Scout organization. In an announcement of his death, *The New World* described Ashenden as the founder and first director of the youth organization.[38] In June 1930, Sheil appointed Ashenden as the first executive director of the CYO, which is probably the reason he was considered by some to be the founder of the organization. Sheil, however, was not the founder of the CYO either. He was, instead, its chief organizer and promoter. It remains unclear who exactly started the organization. Many of the ideas and programs the CYO encompassed had been around and tried by various people many years before its formal organization.[39]

Regardless of who founded the CYO, it is certain that Ashenden was an important element in getting the highly successful organization started.[40] While there is no direct evidence as to why Monsignor Egan decided to build the community center, it seems quite likely that his close relationship with Ashenden influenced his decision. He may also have been influenced by the diocesan paper, *The New World*. In the early 1920s the paper began to urge parishes to provide social activities for young people so they would recreate in the church hall rather than hang out on the streets or be lured over to commercial entertainment centers, "even if it meant going as far as putting pool tables, bowling alleys, and even skating rinks in the church basement."[41] Throughout the 1930s, Bishop Sheil encouraged pastors to establish social and athletic centers in their parishes, which he believed were crucial to the success of CYO sports leagues. Monsignor Egan was one of the few pastors to respond to Sheil's call. This gave St. Sabina's a unique attraction among the parishes of Chicago.[42]

The two-story building housed a college-sized basketball court, which could also be split into two smaller courts. Its folding bleachers sat 1,800 people. In the basement were locker-rooms, showers, handball courts, a kitchen and dining room, and meeting rooms for the various parish societies. The cavernous building was valued at $150,000. Through the fund-raising efforts of the Holy Name Society and proceeds taken in from the community center's activities, the center was paid for in full by 1940.[43]

Under Monsignor Egan and his successor, Monsignor Gorey, the St. Sabina community center grew to be a major attraction for Catholics at St. Sabina's and throughout the South Side. Like Egan, Gorey was concerned for "the right recreational environment for his young people, because he knew full well the dangers which lurk in the commercialized recreational center in our community."[44]

In July 1939, Father Thomas S. McMahon was assigned to St. Sabina's. He had previously been posted at Bishop Sheil's parish, St. Andrew's, on the North Side of Chicago. His experience under Sheil helped make him an ideal candidate for director of St. Sabina's new center. Father Tom, as he was fondly called, proved to be a virtual Bing Crosby–style priest. Under his tutelage the center became an expression of CYO philosophy.

Father McMahon thought his mission to the young people of the parish was quite simple. The pastors "gave me carte blanche permission. . . . I could do what I wanted. . . . I always kind of tended towards athletics. I played all the sports and I liked priests who played sports. Priests used to coach teams when I was a kid. . . . I'm a priest because of some others that I wanted to emulate. I wanted to be like they were." He intended for the center to be an instrument "to save souls and . . . to keep those kids in the formative years out of trouble. . . . Get them right after school. Have something for them and keep them nice . . . athletics or dancing. . . . that's what I thought I should do as a priest."[45]

Irish Americans had a close association with sports in this country in the nineteenth and early twentieth century. Sports provided heroes and an avenue for upward mobility for a group with often limited opportunities. This affinity for sports was also a product of Irish culture. After the Great Famine of the 1840s a bachelor subculture developed. Delayed marriages and stricter sexual morals were intended to protect the Irish against another similar calamity. This prompted a large number of men to find release in drinking and sport. This eased loneliness and provided camaraderie. These bachelor groups, which evolved into sporting fraternities, prized politics, violence, and sports.[46] This sporting tradition was coopted by the parish. In St. Sabina's, it was harnessed by Father McMahon and the community center to create a Catholic haven in the midst of the temptations of the big city.

Father McMahon was aided by a dedicated parishioner, Merlin X. Mungovan, a juvenile officer. Mungovan had been volunteering his services to the community center since it opened. He had already begun a St. Sabina tradition of hosting an Amateur Athletic Union (AAU) basketball tournament, and he coached the CYO and grade-school teams. His talent for directing young people helped the St. Sabina grade-school team bring home the city championship in 1938. Recognizing a great asset, Father McMahon encouraged Monsignor Egan to hire him as the full-time athletic instructor during and after school hours. The pair expanded the community center activities to include such events as a preseason grade-school basketball tournament and a house league for high-school teens who could not make either their school or the CYO team. St. Sabina also staged CYO boxing bouts. These various events drew capacity crowds.[47] J. Nelligan remembered the excitement of the AAU tournaments. "Even if you were small and you had to be in bed at eight o'clock," he said, "that was a special occasion. And you'd be allowed to go and . . . stay out until it was over."[48]

Among the most popular and enduring programs that started during these early years of the community center was weekend roller skating. Father Tom had been unhappy with the lack of decorum at the local roller skating rink. The low lights and song selections, he felt, were not suitable for young Catholic children. He thought it was quite likely that the community center floor could take the quick stops of skates. To test this theory Father McMahon and some friends donned roller skates and took to the gym floor. They found it was quite capable of withstanding the abuse and silenced critics in the parish who feared the destruction of their new floor. Within the first year of operation the receipts from roller skating more than covered the cost of the floor. Twelve hundred skates were available for rent in sizes ranging from one to twelve. The more dedicated skaters eventually bought their own.[49]

Boys with shoe skates hanging around their necks and girls with their skates in multicolored cases became a frequent sight on the streets of the neighborhood as they walked to the center. Friday evenings from five until seven was Twilight Skating for seventh and eighth graders. From 7:30 until 10:30 was reserved for high-school students. On Saturday afternoons the community center opened its doors to the younger children, who participated in games and races. The winners received free bottles of pop. Special skating parties for high-school students were held at the rink on Saturday night. Nearly every high school on the South Side held a skating party regularly. One evening, 728 teenagers paid their way into St. Ignatius High School's party.[50]

The children of the parish were not the only ones to enjoy roller skating. After the community center's doors were closed for the night, Father Tom and his staff took their turn at skating across the floor. "We'd go skating around there and play crack the whip. We didn't allow the kids to do it, but we were racing and jumping over chairs." He also bought skates for all the nuns, who used them during their free time.[51]

Among the most notable events Father McMahon helped orchestrate during his tenure at St. Sabina's were the annual St. Sabina Roller Varieties. He received the inspiration from watching the young people skating. "Once I opened up the gym for skating, they began doing things that they saw in shows—at the Stadium, the Sonia Henie show, or the Ice Capades. And they were doing little twists and jumps and spins, and before long, we'd play a waltz number and they were waltzing. And they would learn how to eagle to the right and the left. . . . And we thought, 'Golly, we could put on a show because they're so good.' "[52]

To put this idea into action, Father McMahon took a group to the Arcadia on the North Side of Chicago to learn dance steps on skates. They, in turn, taught the youngsters at St. Sabina's the waltz, the fox trot, the fourteen step, and other skating numbers. During the summer, then, the children were told to think of an act they would like to do based on a theme Father Tom had given them. Through the fall, up to thirty acts and over five hundred participants worked on their various numbers and the myriad tasks. Well over a hundred parishioners joined the production staff. "We had everybody doing something," Father McMahon proclaimed. "It was a community event."[53]

The boys and girls skated to songs such as 'Swinging on a Star' or enacted fairy tales such as Snow White and the Seven Dwarfs. No roller variety, however, was complete without an Irish number with a "song dear to the hearts of Erin's sons and daughters." Some brave and talented skaters did the Irish jig on skates.[54] Roller varieties sometimes had a religious theme. In 1950, a Holy Year, the subject was a pilgrimage to Rome. The Holy Name Society hoped it would "convey a lesson to each of us in our pilgrimage though life."[55]

When the roller varieties first started, the performances were scheduled for just a few evenings. As their popularity grew, St. Sabina's began staging them for a week and advertising them on billboards throughout the city and had colorful programs printed. Approximately forty billboards around the city heralded the coming of St. Sabina's Roller Varieties. In 1948 over ten thousand people came to watch the show.[56]

Next to roller skating, St. Sabina dances were the most memorable feature of the parish and community center. St. Sabina's Young Peoples Club had already been holding occasional dances when Father Tom arrived. Since he had run dances at St. Andrew's and realized their popularity at St. Sabina's, Father Tom decided to hold them every Sunday. "They were teenage dances to keep those kids in the formative years out of trouble."[57]

To get into the dances, the children had to comply with certain rules. "All you had to do was dress decently," Father Tom explained. "The boys had to have a jacket and tie on. The girls had to have a decent dress. And that was it—decency."[58] To enforce the rules, the community center hired two policemen and several Andy Frain ushers and enlisted the assistance of parish chaperones. "If they would smell anything on their breath—out! They'd never get in again. We had a woman in the girls' room and a man in the boys' washroom. And if they noticed anything, a drink or anything—out!. . . . We were strict, and that's what the kids liked. . . . They like to be gentlemen and ladies, and they wanted to be treated as such."[59]

Father McMahon's strictness did not subdue the popularity of these dances. On an average Sunday the dances drew 1,200 teenagers, with a record attendance set at 1,600. The dances were held forty-six weeks a year and discontinued only during Lent, with the exception of a St. Patrick's Day dance. Teens from as many as ninety-one other parishes came to St. Sabina's on Sunday, for over the forty years the dances were held.[60]

The selection of the band was carefully considered. "We'd give the orchestra what they called a one-night stand. You could play this night. . . . We'd have the kids vote on them. If they liked them, we'd give them four Sundays in a row. . . . We had union organists. All union bands." Dance numbers were worked out in advance. There were twelve sets of dances with three songs for each dance. Girls had dance cards that they filled out all week. Ballroom dancing was taught during intermissions. "We had people come in from the Aragon Ballroom and teach these young people how to dance at the intermission, and our organist would play for them. . . . The priests would walk around the hall encouraging the bashful ones to take those free lessons."[61]

The Sunday night dances were primarily for young adults. High-school freshmen were not allowed in until the end of the school year, when they were almost sophomores. "They were just aching to get there," related Father Tom. When many people returned from World War II, the Sunday dances were too young for them, so Father McMahon began a Wednesday night dance for the more mature crowd. These dances were just as popular. One evening drew 1,700.[62] On Thursday evening Father Tom occasionally hosted a dance for adults.[63]

How did the young people of the parish feel about the dances? "It was *the* thing to be at," recalled G. Hendry.[64] "Probably my best memory of Sabina's after school," B. DesChatelets recounted, "was when I started to go to the dances. And the dances were great." He recalled Father McMahon's rules. "They had Andy Frain ushers. There'd be three of them and I don't know how many hundreds of people would be at the dances. You probably had an area about as big as a table to dance in. . . . It was in the days of jitterbugging. They'd say *no* breaking, because then you used to throw them out pretty far. These three would walk around and if they came up and tapped you on the shoulder and said 'Go sit down,' you'd go sit down; or they'd say 'Go on outside, you've had it for the night,' you might put up and say 'Give us a break,' but that's the way it was. . . . If you were holding a girl too close, the nuns would come and walk between you!"[65] G. Hendry agreed. "It was very, very, strictly run." Although he admitted to testing the limits of the rules by smuggling in some liquor, he also said, "There was a sense that you didn't want to defile it—especially coming from the parish."[66]

B. Deschatelets also remembered the inflexible dress code. "You had to wear in those days a suit coat—no air conditioning. And I can remember the gyrations that we went through. You worked up a good sweat. I remember this one used to go between dances and wring his coat out. And you'd ask if you could take the coat off. They'd say 'No, no, no!' "[67]

The uncompromising regulations, however, did not hinder the dance's popularity or stifle amorous feelings. "You'd make dates there. . . . You'd get a date and then you'd go to the Highland Theater, which was at one end of Sabina's, or we'd go to the Capitol Theater." St. Sabina's community center became the premiere Catholic match-maker on the South Side. "I met my wife there," related B. DesChatelets. "I asked her to dance. We were dancing around and I said 'Some day I'm going to marry you.' "[68] Mr. DesChatelets romantic hopes were not unique. G. Hendry said, "My marriage came out of there."[69] T. O'Rourke, who is retired and winters in the sunbelt, said, "I meet people down in Florida who say 'I met my husband dancing at Sabina's.' "[70]

Perhaps the most famous story of St. Sabina's matchmaking came from a WGN radio broadcast in June 1939. A local milk company sponsored a special show on which Quin Ryan of WGN interviewed young couples applying for marriage licenses at City Hall. Ryan interviewed three couples a day. One afternoon, in conversation with a couple, he found out that they had met at the St. Sabina dances. In turn, the second couple revealed that they had met at this St. Sabina activity. Ryan, then, turned to the third couple and said, " 'I suppose you met at St. Sabina's also,' " and they replied, " 'Yes, we did.' "[71]

"No doubt having the three couples on the program was a coincidence," Merlin Mungovan wrote, "but practically every Catholic young person on the Far South Side has at some time or other attended the St. Sabina Sunday Evening Dance. It is hard to say just how much this event has contributed to Catholic Action."[72]

Father McMahon confirmed these results of his activities. "Every place I go, I meet people—yes, every place—no matter where I go on the South Side of Chicago, I'll meet them. 'You married me,' or 'I met my husband or wife at St. Sabina's skating or at the dance.' This thing happens so often. It makes you feel good that you had a part in it."[73]

Father McMahon did not limit his supervision of the young people to the community center. "We used to police the neighborhood," he said. "Mungovan and I would get in the car after the doors were closed and we'd go around and see what was going on in the neighborhood. . . . If we saw anything going on in a car or anything, we'd just pull up and give them a dirty look and away they went and that was it. But there wasn't much of it to tell the truth. We caught them spiking a coke one time in an ice cream parlor, and we did something about that. They never did it again. . . . Sure some of the kids got into trouble. . . . They'd be out with a group in a car or something somewhere, and they'd be drinking beer and they'd get caught doing it . . . If there were any fights going on we'd stop them. And pretty soon we'd have them straightened out."[74] During his years at St. Sabina's, Father McMahon claimed that there was never a boy or girl sent to juvenile court.[75] "I think we gave a good example," he said. "A lot of kids became priests because they wanted to be like the priests of our vintage."[76] J. Kill confirmed that this was part of his inspiration for becoming a priest.[77]

The parents of St. Sabina's enthusiastically supported the supervised activities at the community center. Father Tom was never in short supply of volunteers to assist in his endeavors. "They knew where their kids were on a Sunday night and for the roller skating on Friday nights," Father Tom asserted. "The people love what you're doing when you're interested in their children and keeping them out of trouble."[78] The dances "were very well supervised," concurred H. O'Connor. "There was no trouble. . . . I think that kind of endeared people to the parish."[79]

In 1956 *The Seraph* reminded the parish of the importance of the center to their particular community: "The St. Sabina Sunday Night Dance has been conducted for 30 successful years as a service to the Catholic families of the neighborhood. . . . No other Sunday dance for the high school crowd has such a big band, big hall, or big crowd of fellow Catholics."[80]

Parishioners believed the community center played an important role in their identification with St. Sabina's. "Everything was there for you," G. Hendry related.[81] "The gymnasium had a good influence on [parish identity], because we centered at the gymnasium," said J. Kill. "You didn't center at the local park. . . . You just went over to the gymnasium."[82] K. Clair said, "That's how we identified with the parish as St. Sabina's, because we felt it was the best around because we had the dances."[83]

The center, however, did not have a monopoly on all recreational activities in the parish. Yet some of these other events were still under Father Tom's auspices. He persuaded Monsignor Egan to purchase a corner lot just to the north of the center to be used as a baseball field. Preparing the lot for use turned into a community event. Father Tom enlisted the help of "hundreds of teens, preteens, and young adults" to cut down the weeds and even the ground. He enticed them to do this back-breaking work by treating them to pop and ice cream. To fill in the deep holes and level the ground, a parishioner who worked in the steel mills delivered loads of slag to the new field. To keep the dust from the slag from blowing into the nearby stores of irate shop-owners, Father Tom covered the slag with black dirt excavated by a contractor who was installing a new sidewalk around the church for the pastor. Glad to assist, the contractor hauled the dirt over and rolled the whole field and donated additional dirt. " 'I got kids of my own, Father,' " he explained, " 'and I like the way you are trying to provide a place for them to play and stay out of trouble.' " The Holy Name Society donated seed and within a few weeks the new baseball field had a blanket of green grass.[84]

With the field completed, Father McMahon organized softball leagues. They used sixteen-inch "Chicago style" balls and adhered to slow pitch rules. Children's games were scheduled in the mornings and afternoons, and evenings were reserved for the teens and young adults. The two diamonds at opposite ends of the field were in constant use throughout the summer months. "We took it for granted that everybody played softball," related J. Nelligan.[85] On some occasions four games were played simultaneously out of the four corners of the lot. Local merchants sponsored and outfitted the teams, and proudly displayed trophies in their store windows if their team won.[86]

The children of the parish were not the only ones to take an interest in sporting and social events. Some of the other assistant priests organized an annual St. Sabina Golf Tournament. In its first year, 1942, the outing attracted 89 men and eventually grew to 237 annual participants. More came to the dinner that followed the event to socialize with their fellow parishioners. This brought the annual total number of participants to 400.[87]

Adults also socialized in the "Mr. & Mrs. Club" at their monthly dances or get-togethers. In 1949 they had a membership of 311.[88] Single adults could join the Catholic Adult Social Club. And those out of high school had the Young People's Club, whose aim was "to foster Catholic fellowship among its members."[89]

"One of the biggest and best social events of the year" at St. Sabina's, though, was an annual parish picnic. In 1941 over ten thousand people made their way to a nearby forest preserve for the bucolic celebration of their parish's twenty-fifth anniversary. Picnics in subsequent years were also successful. Busloads of people had to be shuttled back and forth between St. Sabina's and the picnic groves. "The pastor and priests think this is a marvelous way to bring our people together and to solidify the parish spirit," *The Seraph* reported.[90]

Children of the parish also could join the active Scouting program. St. Sabina Scouting dated back to the founding of the Catholic Boy Scout organization in 1930. Father Ashenden, along with a lawyer from Our Lady Help of Christians, laid the foundation for a Catholic Scouting league. Although affiliated with Boy Scouts of America, Chicago Catholics continued the Catholic tradition in America of "separate but equal" institutions by putting their scouting program under their own religious auspices. Although Ashenden obtained permission to use the Boy Scout name and follow their rules, Catholic Scouts were affiliated with a parish and had a priest serve as their spiritual director. Scout leaders were obligated to join the parish Holy Name Society and the Scouts were initiated into the junior branch.[91] Bishops Sheil's enthusiastic promotion of Catholic Scouting engendered 243 parish-affiliated Scout troops in Chicago by 1934. Sheil had hoped to nationalize the Catholic Scout program. He never had the same success elsewhere.

Besides Boy Scouts, St. Sabina's scouting program came to include the Cub Scouts, the Brownies, and the Girl Scouts. Each pack had up to 150 children.[92] Because of their parish affiliation, scouting focused impressionable minds toward a Catholic-centered world. Scout rituals usually included some religious component. The following description of the closing ritual from *The Seraph* illustrates this aspect to Catholic scouting: "The entire St. Sabina Scout Organization consisting of Cubs, Brownies, Girl Scouts, Boy Scouts, leaders, officers, parents and friends . . . convened at our Scout Hall and bearing our national colors and the various Scout flags marched in orderly uniformed ranks to St. Sabina Church for the religious services that bring each year of scouting to a close."[93] Scouts were led in prayer by their Spiritual Director, Father William J. Quinlan, and Monsignor Gorey offered benediction. Girl Scouts also attended mass with their parents and leaders on first Saturdays of the month, Our Lady of Fatima Day.[94]

The neighborhood also continued to be intertwined with the parish. "It was home," D. Foertsch said of the neighborhood. "It was comfortable."[95] In an area of two- and three-flats and small bungalows populated by large families, most belonging to St. Sabina's, socializing was quite easy. "At night there were a lot of children out," J. Nelligan recalled, "so if you wanted a bottle of pop, you could walk up to the corner, get a drink of pop, and talk to twenty kids on your way over. . . . It was very safe. Everybody knew everybody. It was very friendly."[96]

An integral part of neighborhood social life were the local taverns. In traditional, peasant Ireland the sharing of "drink" was a courtesy and symbolized the bonds of friendship.[97] Its associations with hospitality and sociability persisted in the Irish subculture in Chicago and St. Sabina's.[98] The Irish showed a great deal of interest in the saloon business from the time they arrived in the city. Unlike other ethnic groups, who showed decreasing interest in the enterprise in succeeding generations, the Irish tended to increase their involvement in the liquor trade.[99] "There were tons of taverns on 79th Street," recalled D. Foertsch. "Different groups would go to different ones. . . . I'd say almost all men [went]. Sometimes in the evening, some of the women would go with their men as kind of a social place to go."[100]

"There were taverns on every block," B. DesChatelets recalled. "There was a place at 79th and Ada. . . . They'd have spontaneous entertainment, singing, dancing. . . . There was a place at 79th and Bishop that all the "greenies" went. . . . They're Irish wetbacks—a bucket of blood, a fight a minute in there! The Irish love to fight. They just do. . . . It's just a fight to see who wins."[101] The association between fighting and drinking in Irish culture dates back to pre-famine Ireland and faction fights between extended clans. Gradually, fights evolved among men into a form of " 'popular recreation . . . that were held so dear and enjoyed so much.' "[102]

On the corner of 79th and Laflin, outside a tavern, some of the more "notable" characters of the neighborhood used to sit on chairs and play cards. Among them were Edward "Spike" O'Donnell, of the South Side O'Donnell family bootleggers, who had tangled with and had been subdued by Al Capone.[103] "We'd call him 'Mister' O'Donnell," J. Nelligan recalled.[104] Next to him sat Buck Weaver, the White Sox third baseman who, along with seven others, had been blacklisted for throwing the 1919 World Series. The only evidence against Weaver was that he had heard of the conspiracy but did not report it. He spent the rest of his life a defeated man trying to clear his name—and playing cards on 79th Street still sporting a White Sox jacket. Although he was not a Catholic, when Weaver died and was laid out in a chapel at 79th and Emerald Avenue, kneelers were placed before his coffin so his Catholic friends in the area could pay tribute to him.[105]

Along with O'Donnell and Weaver "was a card dealer," related J. Nelligan. "He wore a summer straw and he used to have a long-sleeved shirt with the garter belts so he could deal. And there was a guy named John Duffy—that was the hierarchy. And they used to bring these kitchen chairs out on the corner. These gentlemen were 'retired.' " They made sitting on chairs on the street corner such a distinguished affair that young Nelligan looked forward to the day when he grew up and retired so he could finally sit on the chairs.[106]

Seventy-ninth Street continued to be a lively thoroughfare. Neighborhood businesses continued to prosper. "The stores in the area were great," recalled D. Foertsch.[107] Since most needs were met in the neighborhood, venturing beyond it was a special occasion. J. Nelligan reminisced, "Going around the other half of the world would be going to 63rd and Halsted where they had a big dime store." A big excursion for kids would be to take the 79th streetcar to Rainbow Beach on the shores of Lake Michigan. "The only problem," he said, "was we were all fair. We'd go . . . once a month and we'd get burned. Then we couldn't go back."[108]

The abundance of shops gave kids the opportunity for local jobs. "Your jobs were . . . in the parish," said G. Hendry. "I worked for a supermarket . . . two blocks away [from home]. I was a delivery boy."[109] As the parish children got older, their jobs may have extended beyond the neighborhood, but they often fit a similar pattern. "In high school, you got to be an Andy Frain usher at White Sox park," said J. Nelligan. "This was basically what everybody did."[110]

Besides job opportunities within the parish, the parish network also gave individuals access to jobs. St. Sabina's "was in the eighteenth ward and getting a job [was through] who you knew and who you were related to. . . . [I got a job with Streets and Sanitation] through my wife's aunt. She said, 'George, would you like a job to make money to go back to school?' And through her intercession, she got the job for me."[111]

In all respects, the parish of St. Sabina's remained a vital center of community life for Catholics in the two decades following the start of the Second World War. "It was a community. It was very good spirited," said Father McMahon. "I think because of the priests and the sisters and the school. Everything was centered around the parish."[112] St. Sabina's varied activities led *The Seraph* to boast that "this spirit of cooperation is the earmark that has made Saint Sabina the parish everyone wants to live in."[113]

Although there were forces at work, such as the growth of industrial unions, political coalitions, and the spread of mass popular culture and consumerism, in Chicago and across the nation to help ethnic and racial groups recognize common interests, there were still limits as to how much people were willing to move in this direction. None of these forces, many in the Church felt, could substitute for the deep spiritual and psychological needs that were satisfied within a Catholic subculture. Indeed, some of these things were seen to be direct threats to fundamental values. While in the political arena or at work, Catholics pursued common objectives with others; the intimate aspects of their lives were still expressed in this subculture.

This made the parish community exclusive and insulated its members in a "Catholic" world. "There was no reason to stretch out to any other place," said Mildred Joyce, "because you had that wide territory of your own people. And naturally, you feel towards your own kind."[114] People "were proud of that when they were living there," recalled H. O'Connor.[115] The parish as a way of life was not unique to St. Sabina's, but extended through many Chicago neighborhoods. The "City of Neighborhoods" was in certain areas more a "City of Parishes."

The parish community was defined by locality and mutual devotions, values, and sentiments. Some sociologists have emphasized territorial aspects to community, while other scholars have thought it more profitable to think of community as an experience, a sense of "we-ness," rather than merely of people living in the same locality.[116] Whatever their emphasis, historians and sociologists have often decried the urban, industrial world as an enemy of community. This much-heralded demise of community has perplexed old parishioners of St. Sabina's. "They keep talking about community and how there isn't any," complained T. O'Rourke. "Well, we had it back then!"[117]

More recently sociologists and ethnic historians have come to better understand the regeneration of community in immigrant America. Thomas Bender argues that scholars must look to the historical record to reformulate models of "community" and must reject theories that argue for static or debilitated communities. Recent works have demonstrated that individuals are continually adapting and readapting themselves to the various changes in the modern world to meet their personal needs for intimacy and a sense of belonging.[118] In his impressive synthesis of immigration and ethnic history, John Bodnar argues that immigrants successfully adapted traditional building blocks of community, such as the family and churches, to the modern world as a means to better cope with the vast changes confronting the individual.[119]

St. Sabina's was a re-creation of the Old World parish community adapted to urban America. It was a vital and dynamic parish that provided a positive experience of living in a large city. For the individual, life in St. Sabina's was more of a small-town affair than the impersonal, detached existence often attributed to those who inhabit our great cites. Catholicism provided the meaningful beliefs, values, institutions, and rituals necessary to bind members of a community. The devotional style of Catholicism that persisted during this time in St. Sabina's continually called people over to the church. The school centralized children's experiences toward a parish world. The belief that children and adults needed wholesome and Catholic-influenced social activities and recreation further extended and enhanced the parish's function in the community. In many respects, the parish nurtured and strengthened the individual and the family spiritually, intellectually, physically, and socially. It was a place were people looked out for each other and supported one another.

The need for community is an essential part of the human condition. However, a community can become exclusive and defensive if interlopers threaten to change its nature. While St. Sabina's sought to create a positive Christian environment for its parishioners and basically did, it also created a protected and defensive world. Parish members could accept the presence of others not of their community up to a point and could live with others not of their kind as long as their community was not encroached upon. But the parish could also become defensive toward any threats, real or perceived, that might pollute or destroy their parish, whether it was the YMCA, too many Protestants, dimly lit roller rinks, or other people with whom they were too unfamiliar, who threatened to overrun their neighborhood.

The Irish of Chicago's South Side entered the decade of the 1960s secure in the knowledge that one of their own controlled city hall, that John F. Kennedy was on his way to the White House, and that their network of parishes provided security and solidarity. But waves of change within the Church, within the parish, and, most significant, within the city were already washing against the borders of St. Sabina's and its sister parishes. Racial change would threaten the comfortable, existing definitions of community and offer an opportunity to enrich and broaden the religious and social vision of the parish.

6

The Troubles: Racial Tension and the Parish Community

While the parish continued to be a vital force within the Irish-American community after World War II, external forces were at work to challenge it physically, intellectually, and spiritually. Chicago's black belt began to explode in population as the Great Migration of black refugees from the South poured into the city during these years. This forced many blacks to seek homes in many traditionally all-white neighborhoods and parishes. In addition, new ideas, partly brought on by this crisis and partly by American Catholicism's maturation, would challenge popular notions of Catholicism's role in parish communities. Some clergy and laity made tremendous efforts to broaden the Church's vision beyond its traditional parameters, while others clung to the old ways.

Breaking down barriers between ethnic and racial groups in Chicago has been a slow and painful process. Even within Catholic ranks there were always sharp and bitter divisions. Finley Peter Dunne's Mr. Dooley was not the only Irish American to regard the influx of other immigrants into his domain as similar to the barbarian descent upon ancient Rome. St. Gregory's, a German parish on Chicago's North Side, described the arrival of the Irish after World War I in similar unflattering terms: " 'The great influx of our Celtic parishioners was the finishing blow, of course, and the old ways were swept away by the new as St. Gregory grew and grew and grew.' "[1]

National parishes segregated Catholics and facilitated deep cleavages between co-religionists. Bridgeport, for example, which was only two miles long and a half-mile wide, had four territorial parishes (read Irish) and nine national churches.[2] People segregated themselves residentially even within this single neighborhood around their national parishes.[3] The *Chicago Tribune* commented upon the relations between the Irish and the Germans, who had been the original settlers: "Their characteristics are totally antagonistic, as much so as oil and water, and with a still further difference, that no agent is known which will cause their bases to coalesce and form a new substance."[4] Even as late as the 1930s priests from different national parishes would cross the street rather than be forced to acknowledge each other.[5] Parents and priests often pressured their children to marry within their nationality group. One woman whose Irish mother grew up in a predominantly Italian neighborhood said she never forgot the intense loneliness and isolation of her childhood. She swore all Italians were connected to the Mafia and continually warned her daughters never to marry one.[6]

In the suburb of Cicero, similar feelings existed. Roman Catholic Poles and Czechs made no effort to hide their wariness of Protestant newcomers, who for years were considered an "out group." There was not, however, any reported violence and their presence was tolerated if it was not welcomed.[7] Nearby in Berwyn, where Bohemians predominated, resentment was directed against Irish and Italians when they began to move into the area in the 1950s. When Irish priests "took over" St. Odilo's, there were many protests, which led to some Irish families being forced to leave because of "unfriendly attitudes."[8]

The fiery crosses of the Ku Klux Klan greeted the establishment of a Catholic church in the upscale, WASP community of Beverly Hills in the 1920s. Although anti-Catholic sentiment remained strong for many years, it did not prevent the growth of St. Barnabas or any other Catholic parish in the community.[9] Priests in Back of the Yards eventually learned to work with each other in the Neighborhood Council, and "mixed" marriages between Catholic ethnic groups became more common.[10] However, in middle-class communities such as Auburn-Gresham, institutional separation of religious groups still persisted. White ethnics generally were able to take advantage of housing opportunities in new real estate developments as their economic situation improved.

Many whites in Chicago liked to think that the same process of assimilation applied to blacks as well. Mayor Richard J. Daley, for example, liked to consider the black community as simply one more group that would follow the same pattern of material success and accommodation of white ethnics. This view, however, was willfully blind to other realities facing the African-American community. As the black population grew and their demands for housing and jobs increased, white hostility mounted. On the eve of the First World War a black ghetto was taking definite shape. White hostility and clashes between the races made separate spheres appear to be the only peaceable solution to race relations.[11]

Chicago's black community dates back to the city's earliest days. In the late 1840s fugitive slaves and freed blacks settled in the area. Like the Irish, they tended to live for the most part on the South Side and to a certain extent west of the downtown business district. However, during the nineteenth century their numbers remained small compared with the growing immigrant population. In 1860 blacks numbered only a thousand. By 1890 their numbers had increased to fifteen thousand, which was only 1.3 percent of the total population.[12]

By the 1870s Illinois law guaranteed blacks basic civil rights such as the right to vote and the right to attend any school. By the 1880s public places were legally forbidden to discriminate against them. Initially, blacks were not residentially segregated. Like other ethnic groups, they tended to group themselves, but most lived in mixed neighborhoods. Black businessmen and professionals enjoyed social and economic good will in their relations with whites. Black leaders championed integration in all civic institutions.[13]

Yet the historical experience of blacks in Chicago would differ from other ethnic groups in several respects. Although immigrants faced problems of discrimination in housing and employment, blacks had an even more difficult time. Public places were not always open to them regardless of the law. The city was growing rapidly and offered scores of new industrial jobs; blacks, however, were often barred from these new opportunities. While the Irish and other immigrants were able to take advantage of opportunities in the new growth enterprises of construction, transportation, and industry, blacks had a much harder time getting these jobs. As long as there was a continuous supply of white immigrants, employers were reluctant to create strife in the workplace by hiring blacks. If they did employ them, they were usually the last hired and the first fired, or they were taken on as scabs, which further aggravated white workers. Many unions refused to admit blacks, while others segregated them into separate and subordinate locals and seldom took their needs seriously. Blacks did not fare much better in the civil service, an Irish preserve, although it was theoretically open to all. Blacks were forced into domestic and personal service for lack of other alternatives. There they were separated from the growing opportunities of the burgeoning metropolis, confined to dead-end jobs.[14]

World War I opened up new economic opportunities for blacks. Immigration was drastically reduced due to the conflict, and American businesses faced labor shortages at a time when demands for production were great. Employers had no choice but to depend upon home labor. Race and sex were overlooked as impediments to employment. Labor agents began combing the South for job recruits for the steel mills, railroads, and stockyards. These new openings arose at the same time Southern agriculture collapsed. The lure of greater opportunities and the possibility of making a new life enticed many Southern blacks to the North. "Northern fever" rather than the immigrant's "American fever" met the manpower for America's industrial needs during the war. Chicago was also renowned as the home of the *Defender*—the most popular and outspoken champion of black America, which also encouraged blacks to come northward, particularly to Chicago, to escape Southern Jim Crow laws. Between 1916 and 1919 over 50,000 blacks came to Chicago.[15]

Blacks migrated to the industrial states of Illinois, Ohio, Pennsylvania, New York, and Michigan. Chicago, however, was the Mecca for many black migrants. The Illinois Central Railroad provided easy access to the city for blacks from Louisiana, Arkansas, and Mississippi. The 12th Street Station on the South Side was the terminus of the Illinois Central. Blacks found homes nearby in the increasingly congested black belt.[16]

Whites responded by trying to impose upon them legal restrictions in housing, schools, and public accommodations. When unsuccessful at that, some resorted to violence. During these years after the war a kind of guerrilla warfare was waged against blacks. They were assaulted on the streets, playgrounds, and beaches, and their homes were bombed. When servicemen returned from the war, the situation was aggravated by a shortage in housing and jobs in a recessionary economy.[17]

A full-scale riot occurred in the summer of 1919 when, at a beach, a black youth was stoned by whites and subsequently drowned for failing to respect the "imaginary" line whites had drawn to divide the races in the water. When the police failed to make any arrests, some blacks attacked several white men. Whites retaliated by beating or stabbing any black they found in their neighborhoods. The rioting continued throughout the South Side for the next week. While both sides committed the atrocities, it was the black community that suffered the most casualties. And the end result was to harden the lines of segregation in Chicago.[18]

Any chance for peaceful integration in Chicago was dealt a mortal blow by the riot. The experience confirmed for the black community the importance of self-reliance and the need to develop their own internal resources. After the Great Migration abated at the onset of the Great Depression, the black belt had very specific boundaries ranging from 22nd to 55th Streets and Wentworth Avenue to Cottage Grove. This area was more and more exclusively black, where it once had enjoyed at least a modicum of racial mixture. Within this enclosed community blacks strove to reinforce their institutional bases and practically created a city within a city. Yet poverty, inexperience with urban, industrial skills, and lack of financial resources hampered the development of a solid and stable black economy and community. Their community was the product of discrimination, not choice, and remained dependent on the white world beyond its borders for services and goods.[19]

No other group was as restricted to a certain location in the city as blacks were. Those who had achieved economic success were unable to move beyond these racial boundaries. Neither housing agencies on the local or national level nor slum reformers were interested in altering the status quo between the races.[20]

The Great Depression eased the pressure on the black belt as jobs dried up and migration slowed down. Clashes between whites and blacks temporarily abated. By the Second World War, however, black migration resumed as wartime jobs once again lured them from the South to the North. Blacks were also "pushed" northward by the invention of the cotton picker, which made the sharecropping system obsolete and made thousands of black agricultural laborers jobless. By 1950 the black population reached 13.6 percent of Chicago's residents, and by 1960 it had grown to 22.9 percent. The black belt, with its aging and deteriorating homes, could no longer contain all the blacks who were forced to live in it. For some blacks, poverty was no longer an obstacle to better housing. As middle-class whites moved to the sub-urbs with the postwar housing boom, the black middle class was able to move into the areas they vacated. However, as the boundaries of the black belt expanded block by block, fear spread through many nearby white neighborhoods. Many formed neighborhood organizations in which members pledged not to sell to blacks. In 1948, the Supreme Court ruled that these restrictive covenants were illegal. When white communities had no legal means to keep blacks out of their neighbor-hoods, some people resorted to violence.[21]

Racial succession from the expanding black belt into contiguous areas, rather than a more random pattern of integration, came to be the standard form of population transfer within Chicago. This practice was abetted by lending institutions and the real estate industry. Banks were loath to invest in mortgages in "threatened" white neighborhoods. It was difficult, then, for blacks to buy in these area. To keep whites in the neighborhood, landlords and realtors lowered costs. Despite these efforts, realtors were pessimistic about the future of the neigh-borhood and were reluctant to invest in maintenance. These areas, then, began showing signs of deterioration before blacks even reached them. Whites interpreted this decline to be due to the encroaching black belt and subsequently left.[22]

Real estate speculators or "blockbusters" played a crucial role in this changeover process. Some "panic peddlers" had no qualms about spreading rumors, encouraging fear, or in harassing white homeown-ers about the prospect of having black neighbors. Other realtors tried to maintain some degree of "respectability" by not selling to blacks until they composed at least 50 percent of the neighborhood population. Others used lower percentages. These brokers, though, stood to gain by the activities of less scrupulous realtors. Whites, who were too ashamed to "break" the neighborhood by selling to blacks, were easy prey for these speculators. For fear of losing all the value of their homes if blacks moved in, they would sell to a speculator at reduced market value, but higher than if they sold to blacks directly. Blacks, then, who were unable to obtain financing through conventional methods, went through these speculators to get money needed to purchase a home. They were generally forced to pay a much higher price than the speculator paid for the property. Although they only needed a small down-payment, monthly costs were very high. This left little money for maintenance and forced some to "double up"—taking in more people to help meet the payments. Those blacks who rented in these newer areas also faced deteriorating buildings. Many apartments were converted into "kitchenettes," which caused overcrowding in the facilities, or blacks were forced to pay higher rents, which were not reinvested in the building. As these areas deteriorated, white fear of black property destruction was reinforced.[23]

This process of neighborhood succession seemed inevitable. However, after the war the federal government began to exert some pressure on cities to end segregated ghettoes. Mayor Kelly's administration also worked to alleviate pressure in the black belt. The Chicago Housing Authority (CHA), under the direction of Elizabeth Wood, tried to build scattered site homes for blacks as well as veterans. However, whites in outlying districts responded with violence. White politicians brought the agency under the jurisdiction of the city council, thereby ending any integration hopes. By 1947, Kelly had been succeeded by Martin H. Kennelly as mayor, and by 1954 Wood had been fired for her liberal policies. The CHA stopped experimenting with progressive policies, and once again the status quo was in place. High-rise public housing was built to keep the growing black population within its traditional confines. By 1960, the black ghetto was much larger than in 1919, and it was more firmly entrenched in the city's landscape.[24]

When blacks came North, they were not just moving into urban America, they were also invading the heartland of Catholic America. Catholics were not unique in their fear and resentment of blacks. It took city-wide resentment of blacks to create the first ghetto. The power elite of the city were content to keep blacks in a subordinate social, economic, and political position. Since so many Catholics and blacks competed for similar jobs and neighborhoods, Catholics often stood out as major protagonists in the conflict over neighborhoods, with the Irish often in the front-line trenches.

The Irish themselves were no strangers to resentment and discrimination. Of all immigrants, they had arrived in America with the least amount of skills to offer employers or apply to urban living. Their lowly status and dependence on unskilled work made them more suspicious and resentful of black competition. As one former Chicagoan noted, "Nine-tenths of all immigrants from the Green Isle were at best adapted only to the commonest labor, and so came often not only in close contact, but even in direct competition with blacks, both bond and free."[25] In 1864 the *Chicago Tribune* noted the same propensity among the Irish to resent blacks, saying "It is a little singular that no class of people in Chicago fear the competition of the handful of blacks here except the Irish."[26] Of course, the WASPish *Tribune* had no understanding of the trying circumstances of the Irish laborer. The paper chastised them by arguing that their experience should have made them sympathetic to the black plight: "The Irish are the most illogical people on the face of the earth. Of all nationalities they should be the strongest abolitionists. Possessing but little property, depending on their hands for support, having but few skilled workmen among them, most of them being "raw laborers" they above all men have the deepest interest in making labor *free* and thereby *honorable*."[27] Free black labor, however, meant fewer jobs for the Irish.

Although many thousands of Irishmen fought and died for the Union cause in the Civil War, some Irish had difficulty arousing enthusiasm for a war to free slaves when they considered themselves "wage slaves" in northern factories and had not won much empathy from social reformers to alleviate *their* plight. The race problem in Civil War Chicago is illustrated in the following account. "Whenever there was a notable Union victory, the North Side would burst spontaneously into a furor of enthusiasm, while matters down in the densely populated southwest region would be reduced to a mere simmer. But no sooner was there a Rebel victory than it was the turn of Bridgeport and its appendages to celebrate; and these demonstrations generally took the form of hunting down any poor colored brother who might have strayed inadvertently within those delectable precincts."[28]

The Chicago Irish were not alone in their mixed feelings about blacks and the war. In the summer of 1863, the New York Irish responded to a new Draft Act that would impose a heavy burden on the community with the worst riot in American history. Thousands of working men, already angered by blacks brought to the city as strikebreakers, took to the streets for four days. Eleven blacks and an Indian mistaken for black were killed and a black orphanage was burned. Twelve hundred rioters were killed by police and soldiers.[29]

The South Side of Chicago would continue to be a staging ground between white ethnics and blacks into the twentieth century. It was estimated by the Illinois Commission of Human Relations, which investigated the race riots of 1919, that 41 percent of the conflicts between whites and blacks occurred in the white neighborhoods around the stockyards. Athletic clubs from Bridgeport, including the

Hamburgs, Richard J. Daley's club, roamed streets looking for blacks to beat up. They often formed the core of mob scenes.[30]

As the black belt expanded in the years after the Second World War, it moved west of State Street and then pushed south. By 1950 it had reached 71st Street. Halsted Street, which was now just blocks from the ghetto, had been the thoroughfare that the Irish had taken in their climb to the middle class. For blacks to move into neighborhoods west of Halsted meant a confrontation between old enemies.

During the week of November 7, 1949, a riot broke out at 56th and Peoria Street in Visitation parish. The American Civil Liberties Union (ACLU) of Chicago called this area "one of the most dangerous spots, potentially, in the human relations field in this city."[31] This traditionally Irish neighborhood was reputed to have been growing increasingly apprehensive as the black belt crept closer to its borders. Just a week before the riot a black family purchased a home in the area. When rumors of the sale reached the community, a meeting was held in the parish hall. A block organization was formed to try to "maintain the standards" of the community. Its activities were sanctioned by Visitation's pastor, Monsignor Daniel Byrnes, who had promised to buy property before blacks would have a chance to move in. The block organization distributed signs for all to place in their windows that said, "This property not for sale." "This was to discourage letters coming into the parish offering to 'buy your property at any price.' "[32] This organizational network facilitated the spread of rumors.[33]

On October 15, 1949 a Jewish man by the name of Aaron Bindman moved into a house at 56th and Peoria Street within the boundaries of Visitation parish. He was the secretary-treasurer of a CIO local. On Tuesday, November 8, he held a reception for his local, which included some blacks. When ten to twelve blacks were seen entering the home, people immediately assumed the property was being shown to potential black buyers. "From this simple and harmless occasion," wrote the ACLU, "developed the most violent outbreak of anti-Negro, anti-Semitic feeling in the recent history of Chicago."[34]

As the rumor network went into action on Peoria Street, people began coming out onto their porches and front steps. At 10:30 p.m. the block captain was urged to knock on the door to find out what the situation was. Although Bindman explained the nature of the meeting, the block captain insisted that the blacks leave. Bindman refused and the police were called in. By that time a group of fifty or sixty people were assembled outside the home, hurling taunts and threats at the people inside. Although the priests at Visitation were alerted to the gathering, they made no attempt to quell it. The police also made no effort to disperse the crowd, many of whom were their neighbors, but they did escort the blacks out of the building and neighborhood. That night there was no violence.[35]

On the next evening, however, a crowd nearing two hundred gathered outside Bindman's home. Again no attempt was made to disperse them by the fifteen policemen present as the mob shouted out abuses at the man inside. Some began to throw bricks, but no arrests were made. But besides racial fears, anti-Semitism began to pervade the throng. People began shouting insults such as "Let's have a necktie party. Kill the sheenies. Lynch the Jews. Hitler didn't burn enough Jews—let's finish the job."[36]

Many outsiders, particularly students from the University of Chicago, were drawn to the vicinity as news of the conflict spread throughout the South Side. Their presence only exacerbated the situation by encouraging locals to interpret the incident as part of a "Communist plot" directed against their community.[37] A policeman explained to a reporter that "one batch were properly beaten because they were Communists." When asked how he knew they were, he replied, "Because they are Jews."[38]

Despite efforts by the ACLU and the Commission on Human Relations, Mayor Kennelly and the police commissioner took no action to reduce the tension. By Friday night the crowd numbered nearly four hundred and turned violent, not only against those in the Bindman home, but toward all "outsiders." Gangs of youths began roaming through the streets looking for these "troublemakers." To identify them, the youths asked "What parish are you from?" Not being from a parish, many University of Chicago students became victims. Since few blacks lived on the west side of Halsted Street, gangs moved to the thoroughfare, pulled blacks off the streetcars and beat them, and turned over any cars that blacks were driving. The police, many of whom lived in the neighborhood, were sympathetic to the mob. Violence continued on Saturday night. However, the police officer who had quelled a racial incident in Park Manor was assigned to Peoria Street. This action could not have come sooner as more militant members of the black community set out for Peoria Street to retaliate. Arrests were made and the crowd disbanded. By Monday morning fifty-four persons appeared in court to answer for their actions. Most of the cases were eventually dropped because police practices in making arrests were less than exemplary, making prosecutions impossible.[39]

In the weeks that followed the Mayor and the police department were subject to increasing criticism by human relations groups and the press. Their behavior in Englewood was more perplexing in light of another racial incident that had received prompt police action. On the same night that the trouble started on Peoria Street, another crowd assembled at 74th and South Park (now Dr. Martin Luther King Drive) to demonstrate against a black family that was moving into a home in that neighborhood. The police at the Grand Crossing station took immediate action and protected the black family.[40] Nonetheless, Kennelly, considered a reformer, began to lose his prestige in liberal and black communities.

Because of these incidents, along with outbreaks of racial violence in Cicero, which was heavily Catholic, Catholics became increasingly identified with racial violence in Chicago. An article in the *Congress Weekly* stated, "The Catholic Church, itself, appears to be continuing to foster the belief that a man has a right to determine who his neighbors will be."[41] In the South Deering Methodist Church's newsletter, which described the formation of a Ministerial Alliance of four Protestant ministers and a Jewish rabbi, their minister stated, "We also continue to look to the day when the Roman Catholic church will take action locally toward ending the community tension, as the bulk of the problem lies with their constituency."[42]

However, many clergy and laity in the Catholic Church were very concerned with interracial justice and were not idly sitting by while these outbreaks occurred. In 1945, the Catholic Interracial Council (CIC) was founded in Chicago. It was a lay organization not affiliated with the Archdiocese but recognized by it. The Council also had the invaluable assistance of Rev. Daniel Cantwell. Cantwell had been on the faculty of St. Mary of the Lake Seminary. He was dedicated to social, labor, and interracial justice, and strongly advocated lay participation in Church matters.[43]

"The biggest single social phenomenon and social crisis in Chicago," said John McDermott, a former director of CIC, "was the changing neighborhood. . . . The process was chaotic and violent and disastrous. . . . Everyone went away feeling they had lost something of value. . . . It was devastating to many parishes. . . . Blacks were embittered. . . . It was not a pleasant experience to have people walk away from you as if you were a leper"[44]

Within this troubled situation the primary goal of the CIC was "to educate and mold public opinion, particularly the opinion of Catholics in matters calling for the application of the Catholic principles of interracial justice."[45] The CIC took as its mandate a statement by Pope Pius XII on "Human Solidarity" in which he said that racism was the outstanding heresy of the age. "Our motivation in the CIC must be directed by both natural and supernatural objectives in restoring the oneness of the human family."[46] CIC's aim to help end discrimination against minorities encompassed the areas of employment, housing, education, schools, and hospitals. Its methods were to work through existing church organizations and create "cells" in parishes, and to work with civic organizations and official agencies.[47] By 1949 CIC's meetings were attended by 100 to 250 people of both races.[48]

When the race riots broke out in Visitation and in St. Columbanus parish, along with riots at the Airport Homes and in Fernwood, the CIC sadly noted that many of the rioters were Catholic. In February 1950, a CIC member wrote, "It is certainly true that the pastor in the Englewood area where the Peoria Street Riot occurred is not friendly to Negroes and is outspokenly on the side of racial segregation. Even the Cardinal hasn't been able to do anything about him."[49]

Particularly troubling to the CIC was that most pastors were one with their people in their feelings about blacks. Priests schooled in the "brick and mortar" era of American Catholicism naturally ended up putting undue emphasis on the buildings and community they had helped build. They believed that if blacks moved into the parish, it would be "ruined." They "seem to base the success of the parish upon the bank balance," wrote a CIC member.[50] In Berwyn, Father P.J. Buckley, pastor of St. Odilo's parish, claimed that nine out of ten pastors there were more concerned with their property than with human values.[51] Many did not want to loose their fiefdoms.

The beliefs of the pastors and their people fed on each other. Pastors justified their positions by saying, "My people hate the niggers," while parishioners were given the message that it was all right to do so. "The official teaching of the Church was clear," said McDermott, "Pastors and priests, many of them knew better, but they also didn't like to see their parish falling apart. They hoped they wouldn't have to go somewhere else. . . . And people were coming to them with heart-rending tales about what was happening and expecting the Church to be sympathetic."[52] The CIC lamented that "it seems that it has come to the point where Catholics believe our Church condones and approves segregation. . . . Our people seem to think there is nothing wrong in hating, as such, and its outward expression—mob violence. In fact, they seem to act as though it is a holy crusade, and their hate and spleen is not entirely against the Negro but is often anti-Semitic."[53]

McDermott also pointed out that the process became associated not only with racial change but decline in physical and social standards. "This led a lot of white people to think it is perfectly reasonable to resist. They were resisting people who were going to tear down the neighborhood." For over twenty years the CIC tried to convince people that part of the reason for the problem was due to their panicking. "But when you're sitting in a changing neighborhood, you don't want to hear about the whole picture. It sounds academic."[54]

Black Catholics were not any more warmly received in these parishes or in other Catholic institutions such as schools and hospitals than were non-Catholic blacks. In fact, blacks were often outrightly barred from admission to churches, schools, and hospitals, even though white Protestants were permitted in these Catholic establishments. Protestants, however, were not entirely comfortable within this Catholic subculture. Some thought it necessary to lie about their religion to get better care in Catholic hospitals.[55]

Chicago's black Catholic population was quite small. But its experiences in the Church were unique compared to other ethnic Catholics. In 1889, Rev. John Augustine Tolton, who was among the American Catholic Church's first black priests, was appointed to organize St. Monica's parish at 36th and Dearborn. It was the first black Catholic church in Chicago. The small black Catholic community had previously been worshipping in the basement of Old St. Mary's at their own mass. They had asked to have their own parish even though they could attend other masses and churches. When the small congregation could not meet its expenses, the Catholic women of St. James and St. Elizabeth parishes held a fund-raising bazaar for them. In 1924, St. Monica's was consolidated with St. Elizabeth's and became the center for black Catholic Chicago.[56]

When Archbishop Mundelein came to Chicago on the eve of the Great Migration, he designated St. Monica's as reserved exclusively for the black Catholic community. They were not, though, to be excluded from attending other parishes. St. Monica's appeared to be simply another "national" parish. However, white territorial parishes often exercised their prerogative to exclude blacks or treat them as second-class parishioners. If blacks wanted to be full-fledged members of a parish, they had to go to St. Monica's or St. Elizabeth's.[57]

Cardinal Stritch also failed to attend to the needs of black Catholics. However, when racial conflicts began to brew in his parishes after the second wave of black migration, he was called upon to clarify the Church's position on the race issue. In 1946, he declared unequivocally to the Chicago Commission on Human Relations "that the Catholic Churches of this city are open to Catholics from all minority groups and that this held for the parochial schools attached to the parishes." He was also concerned that whites not run from their neighborhoods "but instead . . . remain there and welcome these new community residents."[58] When Cicero exploded with riots, Stritch instructed all the pastors of that suburb to deliver sermons on the equality of all men and on property rights.[59]

Not all parishes were as reactionary and hostile as Visitation. Old St. John's Church, where in the last century Father Waldron chased Irish ruffians with a blackthorn stick, made it its mission to serve the local black community. The pastor, Father William D. O'Brien, wrote the CIC of the positive things Old St. John's was doing for interracial justice. He said, "St. John's congregation consists of about twenty Negro families and not one White family within its borders, although there are perhaps a few score of White people who, in the good weather, come to Mass on Sunday. . . . Cardinal Stritch said that St. John's branch of the St. Vincent De Paul Society was the best in Chicago because your humble servant is personally taking care of its local needs."[60]

At St. Joachim's in Chatham Monsignor William H. Byron insisted his parishioners welcome blacks as their equals. In 1951, the parish school had eighty black pupils out of four hundred enrolled.[61] In 1950 the CIC claimed that at least fifty parishes were integrated on all levels.[62]

The CIC was not the only organized Catholic effort to fight racism in Chicago. Friendship House also played a key role in helping the Catholic Church combat racism on the South Side. Friendship House was founded by the Baroness Catherine de Hueck. Although she was born to the Russian aristocracy, the Bolshevik Revolution plunged her into poverty. After the war she and her husband found employment in Toronto, where she began her first Friendship House. It was originally inspired by her experience with Communism. She believed that if she could help the poor and unemployed, they would be less attracted to Communism.[63]

Friendship House evolved into a Catholic community center similar to settlement houses, except that it was less bureaucratic and strongly religious. In the late 1930s de Hueck opened a Friendship House in Harlem, New York. While there, she saw not only the material deprivation of black people but also that they were being denied basic human justice and love. From that time on Friendship House's primary mission was to work for the advancement of blacks. Martin de Porres, a black saint, became the patron saint of the movement.[64]

De Hueck worked to get the Catholic hierarchy to be more forthright on the question of racial justice. She frequently corresponded with Bishop Sheil in Chicago. Sheil invited her to open a Friendship House in Chicago in St. Elizabeth's parish. By 1942, Chicago opened its House with seven staff workers and twenty volunteers. It later expanded to several hundred volunteers. Father Daniel Cantwell served as their chaplain. The people who made up the movement were convinced that ordinary people could improve society in small but profound ways. Their work involved direct assistance to the needy in the neighborhood. They tried to educate people both at the local and national levels on racial justice and to engage in social action. They were interested in housing, political rights, employment, education, health care, recreation, and worship.[65]

With all of the effort being put forth by members of the Catholic community to deal with racial problems in Chicago, charges against the Church's failure to do so were a real affront to those involved. In 1953, the CIC wrote a letter to the Council Against Discrimination saying that they were "greatly disturbed by what appears to be a failure on the part of some CAD leadership to admit that Catholics have done anything positive."[66]

Changing individual attitudes in the chaotic and fear-ridden neighborhoods and parishes that were one by one being enveloped by the black belt was not an easy task. The pastor of St. Sabina parish, Monsignor John McMahon, was one of a number of Catholics who tried to use the values of the parish community to create an integrated neighborhood and to prepare St. Sabina's for racial change.

7

Make No Small Plans: The Parish Community and the OSC

As the black belt moved further south and west after World War II, neighborhood after neighborhood succumbed to fear, hostility, panic peddling, violence, and ultimately to white flight. Confusion, division, bitterness, and resentment worked their way through succeeding neighborhoods and parishes. Religious groups fought each other as they groped to find solutions for their disintegrating communities. It appeared as though nothing could halt the destructive process that physically and psychologically wounded people and communities.

Monsignor John McMahon, however, who became pastor of St. Sabina's in 1952, refused to submit to the idea that the presence of blacks meant the death knell for a neighborhood. Monsignor McMahon represented a shift in the traditional view of the parish's function. According to his vision the parish should aim to be more than a place to fill the social and spiritual needs of the individual. He hoped to offer a wider vision of the Church's role in society. He knew he needed to prepare his people for the inevitable day when Chicago's growing black population would begin looking for homes in St. Sabina's.[1]

Father McMahon had come from St. Charles Borromeo parish on 12th Street just west of Holy Family parish. During the late 1940s, blacks began moving into the area and their children began attending the parish school. Compared to other parishes on the South and West sides, however, St. Charles managed to remain integrated for nearly twenty years.[2] When he was transferred to St. Sabina's, John McMahon was told that it, too, could expect to change racially, given the migrations that were taking place on the South Side. His plan was to prepare his people to deal with change and to slowly integrate so that the benefits of the community would not be destroyed.[3]

John McMahon was a tall, slim man graced with a gentle, spiritual nature and no particular athletic ability. He enjoyed gardening and watching the young children romp on the playground he had installed outside the rectory dining room windows (except when they got into his periwinkles) rather than being part of the community center's

"jock" culture. Although he did not personally appreciate "jock" Catholicism, he had no desire to disturb the popular activities taking
place at the center. He could see that it was fulfilling a very important
function by generating community spirit, which could provide fertile
ground for the direction in which he wanted to take his parishioners.
Monsignor McMahon regarded community events such as the St.
Patrick's Day parade as good for civic pride rather than as a celebration
of being Irish.[4]

When he arrived in St. Sabina's, Father McMahon was impressed
by the frenetic activities and devotions in his new parish. In July 1952
he expressed the following observations to his parishioners in *The
Seraph*: "Foremost, [the pastor] recognized immediately the amazing
faith of his people. It shows itself in the vast numbers who attend Mass
on Sunday and during the week, your frequenting the Confessional and
Communion rail. It is so evident in the deep respect shown by the
people one meets in the neighborhood."[5] Yet he also hinted that he
would like to challenge the established culture of the parish community. "With people so loyal can there be any limit in parish activity, in
individual and community spiritual growth? What can stop us from
making St. Sabina great in every way and most especially as a school
for Catholic leadership?"[6]

He immediately began to organize new parish groups, such as the
Christian Family Movement, the Legion of Mary, and Young Catholic
Workers, to begin laying the groundwork for his mission. The introduction of these organizations brought St. Sabina's into a different
current of Catholic social and spiritual thought. Midwestern Catholicism had established a more liberal reputation than the Church in the
East. In the nineteenth and early twentieth centuries John Ireland,
Bishop of St. Paul, Minnesota; John L. Spalding, Bishop of Peoria,
Illinois; and John Keane, Bishop of Dubuque, Iowa were staunch allies
of James Cardinal Gibbons of Baltimore, the progressive spokesman
for the Catholic hierarchy. They recognized the unique opportunities
for the Catholic Church in American society. They wholeheartedly
endorsed the American system of separation of church and state—a
notion that was anathema to European Catholicism—as creating the
most conducive environment for religion to flourish. They were advocates of rapid Americanization of immigrants, and they did not view
the modern world with as much suspicion as many of their counterparts. Catholicism, they believed, should be actively engaged in the
social and economic problems of society. They also had a much more
relaxed attitude toward Protestantism. In 1899, however, Pope Leo
XIII condemned what was referred to as "Americanism," which urged
the Catholic Church to adapt its teachings to the modern world.
Catholic intellectual life was severely stifled.[7] However, the American

milieu of freedom and voluntarism would continue to stimulate American Catholic leadership's ideas about the Church's role in society.

Cardinal Mundelein was considered the most liberal leader in the American Church of his day in large part because of his friendship with Franklin D. Roosevelt. Mundelein's subordinates, Bishop Sheil and Monsignor Reynold Hillenbrand in particular, experimented with liberal programs and enhanced the Chicago Archdiocese's reputation as a progressive institution. Mundelein's liberal leanings were stirred more by his sympathy for the poor and the downtrodden than by intellectual musings. His approach to the social and economic concerns of his people was entirely pragmatic and nonideological. The atmosphere he created within his Archdiocese allowed the liberal inclinations of others to flourish.[8]

Sheil's social action, or Catholic Action, was not solely limited to CYO recreational programs. It also included shelters for the homeless and other social services. In 1943 he established the Sheil School of Social Studies to enlighten Catholics on the plight of the poor and persecuted and to provide adult education. However, Sheil's most notable and crucial involvement with social concerns came in 1939 when Back of the Yards Neighborhood Council formed to create a livable environment in "The Jungle."

The Back of the Yards Neighborhood Council was organized by Saul Alinsky, a self-styled radical of Jewish background, and Joseph Meegan, an Irish-Catholic schoolteacher. While the Council was not an official Catholic organization, the neighborhood it represented was nearly 90 percent Catholic. To be effective, the Back of the Yards Council needed the Church's support. Bishop Sheil played an important behind-the-scenes role.

The Neighborhood Council could not effect substantial change in the neighborhood without improving working conditions and wages for the laborers in the meatpacking plants. It was here that Bishop Sheil played a key role by lending his and the Church's prestige to John L. Lewis's CIO. Workers and labor union organizers could not be branded Communists to discredit the movement. Through Sheil's intervention labor unions and community organizing were given more respectability, and he acquired a national reputation as a Catholic liberal leader.[9] Through all of Bishop Sheil's social activism ran a deep commitment to interracial justice. CYO activities welcomed all people, regardless of race or religion. And he opened a social center in St. Elizabeth's old high school to serve the South Side black community.[10]

Monsignor Hillenbrand, rector of St. Mary of the Lake Seminary and a contemporary of Bishop Sheil, developed a more intellectual type of Catholic social action than his more flamboyant colleague. Hillenbrand was inspired by papal encyclicals on the Christian response to modern economic and social problems, and by Dorothy Day's Catholic Worker Movement, which sought to transform the world through the application of Christian values to modern society. It was introduced to Chicago in 1933.[11]

The technique that Hillenbrand and his followers adopted was borrowed from the Jocist movement in Belgium, developed by Father Joseph Cardijn. The basic idea was to organize individuals of similar background into groups or cells to discuss social and economic problems that they encountered in their daily lives, interpret them in light of Christian values, and then try to correct them. This formula was called the inquiry method, which was simply to "observe-judge-act." While many people understood this method in theory, it came to the United States through a man experienced with its application. Louis Putz was a German Holy Cross priest who worked for four years with French youths in an industrial area of Paris. The Second World War forced him to leave. His order gave him a post at the University of Notre Dame, where he continued his work with students.[12]

In 1941 Monsignor Hillenbrand invited Father Putz to the seminary to speak to a group of deacons. He helped Hillenbrand teach his method to the Chicago Archdiocese through seminars, training sessions, and a summer-school program for seminarians, clergy, and laity. A whole generation of seminarians and laity were excited by this innovative approach. New organizations, such as the Catholic Interracial Council and the Catholic Labor Alliance, sprang up in areas ranging from liturgical reform to interracial justice. Catholic laity organized the Christian Family Movement (CFM), the Young Christian Workers (YCW), and the Young Christian Students. The Chicago Archdiocese program prefigured the spirit and teaching of Vatican II.[13]

Father McMahon had this rich base to call upon to help him begin his work in St. Sabina's. In 1945, St. Sabina parish had purchased some storefront properties on Racine Avenue across the street from the rectory and community center.[14] Father McMahon planned to use their separate facility for the new groups he introduced into the parish. He was assisted by two of Monsignor Hillenbrand's protégés, Rev. Jerome Riordan and Rev. James Mollohan. Although he himself was taught the traditional path to spirituality, John McMahon, much like Cardinal Mundelein, was open to the experimentation of his subordinates.

Father Riordan had first been introduced to John McMahon at the seminary's summer-school program at the seminary's summer villa in Clearwater Lake, Wisconsin. Father McMahon was the spiritual director the summer Riordan was there. Although many of the young seminarians thought McMahon was "a bit of an old lady," Jerome Riordan could see that he was an "intensely spiritual person." In 1953 Father Riordan was transferred from St. Mel's on the West Side to St.

Sabina's. He recalled his first impressions of the parish. "It was the grandest example of [the old Church]. This was it in its acme of perfection," he explained. Yet he was aware, like Father McMahon, that "a new day was coming." And John McMahon was the type of pastor he had hoped to work for so he could implement what he had learned at the Hillenbrand-run seminary. "He displayed a universal church mission," he said of his new pastor, "the one that I thought I was a part of, having come out of the seminary that Hillenbrand ran. . . . We thought we were out to change the world."[15]

However, convincing his new parish of the importance of a new outlook was not easy. In some eyes, the new pastor got off to a bad start. Since he did not become a monsignor until 1953, with Father Thomas McMahon still in residence, there were now two Father McMahons in St. Sabina's. This situation caused some confusion at the rectory. Visitors would often ask to see Father McMahon. When asked, "Which one?" the reply would be, "*Our* Father McMahon," meaning Father Tom. Father Tom was, of course, the personification of St. Sabina parish. His work in the community center made him extraordinarily popular and loved among the parishioners, and many people expected that he would be the next pastor. John McMahon "was going uphill against a legend."[16]

When Father Tom was suddenly transferred in August 1953—June was the usual month for priests to be moved—to St. Mel's and Father Riordan was sent from there to St. Sabina's, people began speculating "who did what to whom to cause this to happen." John McMahon seemed to be the likely villain, jealous of the other Father McMahon's popularity. The reason for the switch, however, was that the pastor at St. Mel's needed a first assistant and was told that Tom McMahon would be a good one. However, some people continued to harbor suspicions of ulterior motives, which clouded John McMahon's first years at St. Sabina's. Resentment against him was compounded because he brought in his own secretary and let go the very well-liked parishioner who previously held the job.[17]

Although he was trained in the traditional model for parish priests, John McMahon's ideas and approach were a bit different from the more simple "people" philosophy and devotional Catholicism of parish life. Different enough to make some of the parishioners a bit wary of what he was trying to do. "He seemed to be kind of socially active," recalled J. Hagerty. "Trying to steer people's minds into some other area of thinking than what they had been used to."[18]

When Father Riordan came to St. Sabina's in 1953, Father McMahon made him chaplain of the CFM chapter that he had started. Father Riordan actually began his work with St. Sabina's CFM group before he formally arrived in the parish. The morning he received the letter informing him of his transfer he had a call from Father McMahon, who welcomed him to the parish and said he remembered them meeting at the seminary. He then explained that he was looking for a chaplain for the CFM chapter and had heard he was an expert on the subject. Father Riordan replied that he was "a theoretical expert on the subject." He had not done it yet. Father McMahon did not hesitate. He told him that the group was already formed and that they were having a picnic at Palos Woods and it would be great if he went out to meet them. "That was the beginning of a very wonderful relationship," Father Riordan recalled. "We had thirty to forty families influenced by that."[19]

The CFM was quite different in organization, membership, and format from traditional parish confraternities or sodalities. Men *and* women met together, not only for spiritual enhancement or charitable work but also to discuss social conditions and problems that impinged upon the family. Like the modernists of the last century, CFM did not reject the modern world, but sought to influence it and shape it in a way that was more in keeping with Christian values. CFM was also very much a lay-directed organization. It was begun in Chicago in 1949 by couples influenced by Hillenbrand and Putz. They formed a national organization, with Chicago serving as its headquarters. A coordinating committee was established to provide direction and cohesion to the various cells. By 1958, thirty thousand couples in over two hundred cities and seven foreign countries had CFM cells.[20] Chicago had nearly three thousand couples in the movement.[21]

The introduction of CFM into American Catholicism marked a significant shift in its character. No longer was it predominantly a working-class, urban, ethnic church dominated by the clergy. The new urban and suburban middle-class laity, independent of ethnic bonds, was beginning to acquire greater prominence in the Church.[22] CFM interpreted its work to be a part of the Mystical Body of Christ, in which the Church was a living organism. Christ was the head and his followers were the members. Viewed in this manner, the laity had a great sense of responsibility, which they could no longer relinquish to the hierarchy. They had to act themselves.[23]

Throughout the 1950s CFM's focus was to encourage Christian values in the family, neighboring families, and in institutions affecting these. Although it was a family organization, a husband's and wife's concerns were not to be limited just to each other and their family, and not even just to their parish, but should extend to their community and even their national and international communities. A family could not be well ordered if the world in which it had to engage was not just and humane.[24]

CFM sections comprised six couples and a chaplain who met every two weeks. The first fifteen minutes of their gathering was spent on the gospel and the next fifteen on examining the liturgy or Mystical Body. This exercise prepared them for the remaining forty-five minutes, which were spent on social inquiry. The topic for the section meeting was established by the national coordination committee. CFM prided itself on action not ideology. These sections were supposed to think up an action that could be done before they next met. Originally, they were supposed to be small actions that could be accomplished within that time frame. For instance, how might they follow Jesus' teachings to clothe the naked within their own parish or neighborhood? This might result in a clothing drive.[25] CFM's very nature of looking to change the external world, however, inevitably led to broader social issues. By 1960, the national goals had changed direction. Strictly family concerns were subordinated to broader social concerns. This philosophy forced CFMers to look beyond the confines of Catholic ghetto life.[26]

Besides several active CFM sections, St. Sabina's also started a YCW chapter in 1956 that was modeled according to the same basic idea as CFM. Its purpose was to bring young men and women together to talk about friendship, work, leisure, preparation for marriage, parish life, and neighborhood problems. They, too, searched for small, practical ways to become active for Christ in their parish and at their places of employment.[27] "Talk is converted into action. Practical projects are planned."[28]

Monsignor McMahon established his own spiritual development group, the Legion of Mary, which was more in keeping with his own style of spiritual enhancement. The Legion of Mary was an Irish spiritual movement initiated in Dublin. Members had a program to promote their own spiritual growth. Their meetings were intended to energize them to go out in an organized manner to perform spiritual and corporal works of mercy. St. Sabina's came to have five groups of the Legion for different age groups and sexes. Their actions, though, mostly involved visiting people. Father Riordan also was chaplain for the young ladies' Legion group.[29]

As the black belt crept closer to 79th and Halsted through the 1950s, Monsignor McMahon realized that more practical and pragmatic things needed to be done to deal with the great challenge that his parish faced. In 1952 he encouraged the Holy Name Society to establish a neighborhood stabilizing committee.[30] The St. Sabina Credit Union was in large part a product of the Holy Name Society's stabilization committee. Through the next decade parishioners were encouraged to use credit funds to make improvements on the interior and exterior of their homes. These renovations were intended to maintain the appearance of the community so it would not look like it was declining.[31] In 1958 the Credit Union announced: "Parishioners of

St. Sabina have always felt, and with pride, that they belong to the best parish in a neighborhood that is most desirable and appealing in the pursuit of happiness and spiritual development. Our pastor has worked hard and diligently to maintain the high caliber and correct standards of our community and parish, and we feel that this work should continue unabated for the good of all concerned. . . . Attend to those nicks and dents before they turn into major repair jobs."[32]

By 1958 the Archdiocesan Council of Catholic Women had added a civic committee to their organization. It followed the CFM method. Among its duties were welcoming new neighbors, whether they were Catholic or non-Catholic, reporting need of physical improvement in the neighborhood, and teaching, by work, example, and literature, the basic Christian principles of neighborliness.[33]

Monsignor McMahon became a familiar sight as he walked through the neighborhood with his dog checking for signs of neglect, deterioration, or illegal use of buildings in his parish. He wrote to his parishioners: "In our own neighborhood, there have been many "sneak" illegal conversions. The people who paid for the construction work, the construction company, and the neglectful neighbors—all have a share in the wrong-doing. Illegal conversions in a fine neighborhood do not produce bad fruit immediately but what will happen in the future cannot be laid only at the doorstep of judges or future owners. Keeping up a neighborhood is everyone's responsibility."[34]

He also warned his people of being susceptible to gossip about what direction the neighborhood was going: "Neighborhoods have been wrecked because of idle conversations in supermarkets, beauty parlors, taverns, or street corners. . . . To start a rumor is criminal, to pass it on is no less so. To make a false judgement is wrong, to make it a part of conversation is diabolic."[35] On another occasion he wrote: "A wise person will not accept the opinion of a salesman or idle gossip particularly in regard to problems or a neighborhood. A charitable person will not spread rumors because he knows the great harm they cause. . . . An interested person will consult with those who are responsible, those who are interested not in making "the easy buck" but in preserving the rights and good of a community."[36]

Yet all these attempts, he knew, could not adequately deal with the burgeoning black population on Chicago's South Side. Their vast numbers and pressing need for good housing could easily destabilize the best of neighborhoods with the best of intentions. Monsignor McMahon was determined to maintain the integrity of his own parish, while graciously welcoming newcomers. To do this, he realized he would need more help and great organization to combat real estate panic peddlers as well as fear and prejudice.

McMahon had been a member of the Archdiocesan Conservation

Council since 1953. It was established by Cardinal Stritch to study the relationship between the Church and urban renewal and neighborhood preservation. Stritch was very concerned about urban renewal projects, expressway construction, and the largely non-Catholic poor blacks that threatened to displace his constituents. With its 262 churches and 1.4 million Catholics in 1940, the Church had a huge investment in the city and Catholic Chicago had a high profile in the nation. It did not want to see its people and resources scattered to the far reaches of the Archdiocese. Stritch, however, never overcame his Southern roots on race and failed to provide leadership on racial matters, even when it directly involved Catholics and the Church. Despite his disappointing handling of race issues, Stritch, like his predecessor, allowed his subordinates a measure of freedom to pursue their interests.[37]

Through his involvement in the Council, McMahon met Monsignor John J. Egan. Egan had been a student of Hillenbrand and a follower of Saul Alinsky, whom he met in 1954. In 1956 and 1957, Egan was trained by him at the Industrial Areas Foundation (IAF), a school for community organizers. The Archdiocese gave IAF $118,000 for a study on the rapid social changes occurring in the city. Egan then went ahead and studied the black housing situation in South Side neighborhoods. The deplorable conditions he found prompted him to write a report to Cardinal Stritch, who in turn asked him to be on the Archdiocesan Conservation Council that dealt with city and neighborhood problems. It was through the Conservation Council (later renamed Archdiocesan Office of Urban Affairs) that Egan came to know Monsignor McMahon and his efforts to prepare his parish for integration. McMahon discussed large-scale community-organizing strategy with Egan, and he talked with Monsignor Vincent Cooke at Catholic Charities about money. He also was willing to use parish funds for an organizing effort. In 1959 Egan then helped bring together Alinsky and people from the Southwest Side community to discuss the problems facing that area and to help them form a community organization. [38]

Many people in the Catholic Church did work hard to dispel the racist image it had acquired during the previous fifteen years, and played a prominent role in the formation of the Organization of the Southwest Communities. While McMahon made the initial overtures to pastors on the Southwest Side, Egan worked to pull key people together. Peter Martinez said of Egan's role in OSC's birth, "He was the one doing all the talking between Alinsky and all the pastors. . . . Jack had a lot of contacts with Protestants and a very ecumenical relationship. So he was instrumental in bringing the Protestant and Catholic Churches together at the local level and was instrumental in the dialogue between Alinsky and those pastors."[39]

When Albert Meyer became Chicago's Archbishop after Stritch's death in 1958, he was hesitant to get the Church involved in secular politics. Yet he knew he had to become better acquainted with the issues facing his adopted city. Meyer spoke at length with Egan about urban issues and had even asked him to take him on a tour of Chicago. Egan, having been sensitized by Alinksy to see the city in terms of people and neighborhoods instead of its architecture, was careful to point out the social dimensions of the city. Egan convinced Meyer that the Church should provide leadership in urban affairs. What Egan and McMahon wanted most from Meyer was his moral support and financial assistance. Conservative Southwest Side Irish pastors needed a lot of convincing before they lent their support to a community-organizing effort. Although reluctant, Meyer called a meeting of the pastors at Christ the King rectory in Beverly on January 6, 1959. Meyer listened to the presentations of McMahon, Egan, and Nicholas von Hoffman, an Alinsky organizer. At the end of the meeting he unequivocally endorsed the organization.[40] Meyer also censured white communities for failing to accept blacks of equal social and economic backgrounds.[41]

From the beginning Alinsky made it clear that he would have nothing to do with the Provisional Organization of the Southwest Community (POSC) unless it stood on the side of integration. Organizers were realistic enough to know that an effective community organization needed a wide base of support. Racists and moderates, as well as liberals, had to be included. Yet if they were going to include these people and stand for integration, leading activists knew they would have to handle the situation with great delicacy if their organization were to get off the ground. Their strategy, therefore, was geared toward a pragmatic approach. Organizers were under no illusions that they could inspire anyone with talk of brotherly love. "The approach was hard-nosed," Peter Martinez explained. "The idea was to get everybody involved and to pull known racists into the organization. . . . You had to keep all these people in the same arena. . . . That way you'd get a very realistic perspective . . . [otherwise] the solutions that would come out of this would have a narrow basis of support. They would lose their credibility."[42]

POSC aimed to attract a variety of people into the organization by appealing to their self-interest rather than their idealism. Many in the community worried about the aging and obsolescence of neighborhood facilities and sought to keep the community viable. It was on this basis that Alinsky, IAF organizers, and local leaders were able to pull together an interim association. By May 25, 1959 three hundred leaders, representing eighty community groups, established the Provisional Organization of the Southwest Community. Donald O'Toole, president of the Standard State Bank and chairman of POSC said: "We got together first because we were alarmed at the decline of city communities near us, and we had become aware of some disturbing evidences of decline in some parts of our community. So a few of us began to talk to each other. The original small handful grew into a large group that decided there'd been enough talk—it was time for action—and the Provisional Organization for the Southwest Community was born."[43] O'Toole also pointed out that the group aimed to maintain the high standards of the community and did not intend to "try to stop the unstoppable." The *Chicago Daily News* described their Solomon-like policy, saying, "On that somewhat slippery rock, OSC stands."[44]

By the fall of 1959 POSC organizers were ready to present their program to the whole community. However, the issue of boundaries and who was to be included in the organization threatened to sabotage the project before the ratifying convention. Segregationists wanted the border gerrymandered to keep blacks out of OSC's territory, and they hoped out of the South Side. Integrationists, notably the clergy, wanted boundaries that would unequivocally include black neighborhoods. The Boundary Committee decided to simply designate communities rather than streets when they determined OSC's area of operation.[45] This plan was tested a week before the convention when Alinsky's organizers urged a black Methodist church to apply for membership. It was located on OSC's vaguely defined northeastern boundary. Chairing the Credentials Committee was a liberal named Richard Bukacek. He called an emergency meeting to decide on the church's admittance. The vote would be close.

Ironically, the man who saved the day for Alinksy's position was Monsignor Patrick J. Molloy, pastor of St. Leo's. Molloy was not a credit to the Church. He was vulgar and bigoted and allegedly had connections with the mob. He also had powerful friends in city hall and local ward offices. He was willing to work with POSC simply because he did not see any alternative to the pressure put on his parish by the black belt. If he could be urged to endorse the black church's membership application—considering his reputation—he would not risk alienating conservatives and racists. They could not accuse him of being a "bleeding heart." Monsignor McMahon was to act as the back-up advocate for the black church if Molloy fell through. Alinsky and his organizers made it clear they would pull out if the church was not admitted.

Molloy came through for them at the next meeting. He cautiously asked whether the minister was a "jackleg" preacher with a storefront operation. Jackleg preachers had a poor reputation on the South Side among whites and middle-class blacks. This area had an abundant supply of black preachers who occupied abandoned retail space. They had no formal ministerial training. Many were simply interested in money from collections or the authority bestowed on men of the cloth. They also had unsavory reputations for taking sexual liberties with unsuspecting and trusting women followers.[46] When Molloy was assured this was not the case, he proposed that, " 'they haven't got a jackleg preacher, and if they've got a building, and you say they fall within the boundaries of this organization, I move we admit them.' "[47] With this crucial issue settled the provisional organization proceeded with plans for their convention.

On a chilly, blustery Saturday afternoon in October over one thousand people assembled in Calumet High School auditorium, which was festooned with red, white, and blue bunting. The turn-out exceeded the organizers' projections. Among those in attendance were church, civic, and business organizations from the Southwest Side whose endorsement and support was crucial for the OSC.[48] Egan recalled that it was " 'one of the thrills' " of his life when he looked out over the unlikely collection of people gathered that day.[49]

After the color-guard display and the Pledge of Allegiance, the convention faced a tense moment that tested the organization's purpose. The delegation from the black Methodist church arrived and proceeded down the aisle to their seats. Not a word was uttered in the auditorium in those few moments that lasted an eternity. Once the chairman called for the next order of business, however, the tension and silence were broken.[50] One observer optimistically commented that this was "the day the racists lost."[51]

From the beginning, racists, liberals, and moderates vied for control of the fledgling organization. For ten hours delegates discussed and argued over the objectives of the new group. Despite their illegality, Egan estimated that this area supported at least twenty neighborhood protective associations. "They called themselves conservation groups. They called themselves a development group. They called themselves neighborhood block clubs of one kind or another," explained Monsignor Egan. "But they had no other function in life except to keep black people out of the community."[52] Their objectives were to turn OSC into a full-scale protective association. Others felt they could not make a stand against integration but were fearful of the consequences to their community from racial change. Early OSC meetings revealed that blacks had become associated in their minds with crime, slums, and declining property values. These people were interested in finding ways to maintain the quality of the area and keep neighborhoods stable.[53]

Because of the sensitive nature of the issues, the diverse groups they had to organize, and the radical character of their organizer, OSC was born and lived in controversy. "Back at this time," related Peter Martinez, a staff organizer for OSC, "anybody who even thought about creating a relationship between black and white came at it from a very liberal perspective."[54] Just bringing in Alinsky created a stir. "The mere mention of that name out there would be enough to excite [people]," Father Riordan, explained. "That would be like putting a hand grenade in the parking lot and pulling the pin. Everyone would run for shelter."[55]

Alinsky's association with POSC created some image problems for the new organization among many Southwest Siders.[56] In May 1959, Alinsky testified before the Chicago session of the U.S. Commission on Civil Rights and advocated a voluntary block quota for blacks moving into white areas. While he admitted that it was ironic for a Jew to favor quotas, he thought it was the only way to solve the racial stalemate in South Side neighborhoods.[57] This experiment with quotas was an important reason for Alinsky's desire to organize that area. Many people in the Southwest community thought a quota system was practically an open invitation to blacks to move into the neighborhood.[58] Blacks were suspicious of this plan, which would limit their residential mobility. As a consequence, they did not trust Alinsky either. The Back of the Yards Neighborhood Council, which he had helped organize in the late 1930s, had virtually become a neighborhood protective association when blacks tried moving into the area in subsequent years, which horrified Alinsky.[59]

Because OSC tried to be open and pragmatic in its goals and methods, it invited open discussion in the organization. This made OSC's objectives appear confusing to many outsiders. *The Christian Century* claimed that OSC was in reality a segregationist plot, and that racists were trying to manipulate and hoodwink the churches into supporting it. Some Lutheran pastors felt that Alinsky's method of appealing to self-interest was contrary to Christian tenets. They were afraid that OSC's true purpose was to maintain segregation, and they tried to curtail the involvement of other Protestant churches. While they could not do this, Lutherans did not participate in the organization.[60]

A Methodist congregation was also leery of OSC's purpose and goals. Rev. James M. Reed, associate pastor of Trinity Methodist Church, had been elected one of OSC's eleven vice presidents that fall. The pastoral committee of his church, however, felt that Reed's affiliation with OSC was embarrassing because it was not clear where the organization stood on integration. They asked him to resign or request a transfer to another church. He replied that he could not in good conscience do either. Donald O'Toole stepped in to clarify for the church members that OSC was against segregation. Sixteen local ministers issued a statement supporting Rev. Reed's position. However, the Bishop of the Rock River Methodist Conference removed Reed from his post and sent him to a new church on Chicago's North Side. While it initially seemed a major blow to the organization, Rev. Reed's courageous stand inspired other local churchmen to be even more adamant that OSC be on the side of integration.[61]

Right-wing groups also attacked OSC. In March 1960, Harry T. Everingham, a local resident and editor and publisher of the *Free Enterprise* and vice president of "We, the People," made charges at a meeting of the Civic Council of the Eighteenth Ward that the OSC was a tool of the Communist Party.[62] He had also distributed pamphlets before the first congress making the same accusations. He claimed that the "super civic organization, which seeks to impose its will over all neighborhood improvement organizations and other civic groups, was organized with the help of radicals and members of Communist fronts," and that the clergymen in OSC were at best dupes and at worst "pinks" and left-wingers. Everingham also misinterpreted Alinsky's quota plan, believing that OSC favored forced integration. While he claimed not to be a bigot, Everingham maintained that mixing the races would only be possible after an extensive period of education and "moral training for the newcomers to the neighborhood."[63]

Monsignor McMahon and Monsignor Molloy were both members of the 18th Ward Civic Council and present at the meeting when Everingham made his offensive remarks. The two pastors immediately demanded a public apology from the council's president, John Owl, since Everingham's views of OSC had been no secret. The pastors felt Everingham had insulted them and their work. In a letter of protest to Mr. Owl, they wrote: "We condemn segregation, bigotry, and racism, disguised or undisguised, as being against the basic principles of religion and American democracy. As far as we are concerned, the major responsibility of the OSC is to safeguard the rights of all people regardless of race, creed or color. As Catholic priests, we are forbidden by the teachings of the Church, by the Holy Father himself, and by the Cardinal Archbishop of Chicago to take any other position than that of complete uncompromising and relentless opposition to men such as Mr. Everingham."[64]

Owl made a weak reply, saying that the council had passed a motion to have speakers present various opinions of the new group. As far as McMahon and Molloy were concerned, however, Everingham had completely distorted the nature of the organization. They found Owl's response evasive and unsatisfactory and promptly resigned from the ward council.[65]

Two Protestant ministers rallied to McMahon's and Molloy's defense.[66] Rev. Robert Christ, pastor of the Seventh Presbyterian Church, and Rev. William Roberts, pastor of Calvary Methodist Church, were also key leaders in OSC. They supported the monsignors' action, saying they were courageous and exposed Everingham's true objections to OSC—that it was not a segregationist outfit. "With our Roman Catholic brethren we make common cause against every expression of racism, and we vow that the Everinghams of the community shall neither intimidate nor silence the Christian church."[66]

McMahon agreed that Everingham was a racist "hiding under the robes of a crusader against communism." And he reaffirmed the common cause of Catholics, Protestants, and Jews in the fight against racism and the lies spread against their work in OSC.[67] By April 20, the two monsignors received a formal apology from the 18th Ward Civic Council for their slanderous speaker.[68]

Alinsky did claim to be a reformed Communist. However, his past or present political affiliations were of little interest to many involved in OSC's formation. As far as Cardinal Meyer, Monsignor Egan, and others were concerned, Alinsky's style of organizing adhered to democratic principles and Christian morality.[69] However, to avoid controversy, OSC officially terminated its relationship with Alinsky in August 1959, well before the first congress.[70] But Alinsky continued to play an important behind-the-scenes role. To show the absurdity of Alinsky's Communism, some delegates wore signs at the congress labeling themselves "Reds."[71]

From its inception the local Protestant and Catholic churches played a key role in OSC, helping to shape its policy. The moral aspects of the race issue prompted most, but not necessarily all, of the clergy to be integrationists. "With few notable exceptions," Rev. Christ wrote, "the firm stands on integration have been taken by the clergy rather than by business, social, political or traditional community leaders."[72] Ed Chambers, an IAF organizer and the first staff director of OSC, claimed OSC would never have existed as a liberal organization without the churches, and perhaps might have turned into just another antiblack group.[73]

These leading churchmen, however, were not always satisfied with the responses of some of their colleagues. Protestant ministers complained that some of their co-religionists were myopic in their vision of the churches' challenge in the city, or that they were afraid of controversy and divisiveness in their congregation if they took a position on race.[74] In their attitudes on race Protestants were not much different than Catholics.[75]

Not all Catholic priests were ardent integrationists either. "There were some Catholic priests who were notorious racists," P. Martinez said.[76] "St. Leo's went along," related Father Riordan, "but didn't know why. Monsignor Molloy ... was just philosophically and internally incapable of dealing with the situation himself. When a black moved into part of St. Leo's, he [transferred] that block over to St. Carthage to the north. He just kept chopping off parts of his parish."[77] His advice to his parishioners was, "If you don't move out, they can't get in."[78] However, Monsignor Molloy did play a prominent role in OSC. His main objective, though, was to keep the area stable and appealing to whites so they would stay in his parish. Monsignor Stephen McMahon, pastor of Little Flower parish, was also very negative in his approach to the issue. The extent of his involvement was to advise his parishioners to keep up their houses and yards as a way to maintain the status quo. St. Brendan's had little interest in OSC, and the pastor of St. Justin Martyr's repeatedly put their OSC delegation in racist hands.[79]

The most notable racist Catholic priest was Father Francis X. Lawlor, an Augustinian who taught at St. Rita High School. Father Lawlor had formed his own civic group called the Better Communities Organization, which protested the proposed extension of the Englewood elevated train line west of Ashland out of fear that blacks would migrate along it. He also organized block clubs along the periphery of the black belt and proposed an imaginary wall down Ashland to contain the black community to the east. He was quoted as saying, " 'If the line can't be held at Ashland, Chicago is doomed.' " John Cardinal Cody, who succeeded Meyer in 1965, finally ousted Lawlor from the Chicago Archdiocese in 1968 for his negative activities. However, this did not keep Lawlor away from Chicago. He probably had more media attention than the liberal clergy and helped shape the public image of Catholic-black relations as mostly negative.[80]

Despite these problems, this religious alliance under OSC auspices outmatched any other group or combination of groups. While only approximately fifteen churches provided significant leadership, those that were involved shaped OSC policy. They already had well-established congregations of people from which to draw workers and leaders, and they had existing networks for disseminating information. The churches were also able to supply most of the financial backing to adequately staff OSC.[81]

The churches' involvement in OSC often provoked hostility and resentment in the community. Many residents felt abandoned when their church took a stand on integration. It seemed to forsake its own people and their interests. A local political leader charged that the churches were undermining a community that took a lifetime to build. The coalition of the religious faiths and their liberal stand brought charges of there being a "clerical steamroller." However, for others the churches' brave stand also led to admiration and a "deepening of faith."[82]

Despite the need for interfaith cooperation, Protestants and Catholics did not have a history of working together. Peter Martinez explained that, "This was the first time that all these different churches worked together on a day-to-day basis on real problems, pooled money, talked about what was happening in their congregations. . . . To be in this situation where all these people were talking together and actually treating each other as equal human beings was a remarkable situation."[83]

The seriousness and importance of this very basic human rights question was enough to encourage the different Christian churches to close their distance. Rev. Robert Christ of the Seventh Presbyterian Church wrote, "We have seen the churches coming together—rather driven together—by the pressures from the world. . . . [This contact] was substantially the first relationship between clergy of the two faiths in Southwest Chicago."[84] It was important to clergymen on both sides to meet often in private to establish a working relationship so they could present a united front and provide strong leadership for OSC. Bickering and tension between the two religious groups could have easily sabotaged OSC's hopes for a stable community.[85] The Everingham affair illustrates the good will Protestants extended to their Catholic brethren to work toward this end.

This move toward cooperation between religious groups was not unique to the local area. The national scope of the race problem the country faced during these years prompted Protestants, Catholics, and Jews to meet formally on this issue. In January 1963 Chicago hosted the first National Conference on Religion and Race. The purpose was to discuss how religious organizations could provide greater leadership in solving this national crisis. Race, then, not theology, was the issue that brought the major religions together at the discussion table for the first time in American history.[86] This historic gathering added to the optimism and excitement of those on the Southwest Side working for neighborhood stability and good race relations.

The new working relationship between Catholics and Protestants, however, was not without its problems. Rev. Christ wrote that cooperation "developed with restraint and caution exercised by both parties."[87] The stereotypic view Protestants of the 1950s had of Catholics tended to be biased and superficial: "Catholics fought Martin Luther, played bingo, had confession, and were not intellectually respectable."[88] In addition to the strong leadership role they played in OSC, Catholics exceeded Protestant congregations in contributions, prompting some Protestants to suspiciously view OSC as a "Roman Catholic plot."[89]

"There were Protestants who were worried that it would be a Catholic-controlled organization," P. Martinez explained. Catholics "had all the big churches. . . . They had major dollars that they were putting in . . . [and Protestants wondered] 'were they just being used as a front for a Catholic controlled organization?' "[90] The Lutheran Church was reluctant to join OSC when they heard that the seed money for the project had come from Catholic sources. Walter Kloetzli, director of the Lutheran Church's urban programs, was convinced that Alinksy was a lackey of the Archdiocese, whose concern was to serve the large, important Catholic parishes.[91] OSC organizers initially played on this fear to get more Protestants in the organization. Organizers and Protestant leaders "worked for weeks on end to form an effective Protestant voice."[92]

Sensitive to this tension, OSC designed its constitution so as to balance these two power blocs. In the monthly council meetings each congregation was awarded one vote. Since Protestant churches outnumbered Catholic houses of worship two to one and a half, they could easily dominate these meetings. At the Annual Congress, however, delegates were allotted on the basis of how large a member group was. Catholic parishes were much larger than Protestant congregations and Catholics, therefore, outnumbered them there. It was also agreed that the Executive Committee would have a balanced ticket.[93]

Even in 1963 after Catholics and Protestants had been working together for four years, however, Protestant fears still persisted. Rev. Gordon Irvine of the Seventh Presbyterian Church prepared a paper analyzing the OSC roll-call vote of the 1961 Congress "to discount the argument in some Protestant circles that the Catholic Church in the community organization is a monolithic, cohesive voting bloc." Because of the sensitive nature of the issue, the Catholic Archdiocesan Conservation Council was informed that this study was intended for very limited circulation so as not to reflect negatively on the Catholic churches involved; its purpose was more to dispel false notions among Protestants.[94] The evidence was conclusive that "in the three years of the OSC, the Catholics have shown neither the inclination nor the ability to do this. If the Catholics were to assume control of the OSC, it would result from Protestant default, apathy, and irresponsibility."[95]

Catholics and Protestants also had cultural differences, which made gathering together often tense. "Catholics were big and gregarious," related P. Martinez. "You could hustle-up large numbers of people. . . . They were pragmatic, and they didn't have too much standing in their way about going after anything. The Protestants were much more scrupulous in their approach to any strategy, and always very wary about being overwhelmed by this large Catholic number." For instance, Catholics wanted to hold raffles to raise money for OSC.

To many Protestants, raffles were a form of gambling, and this became a significant bone of contention in the organization. Catholics were successful at making raffles one method of fund-raising. Protestant clergymen, however, talked extensively among themselves about what to do about it. They finally decided to either buy a block of tickets or to make a contribution, but refused to sell the chances to their members.[96]

OSC meetings at Protestant and Catholic church halls were tense affairs. The emotional nature of the issues under discussion often made meetings quite heated. At one of the Catholic "smoke-filled" halls, if the meeting became heated, "that was no big deal. And if somebody got up and said 'You're a son of a bitch' or 'shit,' that was not outside of anybody's experience." And, of course, beer was also served along with coffee afterward. "So you got the language, the liquor, the smoke when you went to the Catholic church. Now when you went to the Protestant churches—whoa—entirely different! Everybody's coming in uptight. There can't be any smoking in the basement of this church. If somebody lets out with one of those exclamations, the Protestants would tighten up and the pastor would have to say something about decorum. There was *not* going to be any beer served after the meeting."[97]

These minor irritations were for the most part overcome when people's focus was directed toward achieving similar ends. It is important to realize, however, that OSC not only had the black/white issue to tackle, but also the religious, social, and cultural differences that had historically separated whites in the city.

Most OSC members found it was an illuminating experience to work with members of the other faith. Rev. Christ wrote: "For Protestants it has opened cracks in our image of a monolithic Roman Church. We have seen first-hand that Roman parishes share many of the same problems of our congregations; we have been able to realistically evaluate the Catholic clergy and laymen. We have seen the potential strength in the city of a large denomination with a strategy and the staff and resources to implement that strategy."[98]

The two religious groups, though, did not completely let down their guard or lose their competitiveness with each other. Reverend Christ noticed that the churches began to compete in doing good. "Neither Protestant nor Catholic can permit the image to be created that the other group is the more concerned about the plight of the Negro."[99]

Getting black churches to participate in OSC was also a bit of a problem. Most did not come into the organization until 1961 and 1962. They faced many disadvantages in an organization so heavily influenced by major religious denominations. Generally, most black congregations were Baptist and not very wealthy. Most could not afford to put in more than two to three hundred dollars per year towards OSC's operation, whereas some Catholic churches were giving five thousand dollars.[100] In 1960 St. Sabina's donated ten thousand dollars.[101] It was easy' for small black congregations to feel overwhelmed. Yet their involvement was important to OSC, which wanted all parties working together toward common neighborhood concerns.

Monsignor McMahon and St. Sabina's played a major role in forming OSC and pushing its constituents toward a liberal position. According to many, Sabina's was the "heart of the Catholic communities' involvement and participation" in OSC.[102] "Monsignor McMahon worked night and day with us to develop the OSC," Monsignor Egan recalled. "He was a very spiritual man and he detested evil. He felt that the gospel, the teaching of the Church, and also the best traditions of our land taught that every person has a dignity which comes from the fact that we are created. And, therefore, they are to be treated like every other person, like every other American, like every other Catholic. And I think this was the very simple philosophy and theology that motivated him week after week . . . in season and out of season."[103] McMahon was more modest in stating his philosophy: " 'Our goal is not to induce Negroes to move in or to force integration. But if they do move in, it is their right and they should be treated like anyone else.' "[104] McMahon also gave generously to OSC from the parish treasury. Between 1960 and 1965, he donated over $91,000 to the neighborhood group for its operating costs (Table 16).[105]

Parishioners of St. Sabina's were quite aware of the fact that a portion of their contributions was being diverted toward OSC but did not seem to have resisted this by withholding contributions. Between 1958 and 1965 the number of families in St. Sabina's declined by 36 percent (Table 17), yet the contributions during this period declined by only 22 percent. Clearly the pastor was able to overcome his initial personal unpopularity and build general support among his parishioners despite his controversial policy.[106]

Many other Catholic pastors in the area were also receptive to the effort toward stabilizing their parish neighborhoods.[107] Part of their concern stemmed from self-interest. "Some of them had as their idea to sort of 'build up the neighborhood,' clean up, paint up . . . and also keep the white people in the neighborhoods where they had their parishes."[108] If they left, Catholic churches would be left with large physical plants with no means for support or upkeep.

OSC's first years were filled with enthusiasm and optimism. People felt relieved that something was finally being done to constructively deal with neighborhood stability. "Lots and lots of people would tell you those were days when they were happy," related J. McDermott of the Catholic Interracial Council. "They were learning about issues.

Table 16. Sabina Contributions to OSC, 1960-1965

Year	OSC Contribution	% Total Expenditures	IAF	Total Parish Expenditures
1960	10,000	2	7,530	400,586
1961	19,000	5	- - -	371,524
1962	17,799	6	- - -	321,735
1963	16,713	5	- - -	339,845
1964	12,700	4	- - -	357,956
1965	15,315	5	- - -	313,529
TOTAL	91,713			

Source: St. Sabina Annual Reports.

Table 17. The Aging of Auburn-Gresham, 1930-1960

Age Group	1930	1940	1950	1960
5-	9	6	9	8
5-19	24	22	20	21
20-44	46	42	36	27
45-64	17	23	28	31
65+	4	7	8	14

Source: U.S. Census Reports.

They were organizing. Meeting their neighbors. Protestant and Catholic churches were talking to each other, communicating. . . . There was a euphoria in the neighborhood—that it might be possible that we can stay!"[109]

The organizers of OSC were ambitious in constructing a battle plan for a stable neighborhood open to all races. By bringing in bankers, leading merchants, realtors, and churches, OSC was able to marshall talent and resources. Three full-time staff employees handled the day-to-day business. OSC committees were intentionally mixed with blacks and whites, Protestants and Catholics, racists and integrationists. They were to keep their focus on community maintenance and improvement rather than on talk of lofty ideals. Getting disparate people to work on particular issues would, it was hoped, teach them that it was possible for different groups to work and even live together peaceably.[110] Some people who began as confirmed racists changed their views and even became good friends with members of the other race because of this strategy.[111]

OSC had its work cut out for it. Nearly 85 percent of the homes in the OSC area had been built before World War II. The population was aging, and because of redlining practices, few young, white families were moving into the neighborhood. Young people were needed for the future; in St. Sabina's, however, "retiree" was the most frequently cited occupation.[112]

Father Riordan was keenly aware of the need to establish a new generation in the parish. When counseling young couples for marriage, he found that many wanted to stay in St. Sabina's, but could not afford to buy a home in the parish. "We were in a district that had a red line put around it," he explained. "That meant no mortgages longer than fifteen to twenty years because the real estate people thought that the neighborhood wasn't going to be there in thirty years. . . . That's how these people got out to Oak Lawn, because they'd give them the long-term mortgages out there."[113]

To combat this problem, OSC began its own home-loan program. Since their area was considered risky, few mortgage lenders were willing to advance generous credit. New home buyers had to put 40 to 50 percent cash down-payment on a small home. This made new suburban homes, which required only 10 percent down, more affordable. To keep the area vital and attractive to young married couples, three banks—the Standard State Bank, the Mutual National Bank, and the Amity Federal Savings and Loan—worked with OSC to devise a 10 percent down home-loan program. With the three banks pooling their assets, they created a two-million-dollar fund to provide low down-payments on homes in the southwest community.[114] By January

1960, fifteen loans totaling $102,000 were under contract.[115] At the same time the following year 127 mortgages had been obtained, mostly by newlyweds.[116] By the end of 1963, 457 loans had been made.[117]

Besides luring young couples back to the city, the low down-payment program had the unexpected effect of calming panic in the area. Donald O'Toole, president of the Standard State Bank and OSC's first president, claimed that since they began their program, a large number of homes had been taken off the market. When owners realized that they had options in selling, they no longer felt compelled to do so.[118] O'Toole also maintained that people in the area no longer felt "abandoned" and were, therefore, more willing to "stick it out."[119]

Besides the initial success OSC had in stabilizing the housing market, the organization, according to staff organizer Ed Chambers, also helped curb violence in the north section of their targeted area near the St. Leo area. Residents learned from OSC how to talk the issues over with their neighbors to help stop wholesale panic.[120]

At the forefront of its programs was an "antiblockbusting" campaign intended to stabilize the real estate market and normalize the supply and demand of housing. The goals were to expose and prosecute real estate speculators who peddled fear and panic and manipulated homeowners into selling at a loss.[121] OSC had a real estate practices committee whose first line of action was to distribute 25,000 copies of a 1959 *Daily News* series on the methods used by real estate speculators and panic peddlers. With the community educated, the real estate committee made itself available for complaints.[122]

OSC's committee also drew up a fair play code that set up guidelines to prevent pressured sales. Their chief object of attack were rumor-mongering speculators whose phone solicitations, at times in the middle of the night, frightened and manipulated homeowners into a panic sell. Their real estate code condemned solicitations on the basis of race and the advertising of areas with the implication that there was a mass turnover of real estate there. Repeated mass mailings, door-to-door canvassing, and the use of "sold by" or "serviced by" signs on front lawns were condemned. OSC invited all the local real estate agencies to join the group and adhere to these basic principles of real estate transaction.[123] It was able to get over thirty signatures of local real estate agents.[124]

OSC's get-tough policies continued to embroil the group in controversy. Some South Siders continued to complain about "radicalism and dictatorship."[125] In August 1960 Richard F. Bukacek, chairman of the real estate committee, was awakened in the early morning by a phone call. The voice at the other end threatened to put a bullet through his head if he and OSC continued their work. Bukacek bravely asserted that he was "not going to be frightened out of the neighborhood or out of OSC," and he was going to continue as chairman. He believed that the call came from a local real estate operator.[126]

The real estate committee helped facilitate the indictment and prosecution of two South Side real estate salesmen by the States Attorney's Office. In November 1961, the Criminal Court sentenced them to prison for conspiring to cheat and defraud two families in a house deal in a changing neighborhood.[127] The real estate committee's diligence also caused a real estate salesman to receive a thirty-dollar fine for harassing two white homeowners who refused to sell. OSC president Peter Fitzpatrick boasted that this was the first time a realtor had been convicted for such an offense in the city.[128]

Another component of OSC's neighborhood maintenance program was a housing and zoning committee that carefully monitored the condition of buildings in the neighborhoods. Illegal conversions, zoning variations, and violations of the housing, fire, and health codes were to be reported to the organization, which would then investigate the complaint. By the fall of 1960, O'Toole claimed that "hundreds of illegal conversions have been stopped—the respect for code compliance and the law has been elevated, and hundreds of homes have been modernized."[129]

OSC also had a home remodeling program, offering low-interest loans, and sponsored panel discussions at various churches and civic institutions to encourage South Siders to protect their neighborhoods from blight before it even arrived.[130] They offered helpful suggestions on home improvement, and they encouraged the proper maintenance of property.[131] Local banks and savings and loan institutions claimed to be eager to make these loans because they would be lending to old, established customers. Home improvements increased property values, which made the loan a sound investment for the bank and for the community. In 1962 OSC claimed that through their assistance in obtaining financing, permits, and designs, an average of thirty-seven remodeling jobs were started per month.[132] OSC also had a welfare and safety committee that looked into the problems of law enforcement, juvenile delinquency, and community safety.

By the spring of 1961, OSC had progressed beyond its stated policies on integration to support open occupancy legislation that was pending in the Illinois General Assembly. In October 1960, the OSC congress directed the community relations committee to communicate to city and state legislative bodies that OSC advocated the elimination of discriminatory housing practices. The committee took OSC at its word, and in the spring of 1961 sent letters voicing its support for the open occupancy act to state legislators representing the Southwest area. At the March council meeting, however, a violent debate erupted over this action. Opponents of this initiative said that the committee did not have the authorization to speak for them. They claimed the act would entail a loss of individual constitutional rights of property owners. One opposing member warned, " 'This could result in a split in OSC that will hurt it severely. There is growing objection to the unethical tactics of the hard core group of integrationists.' " Several groups quit OSC when the committee refused to retract the letters of opinion. Monsignor McMahon visited each of the exiting groups to entreat them to return to the ranks but was unsuccessful.[133]

The open occupancy issue split the remaining members into two "parties"—the moderate liberals and the Medium Forum. While the Medium Forum praised OSC's efforts on such issues as blockbusting, they claimed OSC needed a more diverse voice on more delicate matters affecting the community.[134] Throughout the summer Monsignor McMahon worried that the Medium Forum would persuade other member groups to withdraw support from the liberals and put OSC out of business. He had little help from his fellow priests in dealing with this problem.[135]

By the fall of 1961 a floor fight was expected at the annual congress in November. For that day the Gresham police station assigned a detail of uniformed patrolmen. Male ushers were appointed, and a "fully equipped" first-aid station was provided. Delegates arrived early to caucus incoming uncommitted or opposing delegates on open occupancy. Conservative delegates, sporting Uncle Sam hats, used walkie-talkies to lobby representatives during the convention and handed out mimeographed voting instructions.[136]

While open occupancy and integration were the immediate issues and threats to the organization, they were not the subjects openly argued. Instead, members fought over a "liberal" constitutional amendment. The original constitution stated that no officer could succeed himself in the same office for a third consecutive term. The proposed change sought to limit this restriction to the president, executive vice president, secretary, and treasurer. The eleven vice presidents, who also made up the executive board, could remain in office indefinitely.[137] It was apparent to all involved that unless the rules were changed Monsignor McMahon, Monsignor Molloy, and Reverend Christ, who had all served two terms already, would be ineligible for office. As founding members of OSC, they were key leaders in shaping the organization's liberal position on the race issue. While the conservatives claimed their opposition to the amendment change was based on "the principle of succession," they were really opposed to the continued leadership of these three men.[138]

To change the constitution the liberals needed a two thirds majority vote. The conservative effort kept the vote tally to only 62 percent, 4 percent short of the required majority. The liberal members of the congress, realizing what had happened, outmaneuvered the conservatives by electing Monsignor McMahon as executive vice president, Rev. Robert Christ as Secretary, and Monsignor Molloy as treasurer for the ensuing year. They were later elected back to the vice presidencies.[139]

Once the issue of officers was settled, the congress adopted an amendment to the "freedom of residents resolution" from the previous congress. While the first amendment put OSC "four-square behind all the legislative efforts for freedom of residence for all people in our community, city, state and nation, regardless of race, creed, color and national origin," the second amendment advised the OSC committee to study any bills and report their findings to the OSC council.[140] In the following year, some of the defecting neighborhood affiliates had a change of heart and came back to the organization, while a few conservative groups pulled out of OSC because of their defeat.[141]

Another crisis arose a few months later that would also rock OSC's existence. This time the issue was overcrowded and segregated schools. Alinsky had also organized The Woodlawn Organization (TWO) east of OSC's territory. Woodlawn was a black area that abutted the powerful University of Chicago and was targeted for urban renewal projects. Part of Alinsky's purpose in forming TWO was to have it act as a sister organization to OSC. If these black and white areas cooperated, Alinksy's quota plan might have a chance to be implemented. However, TWO was more interested in the empty classrooms in white areas than in quotas limiting where they could live. "Truth Squad" mothers from TWO staged media events to expose the Chicago Public Schools' segregation practices by barging into white schools equipped with newspaper reporters and photographers.

The actions of the Truth Squad outraged members of the Medium Forum. In February 1962 they urged OSC's education committee to pass a resolution condemning the Truth Squad's methods. When a meeting was called by OSC Council to consider the resolution, over three hundred people turned out, even though voting was restricted to delegates. Liberals amended the resolution, calling for an investigation into the issues that prompted the Truth Squads actions. When their measure was voted on and passed, many Medium Forum members turned their back on the organization.[142]

OSC's original strategy of holding liberals, moderates, and conservatives in one organization seemed to be faltering. But this did not necessarily mean OSC was mortally wounded. Many conservatives and violence-prone whites had already been leaving the area, which made moderates and liberals the representative voice in the Southwest Side.

It would now be up to them to keep the organization going and maintain neighborhood viability.[143]

Monsignor McMahon had taken a strong leadership role in the Southwest Side community on race and integration through the formation of OSC and by influencing its liberal course. OSC scored great success in its early years with its innovative programs. This gave the community a feeling of optimism and hope that they could stay in their neighborhoods and parishes, maintain the standards of the community, and live harmoniously with the blacks who moved in. But how successful would McMahon be at convincing his parishioners to support his efforts in OSC and in the parish?

8

Where Two or Three Are Gathered: St. Sabina's in the 1960s

"It was a classic Irish ghetto which saw itself as under threat," recalled R. McClory, who served as assistant priest at St. Sabina's. "When I got there in 1963, the black movement was right at the border. There was one black family that lived in the parish at that time. So it was like a " 'The barbarians are at our border! The Huns are at the wall!' kind of experience."[1]

Persuading parishioners of his philosophy of openness and tolerance was no easy task for Monsignor McMahon. Negative attitudes toward blacks had been passed on from one generation to the next, from neighborhood to neighborhood, and parish to parish. "I remember as a kid [1920s]," said T. O'Rourke, "I'd get in the car with my mother and we'd drive down to St. Elizabeth's—that was all black. And she'd always shake her head and say about her old neighborhood, 'Look at it now.' And, of course, that was probably making a big impression on me. They didn't like what they saw. And they'd read about all these things that go on. . . . Even now when you read about crime, it's always happening at 7917 Bishop or 8000 Bishop—houses that we were in and out of, friends and neighbors, and we can't image what's going on in there. . . . And that's what they were reading about the old neighborhoods."[2]

City jobs often took parishioners into black neighborhoods. From their perspective, they gathered unflattering opinions of blacks. Father Daniel Sullivan, who came to St. Sabina's in 1965, had heard many stories from parishioners of the problems firemen and policemen had in performing their jobs in the black belt. "So many of the ordinary parishioners were policemen and firemen and utility men, streetcar people," he related. "And [they] had injurious associations with some blacks."[3]

T. O'Rourke remembered his parents talking about the race riot in 1919 and the effect it had on city employees in the parish. "I remember the policemen in the neighborhood getting upset. My father . . . was a motorman in a streetcar . . . on the 59th Street line and he told about a black man that got in at his feet to be protected to get through a white couple of blocks. If the white lads saw him sitting in the street car, they'd throw rocks at him. . . . I think that's another reason that we didn't want them around, was that there'd be trouble."[4] Some policemen believed that the blacks who initially moved into white neighborhoods were often all right but claimed it was the relatives and friends who visited that caused problems.[5] Some blacks recently arrived from the South often gave house parties on weekends that were reminiscent of Saturday night plantation jukes. The many guests were treated to eating, drinking, music and dancing, and gambling.[6] South Side whites were not positively disposed toward these get-togethers.

Another complaint Catholics voiced against blacks was that they did not keep up their parishes. Most blacks who moved into white neighborhoods were not Catholic. This left the burden of supporting the parish on the few blacks that were. Their modest resources could not always adequately support the massive physical plant white Catholics left behind.[7] "We stereotyped them," admitted D. Foertsch. "People said that the blacks don't get involved in [parish] organizations."[8]

Some people recognized that part of their resistance to blacks was rooted in their own clannishness and isolation. "I never had to think about a black person," D. Foertsch explained. "I knew they were around. I knew they shoveled the coal in right under my dining room window. . . . So I was in my own ghetto and very protected."[9] Resentment of blacks was compounded by those who had uprooted themselves before. "There are plenty of people who are bitter years later because . . . they have been uprooted two or three times," explained M. Dunne. "They've been burned some place else."[10]

Migration patterns on Chicago's South Side reveal the reluctance of many Irish and Catholics to abandon a parish-based neighborhood. By locating parishes where children who made their first communion in St. Sabina's had been baptized, a map of Catholic migration in Chicago's Southwest Side emerges (Table 15). Twenty-three percent of first communicant families had within a seven-year period left neighborhoods in flux because of racial change.[11]

"I used to think," M. Joyce said, "If they really want to get away, why don't they really make a big jump. . . . Why didn't they go far out? But that just seemed to be the tendency. . . . They came from St. Carthage to Leo, then from Leo to St. Sabina, then from St. Sabina to Little Flower. That's the way they'd jump, saying they were chased out!"[12]

South Side Irish parish-hopping was in part because of their reluctance to stray from parish-centered communities and in part because of their mistaken assumption that the black population would not increase nor would blacks want to move outside their "own" area.

"They thought it would stop at their borders," explained R. McClory. "It was a most unrealistic kind of thinking."[13] "We thought . . . that Sabina's would never go black," said T. O'Rourke. "We thought that the blacks had always moved to State Street, Michigan Avenue, South Park [King Drive]. And they always said they wanted to be near the elevated and buses. We said that about them. And we thought they'd never come west of State Street. . . . We thought we were safe."[14] The "no man's land" between the black belt and the white South Side, however, kept creeping further and further west. For a time State Street was the demarcation line, later it became Halsted Street, then Ashland Avenue, to where it rests in the late 1980s tenuously on Western Avenue.

The experiences and attitudes his parishioners inherited and acquired made it difficult for Monsignor McMahon to persuade St. Sabina parishioners to adopt a more generous and tolerant attitude toward blacks. "They would have thought letting the 'Eyetalians' in was the height of integration," related Father Riordan.[15] Many were dubious of the arguments that blacks, like the Irish, were simply trying to better their lives for themselves and their families. "I don't think they bought that," said T. O'Rourke. "They didn't like what they saw. . . . These stories about the blacks don't keep up their property and all that. We'd see that going down on the el. . . . When whites were there, it was an old neighborhood, but a good neighborhood. And then [blacks] took it over and it was burned out. . . . They were ghettoes right away."[16] "The general notion was that they were not up to snuff," explained J. Hagerty. "It was a general fear of them . . . something you were raised up with somehow. It was never any big issue in our house, but it was something that you just sort of knew—Well, blacks are fine but they should stay by themselves."[17]

Monsignor McMahon's strategy to combat these attitudes was to help whites maintain level heads in the midst of panic peddling by continually reminding them of the strengths and benefits of their present community. "You have one of the best neighborhoods in Chicago and never question that," he wrote. "You have facilities for your spiritual development for the education of your children, for their physical development and your own recreation which are equaled by few parishes in the Archdiocese. The tuition in your school is by far the lowest in the Diocese [sic], the teaching staff, the buildings, etc., are the best. There are no double shifts, no huge building programs, no call for extra ordinary sacrifice to put up new buildings. . . . Count your blessings and realize that many neighborhoods have bigger problems and the newer parishes and suburban areas do have, and will have, the same problems."[18]

Monsignor McMahon's approach was generally understated. While he wrote of OSC in *The Seraph* and spoke on it occasionally from the pulpit, it was mostly through conversation and by example that he sought to influence his flock. His role, as he saw it, and that of the other priests, was to be of personal service in dealing with problems arising in the neighborhood. He said: "The priests are at your beck and call to help you squash any rumors and to advise you on any changes which might take place in your particular neighborhood" and "Remember that it is to the advantage of certain salesmen to spread rumors, to scare you, to make you emotionally upset. They feel that the lie that they tell you will be spread by you and others to their financial advantage. You owe it to yourself and to your neighbors to demand proof from everyone for any statement affecting the neighborhood."[20]

For the most part, McMahon kept the issue on a very simple, spiritual level. "He was low-keyed about everything," explained M. Dunne. "He was a very mild-mannered man. You would not think from his personality that he would have been into this. . . . he tried to keep it on a spiritual level." She could not even recall him speaking about the racial situation from the pulpit.[21]

While they were a bit skeptical of OSC's policies and its ability to maintain the community, parishioners did not try to interfere or stop the involvement of the parish in the organization. "People would say antagonistic things," recalled R. McClory. "But on the whole people would just sit there [in church] and they would contribute. . . . They knew their contributions were going to OSC. There was no boycott of collections. And a lot of people would say, 'I don't like it, but I suppose that's the way we ought to be.' "[22]

Many people, though, had conflicting views of what exactly Monsignor McMahon's goals and motives were. "I think he was trying to preserve his parish," T. O'Rourke argued. "He would like it not to turn overnight."[23] Others were a bit more cynical, believing egotism played a role. "In the back of his mind, he thought he was going to have the first parish that was integrated," B. DesChatelets speculated.[24]

Many parishioners resented Monsignor McMahon's efforts to welcome blacks. "When a black family would move in, he would make a special point to go visit them and welcome them . . . but he wouldn't even say 'hi' to the white family next door," complained B. DesChatelets.[25] "When the first blacks came to the school, the pastor . . . would take them up into the classroom for the first time and welcome them into the neighborhood," concurred T. O'Rourke. "A lot of Irish resented that. They said 'nobody welcomed my child when they came here.' Well, of course, they didn't have to be, but they were very critical of the pastor for that."[26]

R. McClory recalled an incident in which Monsignor McMahon did more than say hello. He showed his irritation at the reluctance of whites to follow his example. "When the first black people moved into the block on Carpenter Street . . . McMahon went down to welcome them," he said. "It was a summer day and people were out on their porches looking to see what was going on. And McMahon shouted 'Come on out, everybody. Welcome your new neighbors!' " McClory said he often heard complaints that McMahon was nicer to blacks than to whites. But McMahon realized he needed to put out the extra effort for blacks, whereas whites were already Catholics—"paying parishioners."[27]

E. Lawrence moved to the area in 1963 and was one of the first African Americans in St. Sabina's. Contrary to the perceptions of whites, in her experience, no one, not even Monsignor McMahon, welcomed her into the parish. No one was ever hostile or disrespectful, but "nobody said anything to" her. It would not be until many years later that she would come to know him and love him.[28]

Others, though, were very moved by the Christian examples of this frail, sometimes cantankerous old priest and began to rethink their attitudes on race. "It was because of Monsignor's teaching rather than his preaching," D. Foertsch claimed, that he inspired her. She had to admit that part of this was due to his unintelligible sermons. "You knew if he was going to say mass that the homily would drag on and as hard as you tried you would not get a thing out of it. . . . It would always start out and end up with the Legion of Mary. But that was okay, [it was] his example. . . . Whenever I think of him, I think of the word 'humility.' He was like Jesus."[29] "I can't recall him making any grandiose statement of any kind about it," reflected M. Joyce. "He was just being a pastor for his flock."[30] Because of his example, G. Benzig attended mass at St. Sabina's and sent her children to the school, although she lived in St. Leo's parish. She often thought, like many people, as she watched him walk through the streets with Champ his dog, that he was a saintly man.[31]

However, many resisted hearing his message. "Many people never forgave Monsignor because he taught us," said Dee Foertsch. "I say taught because I never had to use tolerance. I learned from Monsignor . . . through conversations with him or going to organizations, to accept people and judge them for themselves. . . . other people were putting a wall up, saying 'Don't penetrate that. I do not want to be tolerant. I don't want to live with them. I want things to always be the way they are'. . . . The first ones to move were the first ones that didn't want to hear it at all."[32]

Monsignor McMahon's and OSC's efforts did have a stabilizing effect on the parish. Although people were leery about the prospects of sharing a neighborhood with blacks, most people in St. Sabina's did not begin a wholesale panic when the first black families began to move into the parish. In 1963 and 1964 "the real estate men were making their rounds through the parish, panic peddling," explained R. McClory. "They were moving through the parish ringing doorbells and leafleting. There was a great sense of unease. . . . Life went on anyhow. . . . There was no sense that things were different."[33] The nuns in the school reported the same relaxed attitude toward integration. They wrote to their mother house: "Our school was integrated racially with the coming of the King family of four children in December. Three other families came soon after. On the whole the children were accepted very well."[34]

Monsignor McMahon recruited many volunteers for OSC from the various parish organizations he helped establish at St. Sabina's in the previous decade. "There were a large number, maybe twenty-five or thirty people in the parish," said R. McClory, who thought "there was no reason why this [parish] should not be an integrated community. A lot of these people worked with OSC."[35]

St. Sabina's Christian Family Movement (CFM) chapter stood out in its willingness to face the racial question head on.[36] Its approach to religious and social concerns was designed to encourage a more expansive spiritual view of world problems. In 1964-65 it received added impetus from the national organization when it recommended the race issue for its Social Inquiry.[37]

Besides participating in OSC, St. Sabina's CFM chapter initiated its own activities and turned to Friendship House for guidance on the race issue. In 1955, Friendship House had begun a home visit program between whites and blacks. Its staff arranged for a small group of whites to meet in the home of a black middle-class family, or at least one that was financially secure, to discuss racial issues and prejudices. The black host family would relate their experiences with and consequences of prejudice and discrimination in their lives. Friendship House firmly believed that positive personal contact was crucial to dispelling racial stereotypes. Intellectual arguments, they thought, were generally ineffective because racism was more a product of irrational fears. It was more important to influence the emotions, and this could be best done on a personal basis. By meeting face to face, problems in race relations became less abstract and more human.[38]

Initially, many blacks doubted that these visits would result in substantive changes. Yet, after their first session, they realized that many whites were not so much prejudiced as extremely ignorant of the black experience and needed to be educated. Friendship House's paper, *Community,* described their simple belief: "Visits to Negro homes awaken whites to the simple fact that "Negro" family life is as normal as their own, and that at least *this* Negro's home and property are well kept. This chips away at the mental block of prejudice. . . . As the facts speak for themselves some progress is made toward the ultimate goal of integration: to see everyone as individuals, not as a race."[39]

Friendship House staff also arranged for visits of blacks to white homes. Whites who were unwilling to go to black homes could be reached this way, and blacks would be given the opportunity to meet whites, who would welcome them if they decided to move into the neighborhood. In this situation white hosts invited friends and neighbors. They and their black guests, then, acted as team educators.[40]

Each year the home visit program became more popular throughout Chicago. In 1963 Friendship House sponsored a citywide, one-day home visit program in conjunction with the National Conference on Religion and Race that was held in Chicago from January 14 to 18th. The home visits were a common effort on the part of Catholics, Protestants, and Jews. On January 6 five hundred black host families welcomed three thousand visitors. The success of these visits prompted the various religious denominations to establish the Greater Chicago Interracial Home Visitation Committee. They helped organize a national home visit day on October 27, 1963. Project Friendship won the praise of President John F. Kennedy and received national media coverage. On that day 119 cities and 115,000 people participated in the home visits.[41]

In addition to the home visit program, Friendship House was also interested in using the structure of the Catholic church in their war on racism by developing a parish-to-parish program. White parishes visited black parishes and celebrated the Eucharist together. The staff thought that having whites watch blacks receive Communion would be a powerful image of their common bond in Christ. After mass, participants gathered for luncheon and a panel discussion by both participating parishes. Later black parishes returned the compliment by inviting the white parish to their church.[42]

In January 1965, St. Sabina's CFM chapter visited Friendship House to obtain materials on the home visit program. The parish branch of the Archdiocesan Council of Catholic Women also participated in Friendship House programs. Monsignor McMahon gave them his full support. They began home visits starting with black Catholic families in the parish and then expanded beyond that.[43] "It was kind of a trial period," said M. Joyce. "We would go to families from St. Columbanus, which was black, and we had several come over to our house. . . . It certainly broke the ice. . . . It didn't take as long to perhaps make a breakthrough as it would if we had still just stayed in our little areas. . . . It was just another outlet for us to express ourselves that we were willing to let others come into our lives or communities."[44] D. Foertsch described the growth of vision of St. Sabina's CFM chapter. "We broke from being just a nucleus of Sabina's to the Sabina's community. . . . We had a feeling of ecumenism, and we had religious services that we shared. . . . It was getting to know black people socially, and I kind of liked it. It was exciting times."[45] Those involved in the exchanges claimed that many people's attitudes had been softened by the experience. Most agreed, though, in retrospect, that the visits were awkward and stilted and their influence limited. Most people who participated in the exchanges were generally favorably disposed toward blacks to begin with.[46]

Nor were all parishioners enthusiastic about the visits. "I don't know how some of our neighbors felt about us," M. Joyce commented. "They probably thought we were out on a limb at times."[47] B. DesChatelets recalled the sentiments of many. McMahon, he said, "wanted the whites to have [blacks] for Sunday dinner even . . . before they moved in. . . . The parish and the people resented that."[48]

Attitudes toward crime became the real test for parish resolve. During the decade, increases in crime in the Gresham police district were frequently reported in the local newspaper. This put a strain on the credulity of the integrationists. Initially, the crimes that generated the most concern were located on OSC's eastern boundary, where teenagers engaged in racial harassment. In the first six months of 1961 there were approximately ten attempts to destroy black-owned property through window breaking and fire bombing. Antiblack demonstrations were also staged at the newly purchased homes of black families. White youths beat black teenagers, who retaliated in kind. The tense situation was made even more frightening when four black families in the area armed themselves with guns for protection. OSC helped defuse this explosive situation by promising the black families full protection if they gave up their weapons. Since publicity proved to be the bane of the perpetrators of these crimes, OSC distributed information on these occurrences and increased police vigilance.[49] By August 1961 racial disturbances were considerably reduced.[50] E. Lawrence had been warned by friends not to move into the area because it was white and there would be trouble. However, by the time she moved into the parish in 1963, she encountered no violence. Her sons were occasionally called names, but their general experience was one of benign neglect.[51]

However, as the decade progressed so did fear of crime. Juvenile offenses, such as bicycle thefts and purse-snatchings, along with auto and auto accessory theft, became increasingly common. Gradually, house burglaries became more frequent and soon were the greatest law-and-order concern in the OSC area. During the early 1960s, crime in the Gresham police district rose at a faster rate than in the city as a whole. By 1963 OSC and other community leaders were petitioning the police department for more patrolmen.[52]

"The crime was high enough that we had to nail all the windows shut," explained J. Nelligan. "The house was broken into a couple of times. My father was beaten up a couple of times."[53] Women had their purses snatched at the bank.[54] Just the fear of crime became a problem for people doing business in the community. "The doctors would leave because their other patients would be afraid to come in," related T. O'Rourke. "They'd have trouble with their cars. The blacks would steal their cars or take things."[55]

R. McClory thought that it was the talk of crime itself more than its actuality that heightened people's anxiety. "Everyone talked about it. . . . There were occasional houses broken into. . . . You would hear about burglaries and purse-snatchings. . . . It did go up, but what went up more was the perception of crime . . . but it would often be black on black."[56]

Besides the growing fear of crime, Auburn-Gresham's population increased dramatically, making the area less hospitable. For the previous twenty years it had remained relatively stable, but the population grew from 59,484 to 68,846 between 1960 and 1970. The swell of cars and noise made the area less appealing, and the congestion made safety even more of a problem. "It became more difficult to find a place to park," related M. Dunne. "You couldn't come home late and find a place."[57]

Many people, though, simply could not easily move even if they wanted to. Auburn-Gresham's and St. Sabina's populations were aging. Table 17 reveals this age shift. In 1930 the largest age cohort was that between twenty and forty-four years of age. By 1960 it had shifted to the forty-five to sixty-four years of age group. Those sixty-five and older increased from 4 percent of the population to 14 percent.[58]

Retirees living on a fixed income and those in their middle years could not risk losses from their investments in their homes. "Many could not afford to [leave]," related M. Dunne. "They thought they were going to live there for the rest of their lives."[59] Others felt it was either now or never for them to leave. "The kids were pretty well grown and a lot of them figured it was about the last chance that they'd get to move," explained B. DesChatelets. "They moved out. They could sell their homes and get a pretty good price. . . . Basically, it was a fear of what it would be like. This was a big thing."[60] After years of living in a familiar parish setting, it would be difficult for many to adjust to a new environment.

But through all these trials the majority of parishioners in St. Sabina held tight to their homes. "I was amazed at how calm everybody was," R. McClory reflected. "In '64 and '65 people were talking . . . saying 'I don't know whether it will work.' 'There's so much violence around.' 'We're going to lose a lot of money from selling our house if we don't go.' [But] 'don't worry, Father, we're going to stay if it's at all possible.' Then, just all of sudden . . . everybody was saying they were going to stay and then they all left."[61]

The decisive event that tipped the racial scale in the neighborhood was the fatal shooting of Frank Kelly. On August 16, 1965, Frank lost his life from a bullet shot at him by a black teenager.[62] Father Daniel Sullivan was assigned to St. Sabina's that summer. Although he, himself, was not at the scene of the shooting, he remembered the talk and turmoil in the rectory over the murder. "It was just kids yelling at each other, taunting each other," he said. "It just happened that at least one of the black kids had a gun. It wouldn't have been common that any of those. . . . Sabina's guys to have any weapons like that . . . [but] they used to swagger around."[63] Frank Kelly was not well known in the parish, but after his death his name became a household word. "Instantly, instantly, everybody knew that name—Frank Kelly. The horror that spread! The fear that it engendered! Up to that time people had been figuring they were going to buck it out."[64] The shocked parish rallied behind the Kelly family. Frank's friends collected nearly three thousand dollars, a considerable sum then, for his widowed mother. Hundreds of people turned out for the wake and the funeral.[65]

Despite this showing of community solidarity, many people who had taken pride in their parish began to pull up stakes. "It was that incident, probably more than anything else, that convinced hundreds of people to leave," explained R. McClory. "That event had kind of a symbolic significance. . . . The church was packed [for] the funeral for Kelly."[66]

Tension permeated the neighborhood for the next several weeks. Father White, who had been director of the youth programs, found himself in the position of calming the young people of the parish. "It was the most excruciating time of his life," related Father Sullivan. "These guys saw their friend killed in front of them and they were ordinary people. . . . Everything in their lives was at that moment being threatened. . . . He [White] was trying to prevent a blood bath." Father White was afraid the community center might serve as a staging ground for a reprisal. On the advice of the police, he closed the center for the rest of the summer. No one wanted to go there anyway. Parents were now afraid to let their kids go to a place that now seemed dangerous. The once lively center had become an empty shell. Father White, however, succeeded in defusing this tense situation.[67]

After the shooting, the parish rolls drastically declined. At the end of 1965 the parish reported a drop of one thousand families, and in 1966 St. Sabina lost another thousand (Table 18). For Father Sullivan, who had just arrived in the parish, the mass exodus was a depressing experience. "It was sort of a despairing time for me personally. . . .

Table 18. St. Sabina Parish Enrollment, 1958-1968

Year	Families	Persons
1958	2,965	10,400
1964	2,930	8,932
1965	1,908	6,525
1966	900	2,970
1967	530	1,560
1968 (estimated)	400	

Source: St. Sabina Annual Reports.

Instead of people saying 'hello,' they were saying 'good-bye.' " Parishioners, he recalled, said, " 'Well, I don't know if I should even bother meeting you because I'm going to move.' " He often made sick calls and communion visits to the elderly and home-bound in the parish. They would say to him, "Ah, Father! You seem to be a lovely priest, but this is the last time that you'll be coming over to us because after Frank Kelly, we couldn't be safe around here." Father Sullivan realized that he was witnessing the end of an era, and he tried to "savor a bit of the huge double massing—a mass in the upper church and a mass in the lower church simultaneously. The huge numbers!"[68]

In this fear-ridden situation it would have been difficult for anyone to have stopped the wholesale abandonment of the parish. The Irish proclivity for apartment dwellings proved to be the bane of a stable community. Many people said that the apartment buildings in the neighborhood were the first to let blacks in. "There were so many apartment buildings there," explained B. DesChatelets. "The people just picked up and left."[69]

Blacks and whites had different perceptions of what was happening in the community. E. Lawrence commented that she did not remember the Kelly shooting. She thought it was just the presence of blacks that scared people into moving.[70]

"You did see for sale signs all over," said Ann Gaskin. "Every week someone was moving out. It was constant. It would go from block to block."[71] Rumors and gossip spread through the streets of the parish like fire. "A lot of [fear and panic] was created by people talking on the corners," said M. Dunne. "It was just whispering. . . . They were talking about the movement of the new people coming in."[72] D. Foertsch dryly remarked, "Wherever two or three are gathered, they were talking about who moved out and who was going to move in."[73]

The fear, the doubts, and the anxieties about whether to move or stay, along with seeing old friends and neighbors leaving at a rapid rate, confused, disappointed, and hurt many people. "The sense of wondering what is going to happen. . . . The fundamental attitude was one of fear, mixed with some degree of racism, but not vehemently," explained R. McClory. "They were afraid that they were going to lose the value of their house, and they're going to have to move."[74] In this situation parishioners could sell their homes only to blacks. "The real estate people wouldn't direct any white people toward a home in that neighborhood," explained Monsignor J. Egan. "Then the people got blamed for that."[75] In this situation many people adopted a different mentality than the more philosophic one Monsignor McMahon advocated. "When you talk about blockbusting," explained G. Hendry, "you're talking about economic hardship, not racial or social justice."[76] The economic reality was that the last white family to sell its house in a transitional neighborhood was risking just about all its net worth. In a situation like this, OSC organizer Nick von Hoffman believed the problem became socio-economic rather than purely racial.[77]

As blockbusters made their way through St. Sabina's, parishioners had to deal with their intrusions. "The real estate people would send people to your door saying, 'Did you know a black family moved onto your block?' " said M. Dunne. "We'd say 'Yes, we do' even if we didn't know."[78] "John McMahon reserved his greatest anger for the panic-peddlers," related Monsignor Egan.[79] He personally asked a parishioner in real estate not to come into the area; he was disappointed.[80]

"I don't have any idea what anybody could have done to change that situation to really make it work," R. McClory said dejectedly. "The pressure was there. There was such ingrained fear mixed with prejudice that just fed on itself. . . . Homes were broken into. Real estate people were . . . spreading rumors. And there were enough real things to hear about, shootings and robberies and muggings."[81]

Although the parish collectively voiced its support of integration under Monsignor McMahon's leadership, the decision to leave or go was a painfully lonely and isolated one. People were reluctant to discuss their plans. "People were ashamed to tell you they were selling their house," B. DesChatelets said. "[Sometimes] you never saw signs for sale. They just sold and that was it. . . . It made for a lot of hard feelings."[82] This happened with a neighbor who owned a two-flat. When Mr. DesChatelets asked the neighbor what he was planning to do, the man said he was going to stay. But in fact he had already sold the building and moved out at the end of the week.[83]

"They would often keep quiet about [moving]," concurred T. O'Rourke. He had a similar experience with a family friend and neighbor of thirty-five years. "She sold her house. She didn't say good-bye, like she was ashamed to leave. . . . We never heard from her again." He said they did not hold it against her because "everybody did it."[84] M. Dunne claimed some people moved out in the middle of the night without telling any one. "They actually did that . . . because they were ashamed to admit that they . . . were deceiving people. . . . They were going to stay and they didn't."[85]

Those who resisted the initial impulse to leave St. Sabina's after the Kelly shooting found it hard to maintain their resolve when the racial situation in Chicago began to explode at the same time. St. Sabina's could not remain isolated from national events. By 1963, Chicago blacks, inspired by the civil rights movement, began to agitate to change their second-class citizenship. Even the usually obsequious black politicians began to stir up Chicago politics. In late spring, six black aldermen, generally known as the Silent Six because of their fealty to the mayor, arranged a private meeting with Richard J. Daley. They warned him of the inroads the civil rights movement was making in their wards and advised him to make some showing of intervention and concern for black issues. They needed to prove to their constituents that they were working on their behalf. In order not to upset his coalition, Daley made what seemed to be a bold move toward racial equality but would, in fact, not alter the status quo. He asked James C. Murray, alderman of the 18th ward, which covered much of OSC's territory, including St. Sabina's, to draft a fair housing ordinance. Murray was aghast at the idea. He told the mayor his constituents would destroy him for sponsoring such an ordinance. Daley told him the city needed it and that was that. Murray did sponsor a bill in the city council which prohibited discrimination in real estate listings and sales. It passed into law September 11 over the opposition of sixteen "loyal" aldermen.[86]

Murray tried to explain to his constituents that the new ordinance simply protected homeowners against blockbusters and called for the revocation of city and state brokers licenses of realtors engaging in unfair practices. It did not usurp property owners' rights to sell or rent to whomever they pleased. Murray did not feel he was very convincing, and therefore, did not run for re-election in 1967. He had hoped other Southwest Side aldermen would stand united with him on this issue, but they did not. Several of them actually used their opposition to the ordinance in their re-election campaign. The bill, however, was largely symbolic. Implementing it entailed long, involved hearings with the city's Commission on Human Relations.[87]

In January 1966 Dr. Martin Luther King brought the civil rights movement to the North and made Chicago his headquarters. Initially, his campaign was focused on slum reform. Mayor Daley did not want to be targeted as the enemy of black Chicago so he heaped praise on King and his work and expounded on what the city was doing to address black concerns. Unable to attack the reigning powers directly, King decided to launch a campaign to integrate Chicago neighborhoods by staging nonviolent marches into white neighborhoods to champion open occupancy.[88]

King chose the Southwest Side as the place for his first march. On July 24, 1966, three hundred black and white marchers, holding hands and singing hymns, headed west along 71st Street, then turned north to 67th Street. They crossed Halsted, Ashland, and finally reached Western Avenue. An angry crowd greeted them with bricks, bottles, rocks, and cherry bombs. The violence created sympathy among blacks and whites for the movement. New recruits poured in and inspired King to try again five days later. This second march also took place in the Southwest area in Marquette Park and met the same virulent hatred. There was one more march that September in the suburb of Cicero with the same results.[89]

The violent conflict the marches provoked frightened many residents on the Southwest Side and seemed to confirm the opinion that "there would be trouble" if blacks and whites tried to mix. However, it was King's assassination in Memphis on April 4, 1968 that proved the final blow to St. Sabina's hope for peaceful integration. The shooting unleashed a torrent of black anger throughout the nation. Over one hundred cities, including Chicago, erupted in riots. While most of the rioting and destruction took place on the West Side, the apparent message was not lost on South Siders.

J. McDermott of the Catholic Interracial Council said, "The growing voices of anger and black power . . . all chilled hope that we could have peaceful community relations." At the same time that a small, but growing number of white Catholic communities saw themselves "offering the hand of cooperation . . . they were looking at television and hearing these angry voices. . . . That was another nail in OSC's coffin."[90] It was also the final nail for St. Sabina's. "Once whites accepted blacks," related C. Marble, an African American who moved to the area in 1968, "blacks had their own agenda."[91] By 1970, St. Sabina's was primarily black. Auburn-Gresham was 69 percent black, most being in its eastern section where St. Leo's and St. Sabina's were located.[92]

Some whites did stay, partly out of loyalty to Monsignor McMahon, partly because of their own convictions that whites and blacks could live together, and partly because of their lack of alternatives. Many who stayed often developed good relations with their black neighbors, and had many of their remaining stereotypes challenged. "They always got along with the one next door," T. O'Rourke recollected. "I've heard that from many who stayed a few years. And the old ones that stayed say they [the blacks] looked out for them."[93] J. Nelligan said his parent's neighbors "were very good and looked after them and helped out a lot when they couldn't shovel the snow."[94] "When that huge snow storm occurred, [1967]" said M. Dunne, "those black men on our block got out and shoveled the street from curb to curb. We made huge pots of coffee and took them out. They were wonderful. I would have no complaints about our neighbors."[95] "All of our neighbors were colored," M. Joyce said. "They were just as kindly as they could be. . . . We had a nice block club. . . . In fact, when I left, they presented me with a plaque for our cooperation."[96] "They're the same," D. Foertsch discovered. "They go to work. They're struggling to meet their mortgage payments like I was, and they wanted the same thing for their kids."[97]

Those who took the time to get to know the newcomers learned about the insults and the feelings of rejection that blacks felt when whites fled from them. "I remember one woman saying to me," recalled M. Joyce, " 'you can't imagine, Mrs. Joyce, how it feels to be ignored and disliked just because of your color.' Her white neighbors were moving. She said, 'If we had done anything to them, if we had been dirty, or we had been wrecking anything, doing anything that would be a bad neighbor, but just because my color is black. It hurts.' I'll always remember that."[98] D. Foertsch recalled similar conversations with blacks. "Their experiences of injustices that I could not believe.!"[99]

However, mutual respect was not the whole story of the parish during the period of transition and when it was primarily black. There were conflicts and cultural differences that often made life tense. "The cultural differences were very great," said R. McClory. He noted a gulf between the young people of the parish. "The symbolic thing for me was at the girls' sodality mass. On the left side of the church was all black, the other white. . . . Nobody told them to sit that way. It was the cultural differences. They had nothing to share. While there were white girls that would go out of their way to have black friends, for the most part they found mixing difficult.[100]

Once the Sunday night dances resumed months after the Kelly shooting, only whites attended even though the neighborhood was getting to be more and more black. "There was no possibility of integrating [them]," said R. McClory. "Nobody even gave it a moment's thought. . . . First of all, they didn't dance to the same music."[101] After the Kelly's death just a few feet away from the dance hall, it would have been unlikely that blacks would have been wanted. It was also essentially a Catholic dance, advertised primarily at Catholic high schools, although Protestants were admitted.

K. Kopcinski, who attended the dances in 1967 and 1968, said it was her impression that blacks did not feel welcome. But she also thought the music separated them. Whites listened to the Beatles, the Beach Boys, and even the Supremes and Smokey Robinson, whereas blacks listened to music she could only describe as "funky" and unfamiliar to whites. Although she had never witnessed any confrontations between whites and blacks, problems existed within this dual youth culture.[102] "Black people would be hanging around outside on the street. . . . Whites would be coming out of the dance. . . . The cops would come. . . . Everybody would be nervous."[103]

C. Marble was impressed by the efforts the priests and nuns made toward welcoming blacks, but he felt they lacked the skills to integrate young people from the different races. Some of the religious, while well-intended, were very awkward around blacks and tended to associate more with white children.[104]

R. McClory recalled other incidents that made whites a bit leery of the presence of these "interlopers" in *their* neighborhood. "Black people would be out fighting in the alley amongst themselves . . . not even fighting, cussing at each other. . . . Is that a violent crime? No, but it did have an effect. And loud music playing next door, this goofy music. Folks would think it was jungle music. . . . And people would see blacks walking around with big Dobermans. They're not crimes. . . . They're part of a cultural difference."[105] A. Gaskin felt that people tended to overlook the fact that it was not all that uncommon for there to be fights among the Irish outside the local taverns.[106]

By 1968, many residents considered voting five precincts of Auburn Park dry—an ironic turn for a neighborhood in which the saloon was so important to social life. Taverns and liquor stores had proliferated to the point that residents felt the area had more than it could support. They also worried that the atmosphere would promote "all types of illegal activity." The move, however, was unsuccessful.[107]

Tavern life and etiquette had changed. While the area was Irish, the common practice was to order a drink at the bar and talk to the other patrons. A folk tradition among the Irish maintained that an Irishman could drink more whiskey from a standing position. When blacks started coming in, they tended to order a pint of whiskey and then sit at a table by themselves or with friends. "They're as clannish as the Irish," B. DesChatelets said of the blacks. He did not find their attempts at social interaction very genuine. "They put on an artificial veneer to get by."[108]

"They probably didn't feel welcome," replied C. Marble to the accusation that African Americans were antisocial. When he first moved into the area, Marble would stop in at local drinking establishments and sit at the bar. He was generally ignored. If he had been more of a barfly, he said, he might have been more persistent in his experiment in how the races got along there. "The neighborhood just stopped welcoming newcomers," he said, now that they were black, and blacks generally did not put out the effort to change the attitudes of whites. "They were both wrong," said Marble.[109]

Although the neighborhood was predominantly black in 1971, the ushers at St. Sabina's remained white. Many of these ushers left their new parishes to serve at St. Sabina's on Sunday so strong was their attachment to this parish. "They felt a kind of ownership," R. McClory explained. "Well, the church wasn't full of blacks . . . and they hated blacks. They'd be sneering at them as they walked in."[110] This situation put the pastor in a difficult position. He needed the money the ushers collected so he could not dismiss the white ushers, but to not have black ushers was clearly unjust. All he could do was to let time take its course.

The religious life of the parish had also begun to change. The more pietistic and devotional practices of the Irish did not appeal to some black Catholics. "People resisted the loss of the old structures," said R. McClory. Blacks "did not feel obligated by the same rules. Didn't have the Janesenistic understanding of Catholicism that we had. They didn't quite get the idea that you had to go to mass every Sunday. . . . There was the feeling that these things weren't important."[111]

C. Marble agreed that blacks did not feel obligated to go to church regularly or contribute in a substantial way to the upkeep of the church facilities. Since most African Americans were converts to Catholicism, they were not accustomed to the devotional forms of worship and the confraternities the Irish participated in. The Holy Name and the Altar and Rosary Societies did not have organized commentators at meetings since everyone was acquainted with the procedures and understood their meaning. When blacks started attending, meetings had to have readers and commentators in order to accommodate them. Today the Holy Name Society is called the Men's Club.[112] E. Lawrence converted to Catholicism because "Baptist churches turned [her] off." She did a lot of reading and searching and finally decided that the Catholic Church was where she wanted to worship. While St. Sabina's was primarily a white parish, going "to church was more an appreciation for the fact that God loved me." But when she went home, she did not feel any more fulfilled. She tried to read the English translation of the mass in her prayer books, but "didn't get full benefit from" the Latin mass. Overall, she was indifferent to the service.[113]

St. Sabina school experienced many strains during the transition as well. Since so many white Catholics, who sent their children to the Catholic schools, were leaving the area, the public schools, which were once the domain of Protestants, were not equipped to handle full community enrollment. They quickly became overcrowded. This had a major impact on St. Sabina's school. "Maybe the most important thing was the school," R. McClory asserted. "The public schools in the area had been empty . . . because it was the Protestants who went there. [They] were suddenly jammed with black kids. So these factors made the Catholic schools more desirable [to black parents]. . . . I remember around '68 . . . people were lined up on Throop Street all around the corner to register for our school."[114]

"The greatest attribute to the community, besides praying to God," explained C. Marble, "was the school." This was the primary attraction for blacks for joining the parish. Like the Irish, African Americans appreciated the daily exposure to religion that their children got in Catholic schools, as well as the discipline and the uniforms. The fact that many African Americans stopped attending church once their children graduated from St. Sabina school shows how much the school acted as the attraction for many African-American parents.[115]

Since many of the new black pupils were not Catholic, this created a whole set of issues to deal with. In 1967 the Dominicans reported to the mother house: "School opened on Sept. 6 with an enrollment of 930, the beginning of a significant time change. The lowered enrollment was caused by about 200 transfers of white children and about 100 admissions of Negroes. The great majority of the latter were not Catholic. This marked the beginning of a radical change in the nature of the school.[116]

The curriculum also had to be adjusted "to meet the needs and interests of culturally deprived children."[117] This created anxiety and frustration for nuns in the classroom who did not think standards ought to be compromised and whose white, Catholic, middle-class values made it difficult for them to relate to the children. The open talk of sex among grade-school children shocked the sisters. One nun said it was difficult for her to cope with the fact that many of the students had been raped.[118]

The parish bitterly fought over what to do about religious instruction and whether blacks should be obligated to become Catholics in order to send their children to the school. The mothers' club and the new school board became the staging ground for the conflict. C. Marble, who had officially been baptized a Catholic in St. Sabina's, had participated in the Church most of his life and appreciated the strict demands the Church placed on its members. He and the one other African American on the board were very concerned about not relaxing rules and standards. The Irish Americans involved with the school, he said, were used to having the school filled and wanted to reach out to the broader community to fill the empty space. Eventually, the policy for admitting non-Catholic black children into St. Sabina school was resolved by requiring parents to take instruction in Catholicism so they would know what their children were learning, but they had no obligation to become Catholics. We "hoped for, but did not demand, conversion," explained C. Marble. Priority was given to children within the area. Parents were expected to be churchgoers and were required to present a letter from their pastor confirming their attendance at a congregation of their choosing. Children were not allowed to continue in the school if parents did not cooperate.[119]

Since the parish changed over from white to black so rapidly, the school tuition had to be raised to seven dollars in order to compensate for declining enrollments. This was still not enough to cover all operating expenses. The school board had to sponsor a "Share the Load" program and devised various ways to raise money from bingo games, home parties, and an annual fund-raiser. C. Marble admitted that it was difficult to get enough money out of the parish and parents to meet all the operating expenses.[120]

Other aspects of the parish neighborhood were also changing. The whites who did stay on gradually began to miss the familiar ebbs and flows of traditional parish life. "Perhaps living among our Irish ghetto was a little more comfortable than having people who were nice to each other but yet we had nothing in common with," reflected M. Joyce. "The way they've had to live was so much different than we white middle class. . . . So we would have block meetings. . . . We participated in that way, but it wasn't the same feeling of camaraderie as it is if it's one of your own kind."[121] Some simply felt cut-off from their own culture. B. DesChatelets recalled his mother's reaction to the area becoming predominantly black. "My mother said, 'You know it didn't bother me when they were moving this way. . . . It didn't bother me when they were on the block. . . . But now that they're at the other end—now we're surrounded!' And that's just about the way you felt."[122]

C. Marble agreed that whites who stayed were "culturally submerged" by African-American culture. It was difficult to hold block club barbecues. "Whites ate white food. Blacks ate black food." The mothers' club also had a difficult time satisfying all parties. At that time, most white women did not work and held luncheons where "white" salads were served. Most African-American women did work and could not attend the luncheons. Salads were not a usual part of their meals.[123]

Although she liked her black neighbors, G. Benzig decided to leave St. Sabina's because the area no longer seemed like it was *her* neighborhood.[124] "The new breed was taking over," said M. Joyce wistfully. "It just wouldn't be the same."[125] Many old-timers felt the issue of turf deeply. B. DesChatelets recalled an incident when walking with his wife in the parish. They heard a young black man say about them, " 'What are those honkies doing in my neighborhood?' My wife got *so* mad!. . . . She said, 'What does he mean *our* neighborhood? This is *our* neighborhood!' I never saw her get so upset."[126]

Living in an area that was predominantly black was problematic for the remaining whites. Even blacks sadly realized this. D. Foertsch stayed on in St. Sabina's for many years. She moved when her children grew older and she felt they needed white friends, too. "Everybody understood why we were moving. It wasn't because I didn't like them or the area, but I felt it had served its purpose. . . . I felt we had stayed long enough to teach them [her children] what I wanted to teach them, to see other kinds of people in a normal home life situation."[127] Others left for security reasons. M. Dunne was the last white on her block to move. "We thought we could stay," she said. "But it got to the point where our new neighbors were telling us we better go. There was no problem as far as we were concerned with getting along with them. That was not it, but it was not safe."[128]

Even those who were willing to stay in the parish when it was black eventually retired and moved to a smaller place or in with their children. With their family and friends gone, there was no point in staying.[129]

The feeling that they had "lost" their parish, a place that had been so dear to them, made many people resent blacks all the more. "There were a lot who left and blamed the blacks for [making them] give up everything they had paid for and built up."[130] Many former Sabinaites moved to new suburban developments like Oak Lawn and helped establish new parishes, such as St. Linus's, St. Catherine's, and St. Germaine's. There they tried to create what they had left behind. "Oak Lawn is loaded with them!"[131] "When these guys got out there, they wanted to make Linus's the new Sabina's, because they felt cheated," explained Father Riordan. "They had built and run" St. Sabina's. When they left many felt that "they were out in the desert with nothing."[132] Those who stayed on in St. Sabina's blamed those who left. "I have no resentment in my heart for [blacks] at all," said M. Joyce. "I had more resentment for the whites that ran. . . . I really did."[133]

Monsignor McMahon also took the brunt of the blame for the parish changing hands. "Monsignor McMahon was blamed. . . . A lot of people felt that he encouraged the change," said M. Dunne. "He was a victim of the times . . . but I know he would never change his mind. He was committed to social justice. . . . He would go down fighting."[134] D. Foertsch said many people claim they would still be in St. Sabina's if it were not for Monsignor McMahon. "In 1986, there's still some who blame Monsignor because he had the audacity to welcome them in."[135] "You'd have thought he'd gone out and dragged them in," said M. Joyce of some people's feelings toward Monsignor McMahon. "He was being accused of bringing them in . . . because he welcomed them. . . . He didn't say 'you can't come to my parish'. . . . He went through a great deal. I don't know how it affected him."[136]

It had a devastating effect on him. "One of the last conversations I had with him," recalled Monsignor Egan, "he said, 'You know, Jack, the thing that hurts me the most was when some of our parishioners, who had been loyal parishioners, friends of mine, moved out in the middle of the night without ever saying good-bye. . . . They sold their house to a black family and they were going to get out.' But he said, 'I understood that. I understood there were many, many reasons'. . . . He had married them, baptized their kids. Their kids went through the school . . . and he never heard from them again. Maybe they were ashamed. Maybe they thought they were letting him down. . . . But all through it, Monsignor McMahon . . . was a tower of strength."[137] Some parishioners did not have any qualms about letting him know their negative feelings, and wrote him bitter letters. "It hurt him deeply," said A. Gaskin, his administrative assistant.[138]

Part of the reason Monsignor McMahon became the scapegoat was because of his awkward personality. To a young and energetic priest like Father Sullivan, working for the elderly McMahon was at times frustrating and fraught with misunderstandings. "He was very much an old-style priest," he said. "More interested in saving souls. . . . He was sort of 'spacey'. . . . He wanted to do good . . . and he believed that God made all people, blacks and whites, equal. . . . That's what Jesus was saying. . . . He knew what a Catholic should experience . . . but he could never translate it into the common terms, to the common person. He'd say 'You've got to welcome the black people' without examples or encouragement. . . . People would tell him that he would ruin the parish that way. Well, he didn't quite understand what they meant. . . . He was partly trying to dictate how things should be, and everybody should do it this way. . . . It was his age, too. . . . He [was] a very old sixty-five. And he had this terrible deafness which would hamper anyone, and it certainly hampered him."[139]

Monsignor McMahon also offended some of his parishioners through his own clumsiness. "Monsignor had a lot of idiosyncrasies," admitted D. Foertsch. "He could be klutzy about things. Kind of blurt things out that would have been more discreet not to."[140] Father Sullivan said that at funeral masses when old friends and neighbors returned to St. Sabina's, while trying to praise the deceased, McMahon would say things like " 'John was so good. He stayed here with me. You people ran!' "[141]

Monsignor McMahon and OSC were not able to stop panic peddling completely or to create an integrated community. Although it began with high hopes and pragmatic tactics, in retrospect OSC made some mistakes and some of its problems were too big for it to tackle. Its three-person staff was too small. Alinsky's philosophy of community organizing was to use the talents of local leaders, but the massive amount of illegal conversion, marauding blockbusters, and racial clashes overworked the full-time employees. The Southwest Side needed outside help from local and federal agencies. If open occupancy was truly implemented by both local and federal agencies and if the city had a requirement that all city workers live in its boundaries in those years, white flight might have been curbed.[142]

Federal housing policies also favored suburban developments over city neighborhoods. The Home Owners Loan Corporation (HOLC) reinforced the redlining practices of financial institutions. Homogeneous developments were considered less risky. HOLC, therefore, sanctioned segregation. FHA also worked against integration. It claimed it was not created to help cities but to stimulate home ownership and reduce unemployment. The building industry, anxious for guaranteed government money, ignored the needs of older areas and turned to the development of suburban housing tracts. In addition, new expressways made outlying areas easily accessible.[143] OSC was fighting an uphill battle against the lure of the suburbs.

OSC also felt let down by the leadership of the Archdiocese. The Archdiocese bravely chanced endorsing this Alinsky-inspired project for limited integration, but it failed to provide the sustained leadership that was necessary. Cardinal Meyer did not condemn the immorality of race discrimination as vociferously as he should have, nor did he discipline Catholic pastors for their negligence on this matter. Meyer's interests were more with historic changes in the Church with Vatican II. This left many local leaders, who had taken a chance by going against the tide of community sentiment and who thus had made enemies among family and friends, feeling abandoned. Despite the noble leadership of Reverend Christ and Monsignor McMahon, most Catholic and Protestant religious leaders were halfhearted in their efforts. Nick von Hoffman was disgusted with the bigoted Catholic clergy. He said, "With certain noble exceptions, the pastors of the Southwest Side are practically a caricature, a cartoon, of the sins of omission and commission of the Irish Roman Catholic clergy." Donald O'Toole even criticized John McMahon for being too much of a saint instead of a man of action.[144]

In the late 1960s, with the area becoming predominantly black, school issues and municipal services occupied the time of what remained of OSC. By this time Alinsky himself had abandoned the project and OSC faded into the background of his achievements.[145]

Although it failed to integrate the Southwest Side, OSC did create a more positive experience of racial change for many people, and it helped preserve the physical integrity of the community. By slowing down the transition period, OSC enabled many whites to learn more about their black neighbors and their experiences with racial injustice. "It took ten years," said D. Foertsch of the span of time it took for the first black family to move into St. Sabina's and for whites to leave.

"That's not overnight. And yet it took maybe a year and a half to go through Little Flower because [Father Stephen McMahon] preached as negatively as Monsignor Wolfe did down at Visitation."[146]

"It achieved its goals," concurred C. Marble on OSC's effectiveness. He also felt very positively about the personal experiences the organization afforded him. Monsignor McMahon recruited him to participate in OSC. The Foster Park Community Council's boundaries were practically synonymous with the parish boundaries. With McMahon's support, Marble became the first black to serve as the Community Council's president between 1968 and 1972. This office made him an automatic delegate to OSC. Marble described himself as "an integrationist." His hopes were to have the opportunity to compete on an equal playing field with whites. He felt McMahon, St. Sabina's, and OSC gave him this opportunity. What racist sentiments there were in the neighborhood did not deter him from what he wanted. He was "accepted and allowed to compete." Based on past experience, though, Marble did not expect the area to remain integrated. "People will separate according to their own kind." Although the South Side has gone through the painful process of neighborhood change, Marble sees this as part of the strength of this section of the city. "Those aren't real neighborhoods," he said of the North Side. That is why they escaped the notoriety of neighborhood conflict.[147]

Overall, the racial transition in Auburn-Gresham and the OSC area was marked by a great deal of stability. Although a product of blockbusting and a forced marketing process, it went from a white middle-class area to one that was predominantly black middle class. Twenty-five percent of the new homeowners had previous ownership experience. Fifty-one percent were able to obtain conventional loans. This was an important fact. In many other neighborhoods, especially in Englewood, many FHA and VA loan programs were used by unscrupulous brokers to sell homes to families who did not have adequate incomes. With so much of their salaries going toward their mortgage payments, little went toward upkeep. Foreclosures and neighborhood deterioration were common.[148]

While whites felt they were witnessing a breakdown of their community, the majority of blacks who moved into Auburn-Gresham in the early to mid-1970s were very optimistic about their new neighborhood. Ninety-two percent of black residents rated the quality of the area "good" or "excellent" in terms of housing quality, upkeep and appearance, and crime rate. Few had any anxiety or apprehension about living in an integrated neighborhood. Forty-one percent of blacks actually preferred to live with people of a different race. Fifty-two percent had no preference. Many blacks believed that white neighborhoods had better access to public and private services and goods.

Except for shopping, black residents felt the quality of the neighborhood remained the same.[149]

C. Marble believes his block is better now than when he moved in. The income and educational level of residents is higher. "Whites would have benefited if they stayed."[150] "They didn't want to be in a totally black community," explained Father Sullivan. "They loved it when it was an integrated community."[151] While racial disturbances loomed large in the minds of whites, most blacks did not expect to encounter racial trouble when they moved into the area and 89 percent did not have any problems.[152] "There are some exceptions on the South Side," admitted T. O'Rourke. "Some of them have gone into neighborhoods and they've kept them up very well. . . . And I do say that about Sabina's, the side streets look pretty good. Seventy-ninth Street, though, is a disaster."[155] "Seventy-ninth got to be the gosh awfullest looking place," Father Sullivan conceded. "There'd be a liquor store and then a record store and then another liquor store. . . . But then you'd get off 79th Street and the people were keeping up the homes so nicely."[154]

The work of Monsignor McMahon and the other priests and sisters attracted many blacks to the church, and laid the foundation for St. Sabina's to become one of the premiere black Catholic parishes in Chicago and the country. "Black people never got the impression" that the Church was prejudiced, said R. McClory. They "had the impression that McMahon was pro-black . . . and the OSC was an organization that was trying to integrate, and that made an impression. Therefore, the parish was not looked upon as an institution as being antiblack, although the parishioners were. So because of McMahon, Sabina's is a fairly flourishing black parish."[155] "The people who moved into the parish . . . all came to love monsignor," said A. Gaskin. "They considered him their friend."[156] C. Marble said, "I can't say enough about him!" Although he too realized McMahon could be a dictator with a "like it or lump it" attitude characteristic of many Irish-American priests, Marble said that McMahon recognized the reality of a changing neighborhood and tried to involve African Americans in the church and gave them "100 percent support."[157] The parish was also left with a sound financial base of $800,000 in its treasury.[158] It, therefore, was able to avoid the rapid deterioration of other parishes as its membership dropped.

Monsignor McMahon was aided by a cadre of dedicated and able priests and nuns. "Fumbling though we were, we gave it every moment of every day," said Father Sullivan. "There was such a good group of people, women and men, black and white, sisters and priests. . . . It was a hard time, but it was a good time."[159] "Half our nights in the summer [we spent] going around ringing doorbells at random in black areas saying, 'We have a great school over here, a great church to worship at on Sunday. Come on over!' " recalled R. McClory. The blacks that were attracted to Catholicism, he thought, were more "upper crust" and sophisticated. To them, becoming Catholic meant "rising above their humble black origins." Others were drawn to the richness and complexity of the religion. "I think Southern Baptists tend to be weak on substance and so many were very curious. You'd get a real dialogue at times with people who were hungering." To attract other blacks meant changing some forms of worship, such as using the organ during the sermon to add drama.[160]

Father Sullivan took charge of the community center, which had stood empty and lifeless after the Kelly shooting and the exodus of white parishioners. He developed a plan to use the building for the benefit of the new community by creating a neighborhood youth employment corps. They had hundreds of teenagers employed as recreational counselors and tutors for younger children. They had day camp and sports leagues. With the help of a young white couple who had grown up in the parish, they reestablished Saturday roller skating. The couple said they had gotten so much from the center when they were children that they wanted to give something in return. The most amazing act of Christian love that Father Sullivan witnessed, though, was when Pat Kelly, the sister of Frank, volunteered to sit at the cashier's station to sell tickets for the roller-skating. "One of the most magnificent things I could ever recount about anyone was Pat Kelly," said Father Sullivan. "She was selling tickets . . . inches from where her brother died. . . . She couldn't forget what happened, but she helped the little black kids."[161] In all, Father Sullivan felt the youth program "generated a whole lot of intangible good will. That Church gives a darn!"[162]

Once white families left, St. Sabina's went through an evolutionary process. Monsignor McMahon continued to run the parish as he always did—in a rather old-fashioned, dictatorial way. And he continued to give "thirty minute masses," which pleased Mr. Marble. McMahon was named pastor emeritus in 1971 but continued to live in the rectory until his death a few years later.[163] He "embraced the new community," said E. Lawrence. "They were his people."[164] His replacement was Father Henry J. Pehler.[165] Pehler was an integrationist and accepted the changed situation in the parish. Although he has been described as a "noncharismatic administrator," Pehler was a pastor to his people and was open to changes in the parish. He relied on his assistants and community members for outreach work. Father McClory initiated the celebration of Martin Luther King Day, and Father David Walker worked diligently with people in the community. Mr. Marble said he would "give a lot of credit to" Father Walker for creating a feeling of belonging and community among the more recent parishioners in St. Sabina's.[166] "I loved him!" E. Lawrence said. "He loved people." Mrs. Lawrence had thought about searching for a new Catholic church. The African-American tradition of expressing praise for God through song was something she missed. But she was committed to Catholicism. Then Father Pehler had asked her to be one of the first female readers at mass and she started to become more involved in the parish. "I got into worshipping with Father Pehler."[167] When Father Michael Pfleger arrived in 1980 after Father Pehler's death, he was able to institution-alize many of the things that had been coalescing to make the parish an expression of African-American Catholicism. "The first day Father Pfleger came he was "full of fire and ready to go!" said E. Lawrence. "He's a *preacher*." "Mike's blacker than I am," joked C. Marble about Father Pfleger's pastoral style. Pfleger's services often run two hours with a heavy emphasis on the sermon and music. "Sabina's is some-times called a Protestant church," said C. Marble. "Its either a term of endearment or it upsets people."[168]

Many African Americans have been drawn to the strengths of parish life enjoyed by Catholic ethnics, particularly the nurturing of its children. The school and the community center are major attrac-tions. The paternal interest Father Pfleger takes in the young people of the parish brings to mind Father Waldron of old St. John's, who patrolled the streets with his blackthorn stick. Father Pfleger, no less heedful of the temptations presented to impressionable young minds, has taken up crusades against billboard advertisements of alcohol and tobacco found near the school, as well as drug paraphernalia sold in local stores. Pfleger has even begun a drug-testing program in the school to prevent drug abuse among its five hundred pupils. He defended the program stating, "We're family and we're doing this because of love."[169]

While St. Sabina's priests were ministering to their new commu-nity, former residents searched for new parishes to replace what they had left behind. Many settled in Beverly Hills and Morgan Park. "It was real important to me [to investigate] the philosophy of a parish before I would move," said D. Foertsch. "We found that St. Barnabas was more like what we had thought Sabina's was. We looked at every house that was for sale in Barnabas. If it was across the border, even though we liked the house, we decided on Barnabas. This is definitely family."[170] Today St. Barnabas is heavily Irish American.[171] It has an Irish family mass and recently it began a Mother of Sorrows Novena. "I nearly fell on the floor when I heard that!" exclaimed D. Foertsch.[172] Its parishioners support the resurrected South Side Irish parade, which now marches down Western Avenue. G. Hendry also moved to this area and chose St. Cajetan's parish because he wanted to raise his children in the same kind of environment as he grew up in, with the same values. "This area was appealing because . . . there were so many people that we knew . . . transplants from Sabina's, Little Flower, Leo, Ethelreda. . . . We felt comfortable coming in here the same way I felt comfortable at St. Sabina's as a kid growing up."[173] Ironically, Beverly has become a model for managed integration guided by the Beverly Area Planning Association. Its unique home architecture and city ordinances requiring its employees to live in Chicago have contributed to the neighborhood's stability.

Others tried to recreate St. Sabina's in the suburbs, such as at St. Linus's in Oak Lawn. It resulted in tension between those wanting to rebuild what they had lost and those who realized its impossibility. "It wasn't quite possible. You couldn't rebuild a place like that," said Father Riordan.[174]

Most remembered their days at St. Sabina's with great fondness. Although they may have settled in other parishes, many former parishioners still consider themselves to be "from Sabina's." To a certain extent they feel very possessive of their old parish. Since St. Sabina's has become such a prominent black parish, it is often featured in the news but mispronounced. "It really tees me off," said B. DesChatelets, "when I hear them talking on TV about St. Sabeena's."[175] J. Hagerty is irritated when she hears St. Sabina's referred to as "the black cathedral, as if they built it!"[176]

Over twenty years after the parish changed hands, J. Nelligan still occasionally answers the question "Where are you from?" with "Sabina's." Once when he was on a business trip on a small airplane in Florida, the plane hit a rain storm and some turbulence. To calm the passengers, the stewardess tried to make conversation and asked him where he was from. Smiling to himself, he answered "Sabina's." While he confused the flight attendant, a man in the seat in front of him turned and said "I'm from Little Flower!"[177]

Many still think nostalgically about their old parish and lament their loss. "When we go to wakes or weddings. . . . I hear people say, 'Oh, the good old days! Isn't it too bad what happened to Sabina's?'" said D. Foertsch with exasperation. "That just offends me so much because they don't know what they're talking about. Sabina's is, if not more so, as alive as in its biggest day. It's a wonderful community. It's different, and some people just don't want to accept that things can be different and still be good."[178]

Things were different. St. Sabina's was no longer even called St. Sabina parish. Instead, it is called St. Sabina community, because it accepts membership from people who do not live within its traditional boundaries. Blacks do not see the parish as a universe as Irish-American Catholics did. "People identified with the block club. You could tell the black community by block clubs."[179] "The Church is an anchor of morality in the community," explained C. Marble. But African Americans, he noted, tend to treat priests as equals and not put them on a pedestal the way Irish Americans tended to do. From that height, however, "Irish priests had the full cooperation from the people."[180] St. Sabina's new members have draped the African-American national colors down the nave of the church, and a bust of Martin Luther King rests on what had been St. Joseph's altar. Even those who accepted blacks into the parish had a difficult time accepting these additions. To traditional Catholics, Martin Luther King may have been a good man, but he is not a canonized saint and was not even Catholic. Therefore, placing his bust on an altar seemed very inappropriate to them.[181] "I know people who would die if they knew that," said D. Foertsch. However, she often goes back to St. Sabina's for services. Rather than dwell on the new, she says she sees "the communion rail that I received my first communion at, the aisle I got married at, the aisle I buried my father at. My first love will always be there. Always."[182]

Mrs. Foertsch is not the only white person who goes back to the parish for services. Those who do are continually struck by the warmth and vitality of the community and the innovative liturgies. "I'm so well received when I do go," said a recent visitor. "They go out of their way to extend themselves to you at the sign of peace. I wonder if the situation were reversed in some of the all-white parishes if they would even turn around."[183]

St. Sabina's present pastor, Father Michael Pfleger, received a letter from an old parishioner who enjoyed a similar welcome. "On Sunday we returned with two of our daughters who had never been to Saint Sabina before. We attended the sung Mass celebration by Father Tom Walsh and assisted in so many ways by capable, enthusiastic, parishioners. The ceremony was uplifting, the homily stimulating, the music magnificent, the congregation warm, genuine, and friendly— truly a spiritual and emotional experience for all of us. We found the essence of Saint Sabina as we knew it is very much alive, active, and throbbing. We thank the Lord for what Saint Sabina has given us, and for what she continues to give to her people."[184]

"Well, we turned it over to people who can use it," said J. Hagerty, reflecting on the situation. "I think all the old timers would be happy with that"[185]

Conclusion

Patrick Lonigan confides his feelings to his son Studs on their moving day from the fictional parish of St. Patrick's, which James T. Farrell based upon St. Anselm's in his Studs Lonigan trilogy, saying, "You know, Bill, your mother and I are gettin' old now, and well, we sort of got used to this neighborhood ... The old people ... they were all nearby, and they all knew us, and we knew them, and you see, well, this neighborhood was kind of like home. We sort of felt about it the same way I feel about Ireland, where I was born."[1] As blacks began moving into the parish in the late 1920s, Patrick Lonigan sold his building to a black man and bought a new home for his family in South Shore. "No home will be like this one had been to us," Patrick said to his wife Mary. "We made our home here, raised our children, and spent the best years of our lives here." Mary thinks about their pastor, Father Gilhooley. "He's heartbroken, poor man. Here he built his beautiful church, and two years after it's built, all his parishioners are gone." Patrick replies, "Goddam those niggers!"[2] From this point in the novel Patrick Lonigan and his son are forever displaced persons, without a home in a familiar neighborhood. The move to South Shore for Studs contributes to his failure in life and to his early death.[3]

While Studs's demise may be an extreme version of dislocation, the feelings and sentiments his family experienced on moving day were as true in the 1960s and they were in 1928. Racial animosity on the Southwest Side of Chicago has been fueled by these types of experiences. Ethnic parishes were slowly being transformed through the twentieth century. It is likely that they would have eventually died a slow, natural death, but the sudden shock brought on by the Great Migration accelerated the process. Catholic ethnics were not afforded several generations to slowly psychologically remove themselves from a parish-centered life. Many blamed blacks for the loss of a more intimate, community-oriented lifestyle. Their old neighborhoods, now occupied by blacks, for better or worse, became sore reminders of a much-loved, lost life.

The South Side black community also had its own literary heritage, offering a flip-side view of race relations there. In 1940 Richard Wright published *Native Son*, a shocking story of the plight of a disadvantaged black youth, Bigger Thomas, who kills two white women. Bigger's actions and lack of remorse make for a very harsh and unsentimental view of the effects of racism.

Lorraine Hansberry's *A Raisin in the Sun* is also set on Chicago's South Side, nearly two decades later. Hansberry explores the conflict between blacks and whites over neighborhood turf. The drama portrays the difficulties of the Youngers, a black family that consists of an elderly mother, her spirited daughter, and her son with his wife and son, living in a cramped, two-bedroom apartment. When the mother is to receive a sizable life insurance settlement from her deceased husband's policy, the family is torn by what to do with the windfall. The mother wants to buy a house that happens to be in a white neighborhood. When she does, she comes into conflict with the local residents. She is even paid a visit by Mr. Linder, the chairman of the "Clybourne Park Improvement Association," a neighborhood protection group. Linder tries to explain the sentiments of the people he represents: "Our community is made up of people who've worked hard as the dickens for years to build up that little community. They're not rich and fancy people; just hard-working, honest people who don't really have much but those little homes and a dream of the kind of community they want to raise their children in . . . you've got to admit that a man, right or wrong, had the right to want to have the neighborhood he lives in a certain kind of way. And at the moment the overwhelming majority of our people out there feel that people get along better, take more a common interest in the life of the community, when they share a common background."[4] The Younger family is stunned by this blatant affront to their race and blow to their dream. Linder finds it difficult to understand their reaction, saying: "I don't understand why you people are reacting this way. What do you think you are going to gain by moving into a neighborhood where you just aren't wanted and where some elements—well—people can get awful worked up when they feel that their whole way of life and everything they've worked for is threatened."[5] Linder is promptly shown the door, and despite this slap in the face, the family refuses to be intimidated and moves into their new home. For them, it is a move filled with hope and optimism.

Since Martin Luther King's open-housing marches, Chicago's South Side neighborhoods have been considered to be homes of incorrigible racists. Recently, historians have begun to reevaluate King's strategy. These marches were inconsistent with the civil-rights leader's goals in the North, which were vaguely defined as "ending slums." Frustrated by lack of progress on this front, King decided to proceeded with the marches against the warnings of black leaders in Chicago. They correctly believed that if blacks moved into white neighborhoods at this time, whites would flee and blacks would be no better off. King disregarded local sentiment that what the Chicago African-American community needed most was to strengthen its weak institutional life. In fact, the effect of the marches was actually the opposite of what King had hoped for. Rather than awakening the social consciences of whites, the marches were interpreted by South Siders as a moral judgment against their way of life. King, in turn, condemned them for exhibiting more virulent racism than anything he had seen in the South. Christopher Lasch recently commented that "if he had forced himself to understand the content of this resistance, he might have seen that blacks could not hope to achieve their objectives by demanding the dissolution of white communities whose only crime, as far as anyone could see, was their sense of ethnic solidarity."[6] This book has been an attempt to illuminate this resistance.

Irish Catholics insulated themselves from a world that did not entirely welcome them by finding security in their parishes. The parish was vitally important to maintaining a Catholic subculture in America. It gave the immigrant generation a sense of continuity to their past life in Ireland. In America the parish not only had a religious function, but it ensured the cohesion of the American-Irish community.

As the Irish began their ascent into skilled employment and the middle class, they sought better housing in outlying areas of the city. Their second-class position in American society as Catholics was made readily apparent in Anglo-Protestant communities, where the welcome mat was quickly taken up. Rather than shedding such an integral part of their identity and melding into the dominant host culture, the Irish hung on to their strong affiliation with the Church and clung to the parish for support.

While they did not encounter the hostility of Anglo-Protestants in their neighborhood, St. Sabina's Catholics were reminded of their minority status in America with the revival in the 1920 of the Ku Klux Klan and the 1928 presidential election that resulted in the defeat of Al Smith. Some defensiveness can be detected in St. Sabina's parishioners of that period, yet they clearly cherished their community life. Within it they nourished Catholic pride.

After World War II anti-Catholicism diminished to some extent. At the same time Catholics had grown secure enough to see their separation from Protestant America as a positive thing. St. Sabina parishioners saw the parish as a place to foster religious devotion and shelter their families from secular society, and as a means by which to Christianize the rest of the world. Its devotional life, the school, and its recreational activities all combined to reinforce the parish community.

Although St. Sabina's considered itself an Irish parish, its Catholic identity predominated. While St. Patrick's Day celebrations had wide appeal, Irish Americans did not separate their national and religious identities any more than their counterparts in Ireland did. Most took their Irish heritage for granted but cultivated their Catholicism.

With their conception of themselves inextricably entwined with the parish, fear and resentment were the natural reaction to perceived threats. While most parishioners clung to the old parish philosophy of Catholic isolationism, the Church itself was embarking upon a new era. Chicago became a major center of liberal Catholicism. Many clergy and laity hoped to create a more expansive view of Catholicism's role in society. Msgr. McMahon, with the help of others, tried to introduce a new parish philosophy of openness toward others. The results were mixed. Despite their skepticism, most parishioners went along with his new ventures in community organizing. They hoped OSC would keep their neighborhood stable. McMahon's early success could also be attributed to the considerable power priests still enjoyed at that time. His efforts helped mitigate some of the bitter feelings between whites and his new black parishioners by attempting to turn the process into a forward-looking opportunity to grow, yet, in the end, St. Sabina's did not achieve integration any more than other less socially progressive parishes. Love for the old ways and fear of the new sent many looking to repeat their Sabina's experience in suburbs further south and west. Some of those people found a similar parish environment, but, generally, the ethos of the urban, ethnic neighborhood proved elusive.

By the 1960s, American society had changed. Being Catholic was no longer the handicap it once had been. Even the highest office in the nation was held by Catholic John F. Kennedy. There was no longer the need to take refuge against Protestant society in the parish or a Catholic ghetto.[7] As the Irish moved geographically outward and economically upward, the areas they settled were more diverse. While pockets of Irishness continue to exist, for the most part the Irish no longer live or work in religious and ethnic ghettos. Yet the St. Sabina story indicates people were reluctant to give up their parish heritage. The Second Vatican Council also changed the character and outlook of parishes. The parish was no longer a haven from the secular world. Instead, it was to be a home base where Catholics could experience the faith; it also inspired and energized them to deal with broader community and social concerns in the light of Gospel values. Vatican II also encouraged greater lay participation and leadership in various church activities and programs, such as parish councils, liturgy committees, and peace and justice groups. While still a central figure, the pastor is now often assisted by a pastoral team of lay men and women. People participate out of choice, not from a sense of duty.[8]

Yet something intangibly good was lost in the transition to the "new" parish. A recent University of Notre Dame study of parishes found that just half of practicing Catholics thought the parish provided a real sense of community. Suburban Catholics were the least attached to their parishes. They had fewer close friends within the parish borders and fewer contacts with fellow parishioners.[9] Nor do most parishes have any national identification to provide social cohesion. While he feels that overall the changes in the Church were good, W. Hogan thinks that many of the innovations have had an adverse effect on parish life because of "a breakdown in theology. . . . Back then there was tremendous uniformity in the mass. There was no questioning the faith." Today the form of the mass can vary from parish to parish, resulting in a decline in the shared experience of the mass and the universal Church.[10] Devotionalism has been criticized by some as superstitious, but there has been little in the way of personal spiritual exercises to replace it. The parish does not call people over to the church as much as it used to. St. Sabina's white parishioners would have had to respond to Vatican II changes. Whether they could have maintained such a strong sense of identity with these changes is a matter of speculation.

Because America is composed of so many different ethnic, religious, and racial groups and is such a mobile society, conflict and strife seem to be inevitable. This can be seen in the opposing views of families like the Lonigans and the Youngers in their disputes over Chicago neighborhoods. Sooner or later Americans are forced to accommodate and compromise. In the past twenty years, we have seen a growing celebration of ethnic heritages. Many new immigrant groups no longer feel as compelled as earlier arrivals to assimilate into mainstream American society. These sentiments no doubt arise in part from feelings of loss and dislocation. The Irish were among the first to experience this sense of displacement. Farrell's novels chronicle the material success of the Irish and their movement into the mainstream, but he shows how the long struggle has left many of them spiritually impoverished. Catholic communalism, historically seen as antithetical to American individualism, finally was defeated. With the decline of the parish as a cultural entity, Catholics and the Irish have lost a vital aspect of their ethnic heritage.

Notes

Abbreviations

ACA   Archdiocese of Chicago Archives and Record Center
CIC   Catholic Interracial Council

Note: For complete publication information, see Bibliography, 214-18.

Introduction

1. Dan Rostenkowski, "Chicago," *Vis á Vis* (Oct. 1989), 67.
2. Cogley, *Catholic America*, 135.
3. Andrew M. Greeley, "Catholicism in America: Two Hundred Years and Counting," *Critic* 34, no. 4 (summer 1976): 42.
4. Dolan, *American Catholic Parish,* 1:2-3.
5. Author interview with J. Kill.
6. Author interview with Nathalie Hagerty.
7. Lasch, *True and Only Heaven,* 35-36.
8. "Same Old Stuff," *Southtown Economist* 18 Aug. 1963, 4.
9. Anne Keegan, "Has the Term 'White Ethnic' Lost Its Value?" *Chicago Tribune,* 13 Feb. 1989, 1.

1. The Making of the Irish Parish Community

1. Ellis, *Mr. Dooley's America,* 78, 96, 102-22.
2. Ibid., 104.
3. Schaaf, *Mr. Dooley's Chicago,* 71-72.
4. Ellis, *Mr. Dooley's America,* 3-4, 8.
5. Branch, *Farrell,* 9, 15, 16, 45; Fried, *Makers of the City,* 119, 120-21, 126.
6. Fried, *Makers of the City,* 119-58.
7. Clark, *Hibernia America,* 13-19.
8. Pierce, *History of Chicago,* 1:180.
9. Ibid., 2:49, 179-80.
10. Holt and Pacyga, *Chicago,* 113; Pacyga and Skerrett, *Chicago,* 453.
11. Michael F. Funchion, "The Political and Nationalist Dimensions," in McCaffrey et al., *Irish in Chicago,* 62-63; *People of Chicago*; Shanabruch, *Chicago's Catholics,* 1. Paul Michael Green, "Irish Chicago: The Multiethnic Road to Machine Success," in Holli and Jones, *Ethnic Chicago,* 419-20.
12. Funchion, "Political and Nationalist Dimensions," 63, 70-72.
13. Michael F. Funchion, "Irish Chicago: Church, Homeland, Politics, and Class—The Shaping of an Ethnic Group, 1870-1900," in Holli and Jones, *Ethnic Chicago,* 30. Green, "Irish Chicago," 413.
14. Kantowicz, *Corporation Sole,* 215; Ellen Skerrett, "The Development of Catholic Identity Among Irish Americans in Chicago, 1880 to 1920," in Meagher, *From Paddy to Studs,* 119.

15. Funchion, "Irish Chicago," 19, 24-26; Brown, *Irish-American Nationalism*, 21-24.

16. Funchion, "Irish Chicago," 26-27, and "Political and Nationalist Dimensions," 73-77.

17. Ibid.; Louise Carroll Wade, *Chicago's Pride: The Stockyards, Packingtown, and Environs in the Nineteenth Century* (Urbana: Univ. of Illinois Press, 1987), 145; Fanning, *Mr. Dooley and the Chicago Irish*; 414. St. John's Quarterly, Golden Jubilee Edition, June 1927, ACA.

18. Funchion, "Irish Chicago," 19. Pierce, *History of Chicago*, 1:180-81; Wade, *Chicago's Pride*, 145; Shanabruch, *Chicago's Catholics*, 42-43.

19. See McCaffrey, *Ireland,* for general account of this period, 1-13.

20. Ibid., 13-17.

21. Ibid., 20-29, 43-44.

22. Ibid., 42-54.

23. See Connolly, *Priests and People,* for a more thorough account of religious practices in this period.

24. Ibid., 135-74.

25. Ibid., 264-80.

26. Emmet Larkin, "The Devotional Revolution in Ireland, 1850-1875," *American Historical Review* 77 (June 1972): 625-52. Thesis developed in this work.

27. Ibid.

28. Ibid., 638-45.

29. Ibid., 648-49.

30. See Miller, *Church, State, and Nation,* for a more complete account.

31. Thomas T. McAvoy, "The Formation of the Catholic Minority," in Philip Gleason, ed., *Catholicism in America* (New York: Harper and Row, 1970), 10-27.

32. Kathleen Gavigan, "The Rise and Fall of Parish Cohesiveness in Philadelphia," *Records of the American Catholic Historical Society* 86 (1975): 107-30.

33. Ibid.

34. Patricia K. Good, "Irish Adjustment to American Society: Integration or Separation?" *Records of the American Catholic Historical Society* 86 (1975): 7-21.

35. Dolan, *Immigrant Church*, 4-8, 40.

36. Dolan, *Revivalism*, 32-34.

37. Ibid., xix, 187.

38. Ibid., 36-37, 191-97.

39. Ibid., 192-95.

40. Finke and Stark, *Churching of America.*

41. See Taves, *Household of Faith*, for a thorough and thought-provoking account of devotionalism, 89, 128.

42. Ibid., 126-32. See also chapter 3 of this book for a more detailed explanation of Catholic devotions.

43. Ibid., 133.

44. Paula Marie Kane, *Boston Catholics and Modern American Culture, 1900-1920* (Ph. D. diss., Yale University, 1987), xiv, 3-4.

45. Dolan, *Immigrant Church*, 45-46, and *American Catholic Experience*, 158-94; Shanabruch, *Chicago's Catholics*, 115; Dolores Liptak, *Immigrants and Their Church* (New York: Macmillan, 1989), 82-83.

46. Shanabruch, *Chicago's Catholics*, 1, 17, 33, 41, 107, 110, 176; Kantowicz, *Corporation Sole*, 133, 162. Koenig, *History of the Parishes*, 578-80, 751.

47. Dolan, *American Catholic Experience*, 162-63; Funchion, "Irish Chicago," 19; Shanabruch, *Chicago's Catholics*, 39-42.

48. Shanabruch, *Chicago's Catholics*, 41-42; Funchion, "Irish Chicago," 17-19; Skerrett, "Catholic Dimension," 24-25, 33-34.

49. Fanning, Skerrett, and Corrigan, *Nineteenth Century Chicago Irish*, 2-5. See also Slayton, *Back of the Yards.*

50. Skerrett, "Catholic Dimension," 29-30.

51. Ibid., 34; Koenig, *History of the Parishes*, 373.

52. Sanders, *Education of an Urban Minority*, 91.

53. Taves, *Household of Faith*, 120-25.

54. Saint Gabriel Church Diamond Jubilee, 1880-1955; Saint Gabriel Parish, 1880-1980; both in ACA.

55. Ibid.

56. Ibid.

57. St. John's Quarterly, Golden Jubilee Edition, June 1927, ACA.

58. Ibid.

59. Koenig, *History of the Parishes*, 145-47; Wade, *Chicago's Pride*, 145-46.

60. Len O'Connor, *Clout: Mayor Daley and His City* (New York: Avon Books, 1975), 20.

61. Koenig, *History of the Parishes*, 968-71.

62. Diamond Jubilee, 75 Years, Visitation Parish, ACA.

63. Funchion, "Irish Chicago," 21.

64. Skerrett, "Catholic Dimension," 37.

65. Edward R. Kantowicz, "Polish Chicago: Survival through Solidarity," in Holli and Jones, *Ethnic Chicago*, 218, 228.

66. Skerrett, "Catholic Dimension," 43-44, 50-51.

67. Sanders, *Education of an Urban Minority*, 12-13; Shanabruch, *Chicago's Catholics*, 56-58.

68. Shanabruch, *Chicago's Catholics*, 60; Skerrett, "Catholic Dimension," 44-45.

69. Shanabruch, *Chicago's Catholics*, 40-42, 114-45.

70. Funchion, "Irish Chicago," 36-37; Shanabruch, *Chicago's Catholics*, 29-30.

71. Saint Gabriel Church Diamond Jubilee, 1880-1955, ACA.

72. Skerrett, "Catholic Dimension," 39-40.

73. Koenig, *History of the Parishes*, 353.

74. Skerrett, "Catholic Identity," 123, and "Catholic Dimension," 28, 34.

75. William C. McCready, "The Irish Neighborhood: A Contribution to American Urban Life," in David Noel Doyle and Owen Dudley Edwards, eds., *America and Ireland, 1776-1976: The American Identity and the Irish Connection* (Westport, Conn.: Greenwood, 1980), 247-59.

76. Fanning, *Mr. Dooley and the Chicago Irish*, 167. For a complete discussion and analysis of Mr. Dooley, see Fanning, *Finley Peter Dunne and Mr. Dooley: The Chicago Years* (Lexington: Univ. Press of Kentucky, 1978).

77. Fanning, *Mr. Dooley and the Chicago Irish*, 176-77.

78. Fanning, "The Literary Dimension," in McCaffrey et al., *Irish in Chicago*, 109.

79. Ibid., 108-10.

80. Ibid., 123, 125-26.

81. Ibid., 127.

2. St. Sabina

1. "The Southside's Newest Church: St. Sabina's Church Nearing Completion," *New World*, 30 Aug. 1933.

2. *Community of God and People*, 6.

3. Ibid., 7.

4. "The Southside's Newest Church," *New World*, 16 June 1933.

5. Kitagawa and Taeber, *Local Community Fact Book*, 156.

6. Ibid., 156.

7. Koenig, *History of the Parishes*, 543.

8. Kantowicz, *Corporation Sole*, 36-37, 77, 154.

9. Koenig, *History of the Parishes*, 858; *Community of God and People*, 7; author interview with Rev. Thomas McMahon.

10. Dolan, *American Catholic Experience*, 110-11, 115-16.

11. Ibid., 165, 169.

12. Ibid., 170-71.

13. Ibid., 182-83.

14. Edward Kantowicz, "Church and Neighborhood," *Ethnicity* 7(1980): 349.

15. Barlow, *Auburn-Gresham*, 28-45.

16. Koenig, *History of the Parishes*, 140, 545; Kantowicz, "Church and Neighborhood," 355-56.

17. William L. Yancy, Eugene P. Ericksen, and Richard N. Juliani, "Emergent Ethnicity: A Review and Reformulation," *American Sociological Review* 41, no. 3 (June 1976): 391-92.

18. Funchion, "Irish Chicago," 29-30.

19. Skerrett, "Catholic Dimension," 45-46.

20. Slayton, *Back of the Yards*, 25.

21. Harry M. Beardsley, "Auburn Park's Calm Soothes City-Weary," *Chicago Daily News*, 5 Aug. 1922, 12.

22. Author interview with Terence O'Rourke.

23. Author interview with Julia Hagerty.

24. Author interview with Rev. James Kill.

25. Beardsley, "Auburn Park's Calm," 12.

26. Author interview with Rev. James Kill.

27. Author interview with Mary S. Dunne.

28. Author interview with Helen O'Connor.

29. Author interview with Emmett Clair.

30. Author interview with Terence O'Rourke.

31. Hauser and Kitagawa, *Local Community Fact Book*, 290-91.

32. St. Sabina Annual Reports, 1930 and 1936, ACA.

33. Daniel J. Prosser, "Chicago and the Bungalow Boom of the 1920s," *Chicago History* (summer 1981): 86-95.

34. Wim de Wit, "Apartment Houses and Bungalows: Building the Flat City," *Chicago History* (winter 1983): 23-29.

35. Author interview with Terence O'Rourke.

36. Ibid.

37. Wirth and Furez, "Auburn-Gresham," *Local Community Fact Book*. Foreign stock includes Irish-born and their children.

38. Author interview with Terence O'Rourke.

39. Kantowicz, *Corporation Sole*, 72-73.

40. Melvin G. Holli, "The Great War Sinks Chicago's German Kultur," in Holli and Jones, *Ethnic Chicago*, 473.

41. *Historic City: The Settlement of Chicago* (Department of Development and Planning, 1976), 66.

42. St. Sabina Marriage Records.

43. Author interview with Terence O'Rourke.

44. Ibid.

45. Ibid.

46. Author interview with Julia Hagerty.

47. Parish Annual Reports, Our Lady of Sorrow, 1910, 1915, 1920, 1925, and St. John Baptist, 1920; both in ACA.

48. Koenig, *History of the Parishes*, 373; also based on a random survey of territorial and ethnic parishes at five-year intervals from 1895 to 1925, Parish Annual Reports, Archidiocese of Chicago.

49. Dolan, *American Catholic Experience*, 323.
50. Sanders, *Education of an Urban Minority*, 70-71.
51. Author interview with Julia Hagerty.
52. Author interview with Terence O'Rourke.
53. Author interview with Julia Hagerty.
54. Author interview with Bernard DesChatelets.
55. Sanders, *Education of an Urban Minority*, 108-10.
56. Holli, "Great War," 510.
57. Ibid., 508.
58. Ibid., 511.
59. Ibid., 469.
60. McCaffrey, *Irish Diaspora*, 134-37.
61. Funchion, "Political and Nationalist Dimension," 77.
62. "Parish Activities," *New World*, 23 Jan. 1920, 7.
63. "Parish Activities," *New World*, 30 Jan. 1920, 5.
64. "Parish Activities," *New World*, 13 Feb. 1920, 5.
65. "Parish Activities," *New World*, 20 Feb. 1920, 9.
66. *New World*, 12 Mar. 1920, 2.
67. "Parish Activities," *New World*, 12 Mar. 1920, 7.
68. Author interview with Terence O'Rourke.
69. *Community of God and People*, 19.
70. Skerrett, "Catholic Dimension," 46-47.

3. "I'm from Sabina's"

1. Author interview with Terence O'Rourke.
2. Hagerty, *Family History*, 2-3.
3. Halsey, *Survival of American Innocence*, 17, 53, 57, 60.
4. Dolan, *American Catholic Experience*, 355.
5. Kantowicz, *Corporation Sole*, 1-5.
6. Sanders, *Education of an Urban Minority*, 97-100.
7. Shanabruch, *Chicago's Catholics*, 230-31.
8. St. Sabina Annual Reports, 1928, ACA; *Community of God and People*, 9-11.
9. Dolan, *American Catholic Experience*, 192-93.
10. Parish Annual Reports, ACA.
11. St. Sabina Annual Reports, 1916 to 1928, ACA.
12. Author interview with Mary S. Dunne.
13. "Parish Activities," *New World*, 10 Sept. 1920, 8.
14. Author interview with Terence O'Rourke.
15. "Parish Activities," *New World*, 10 Sept. 1920, 8.
16. Author interview with Terence O'Rourke.
17. Ibid.
18. Wirth and Furel, *Local Community Fact Book*, 71.
19. Author interview with Terence O'Rourke.
20. Author interview with Julia Hagerty.
21. Barlow, *Auburn-Gresham*, 39-40.
22. Author interview with Mary S. Dunne.
23. Author interview with Terence O'Rourke.
24. Author interview with Julia Hagerty.
25. Author interview with Helen O'Connor.
26. Barlow, *Auburn-Gresham*, 39-41.
27. Author interview with Lucille Cavanaugh.
28. Author interview with Rev. James Kill.

29. Author interview with Mary S. Dunne.

30. Author interview with Terence O'Rourke.

31. Author interview with Julia Hagerty.

32. Author interview with Rev. James Kill.

33. Author interview with Julia Hagerty. The Catholic Church had officially condemned the Masons as a suspect society that threatened or perverted the faith of Catholics who joined it.

34. Author interview with Rev. William Hogan, 15 July 1993.

35. Jackson, *Ku Klux Klan*, xi-xii.

36. Ibid., 90.

37. Ibid., 96, 125-26.

38. Ibid., 115.

39. Sanders, *Education of an Urban Minority*, 121-22, 126.

40. Jentz and Hansen, *Rethinking*, 5-7.

41. Jackson, *Ku Klux Klan*, 102-3, 116, 123-24.

42. Author interview with Terence O'Rourke, 30 Sept. 1986.

43. Jackson, *Ku Klux Klan*, 115.

44. Presidential election, Nov. 6, 1928, Board of Election Commissioners of the City of Chicago, 18188 and 19199, 18th and 19th Ward Maps, 1921/31. Chicago Municipal Reference Library.

45. Ibid.

46. Author interview with Terence O'Rourke.

47. Author interview with Julia Hagerty.

48. Ibid.

49. Author interview with Rev. William Hogan.

50. Author interview with Terence O'Rourke.

51. Kane, *Boston Catholics*, viii-xii.

52. Author interview with Terence O'Rourke.

53. Ibid.

54. Ibid.

55. *Community of God and People*, 25; author interviews with Julia Hagerty, Terence O'Rourke, Mary S. Dunne, and James Kill.

56. *Community of God and People*, 25.

57. "Dedication of Magnificent St. Sabina Church, Sunday," *New World*, 16 June 1933, 1; John M. Munroe, "Bringing Down to Date the Histories of the Parishes of the Archdiocese of Chicago: St. Sabina's, 1916," *New World*, 30 Aug. 1935; Parish Annual Reports, St. Sabina, 1932-37.

58. St. Sabina Parish File, Letters from Chancellor dating 16 Apr. 1917, 10 Feb. 1921, 22 Mar. 1921, 24 Oct. 1923, 31 Dec. 1924, 17 June 1927, ACA.

59. Parish Annual Reports, St. Sabina, 1930-37.

60. Author interview with Sister Cecilian, who taught 7th and 8th grade during the 1930s, 5 Jan. 1989.

61. Author interview with Mary S. Dunne.

62. Author interview with Terence O'Rourke.

63. Author interview with Mary S. Dunne.

64. Author interviews with Terence O'Rourke and Rev. James Kill.

65. Roger Biles, *Big City Boss in Depression and War: Mayor Edward J. Kelly of Chicago* (Dekalb, Ill.: Northern Illinois Univ. Press, 1984), 13-20, 156.

66. Author interview with Rev. William Hogan.

67. Author interviews with Emmett Clair and Terence O'Rourke.

68. Author interview with Mary S. Dunne.

69. Parish Annual Reports, St. Sabina, 1916-41.

70. Author interview with Julia Hagerty.
71. Author interview with Mary S. Dunne.
72. *Community of God and People*, 27.
73. Author interview with Mary S. Dunne.
74. Author interview with Julia Hagerty.
75. Author interviews with Terence O'Rourke and Julia Hagerty.
76. Author interview with Mary S. Dunne, Julia Hagerty, and Emmett Clair.
77. Author interview with Helen O'Connor.
78. Author interview with Rev. James Kill.
79. Author interview with Julia Hagerty.
80. Ibid.
81. Author interview with Rev. James Kill.
82. *Community of God and People*, 13.
83. Taves, *Household of Faith*, viii, 428.
84. Ibid., 111, 119.
85. Kane, *Boston Catholics*, 67-71.
86. A novena is nine successive days of prayer to receive special favors or graces. It can be done in private or in public. Novenas can honor certain saints or the Blessed Virgin Mary, and petitioners can request intercession on their behalf. The novena grew out of popular piety. In the nineteenth century the Church recommended the practice by granting indulgences.
87. Author interview with Mary S. Dunne.
88. Author interview with Rev. James Kill.
89. Author interview with Terence O'Rourke.
90. Author interview with Julia Hagerty.
91. Taves, *Household of Faith*, 41.
92. Author interviews with Mary S. Dunne and Rev. James Kill.
93. Author interview with Rev. James Kill.
94. Ibid.
95. Author interview with Rev. William Hogan.
96. Author interview with Mary S. Dunne.
97. "Parish Activities, St. Sabina," *New World*, 14 May, 1920, 7.
98. Author interview with Terence O'Rourke.
99. Taves, *Household of Faith*, 30-32, 45.
100. Ibid., 24, 34-35, 41, 45.
101. Ibid., 35, 39, 53-54; author interview with Rev. William Hogan.
102. Taves, *Household of Faith*, 29, 42, 40, 54; author interview with Rev. William Hogan.
103. Author interview with Rev. William Hogan.
104. Author interview with Mary S. Dunne.
105. Author interview with Rev. William Hogan.
106. Ibid.
107. Both the Altar and Rosary and the Holy Name Societies are confraternities, which means that their intention is to promote public worship. The Altar and Rosary Society is a spiritual association whose members are to say fifteen mysteries of the Rosary once a week. The confraternity is assigned to the Dominican master general, may be established in any church or public oratory for the faithful, and is open to all Catholics who have reached the age of reason. An altar of the church must be designated as the altar of the confraternity. In the United States membership is restricted to women. The Society raises the rosary from a form of private prayer to that of shared or common prayer. The Holy Name Society's mission is to increase the reverence for the name of the Redeemer and to achieve for members self-sanctification by attending monthly Com-

munion in a corporate body on the second Sunday of each month. It also encourages participation in spiritual exercises such as retreats, holy hours, nocturnal adoration, and other special devotions. The Society is a public manifestation of respect for Christ's name.

108. Author interview with Mary S. Dunne.

109. "St. Sabina's Men Seek 1,200 at Rail," *New World*, 12 June 1931, 16.

110. Harry P. Martin, "St. Sabina Men out to Surpass Women's Record," *New World*, 9 Oct. 1931, 12.

111. "800 Men, Boys at Altar Railing at St. Sabina's," *New World*, 13 Nov. 1931, 12.

112. Author interview with Emmett Clair.

113. "St. Sabina's Branch," *New World*, 27 Jan. 1933, 10. "St. Sabina's Holy Name Society," *New World*, 16 Jan. 1920, 7; "St. Sabina's Parish," *New World*, 9 Jan. 1920, 7.

114. Author interview with Julia Hagerty.

115. "St. Sabina Church Notes," *New World*, 13 Feb. 1920, 7.

116. "St. Sabina Church News," *New World*, 19 Dec. 1919, 7; "St. Sabina Church Notes," *New World*, 23 Mar. 1920, 7; "St. Sabina Church News," *New World*, 5 Dec. 1919, 7.

117. Author interviews with Terence O'Rourke, 30 Sept. 1986; Emmett Clair, 30 Sept. 1986; "Knights of Columbus," *New World*, 20 Jan. 1921, 10.

118. Skerrett, "Catholic Dimension," 47-48.

119. Author interview with Rev. James Kill.

120. Brewer, *Nuns*, 31-33.

121. Author interview with Terence O'Rourke.

122. Author interview with Rev. James Kill.

123. Author interview with Helen O'Connor.

124. Author interview with Rev. James Kill.

125. Author interviews with Rev. James Kill, Emmett Clair, and Bernard DesChatelets.

126. Author interview with Julia Hagerty.

127. Author interview with Rev. James Kill.

128. Brewer, *Nuns*, 40-42.

129. Author interview with Sister Cecilian.

130. "Parish Activities, St. Sabina: Parish News," *New World*, 11 June 1920.

131. Author interview with Julia Hagerty.

132. Author interview with Rev. James Kill.

133. Author interview with Julia Hagerty.

134. Author interview with Rev. James Kill.

135. Author interview with Rev. William Hogan.

136. Author interview with Rev. James Kill.

137. Author interviews with Terence O'Rourke and Helen O'Connor.

138. Author interview with Terence O'Rourke.

139. Ibid.

140. Author interview with Bernard DesChatelets.

141. Author interview with Rev. James Kill.

142. Author interview with Rev. William Hogan.

143. Author interview with Emmett Clair.

144. Author interview with Julia Hagerty.

145. Author interview with Mary S. Dunne.

146. Author interview with Rev. James Kill.

147. Author interview with Rev. William Hogan.

148. Author interview with Julia Hagerty.

149. Author interview with Rev. James Kill.

150. Author interview with Emmett Clair.

151. Author interview with Rev. James Kill.

152. Jentz and Hansen, *Rethinking*, 5-7.

4. Ticket to Heaven

1. "Dedication of Memorial Books," *Seraph* 12, no. 3 (May 1954): 17.

2. Dolan, *American Catholic Experience*, 352, 356.

3. Lawrence J. McCaffrey, "The Irish-American Dimension," in McCaffrey et al., *Irish in Chicago*, 16.

4. Msgr. John A. McMahon, "Infiltration," *Seraph* 12, no. 4 (Apr.-May 1954): 1, 3.

5. "The Pastor's Page," *Seraph* 9, no. 4 (May 1951): 1.

6. "The Pastor's Page, *Seraph* 9, no. 6 (July 1951): 1.

7. Father Quinlan, "Souls at Stake," *Seraph* 6, no. 2 (Feb. 1948): 37.

8. "The Younger Set Speaks Out," *Seraph* 7, no. 10 (Nov. 1949): 23, 25.

9. Funchion, "Political and Nationalist Dimensions," 83.

10. Hauser and Kitagawa, *Local Community Fact Book*, 290.

11. Parish Annual Reports, St. Sabina, 1935 and 1957.

12. Ibid., 1930-60. Figures not adjusted for inflation.

13. "Six Years," *Seraph* 16, no. 1 (Jan. 1959): 11.

14. "St. Sabina Credit Union," *Seraph* 10, no. 10 (Nov. 1952): 17.

15. "Six Years," *Seraph* 16, no 1 (Jan. 1959): 1.

16. "A First for St. Sabina," *Seraph* 17, no. 2 (Feb. 1960): 17; "Marion Cotillion," *Seraph* (Jan. 1963): 27.

17. Author interview with Bernard DesChatelets and Terence O'Rourke.

18. Author interview with Terence O'Rourke, 20 Sept. 1986.

19. Author interview with Joseph Nelligan, 14 Jan. 1987.

20. Author interview with George Hendry.

21. Ibid.

22. Author interview with Joseph Nelligan.

23. "Good Reading," *Seraph* 16, no. 5 (May 1959): 11.

24. "The YMCA—Remember?" *Seraph* 9, no. 1 (Feb. 1951): 21.

25. "Excerpts from Pastoral Letter of His Eminence Samuel Cardinal Stritch, Archbishop of Chicago," *Seraph* 12, no. 7 (Aug. 1954): 19.

26. Author interview with Rev. Thomas S. McMahon.

27. Author interview with Joseph Nelligan.

28. *Seraph*.

29. Author interview with George Hendry.

30. Ibid.

31. Author interview with Joseph Nelligan.

32. Author interview with George Hendry.

33. Ibid.

34. *Seraph*; *Southtown Economist*; Dolan, *American Catholic Experience*, 385-86.

35. "Do Yourself a Favor," *Seraph* 14, no. 10 (Oct. 1956): 3.

36. "Confession," *Seraph* 13, no. 1 (Jan. 1955): 5.

37. Author interview with Father Thomas S. McMahon.

38. Author interview with Joseph Nelligan.

39. *Seraph* 7, no. 10 (Nov. 1949): 5.

40. "The Pilgrim Virgin," *Seraph* 16, no. 7 (Sept. 1959): 3, 9.

41. Ibid.

42. Author interview with Bernard DesChatelets.

43. "The Pilgrim Virgin," *Seraph* 16, no. 7 (Sept. 1959): 3.

44. *Seraph* 9, no. 12 (Jan. 1952): 5.

45. "Forty Hours Devotion," *Seraph* 15, no. 19 (Oct. 1958): 7.

46. "Mission," *Seraph* 12, no. 3 (Mar. 1954): 3.

47. "In Defense of Order," *Seraph* 13, no. 2 (Mar. 1955): 3.

48. "The Pastor's Page," *Seraph* 9, no. 7 (Aug. 1951): 3.

49. "To Your Credit," *Seraph* 13, no. 1 (Jan. 1955): 1.

50. Author interview with Dee Foertsch.

51. Author interview with George Hendry.

52. Author interview with Bernard DesChatelets.

53. Author interview with Dee Foertsch, 21 Nov. 1986.

54. *Seraph* 10, no. 9 (Oct. 1952): 9.

55. *Seraph,* 1951.

56. *Seraph* 9, no. 1 (Jan. 1951): 11.

57. S.C. Brophy, "Holy Name News," *Seraph* 13, no. 7 (Aug. 1955): 11.

58. "Holy Name News," *Seraph* 15, no. 9 (Sept. 1958): 11.

59. *Seraph* 8, no. 1 (Jan. 1951): 11.

60. *Seraph* 10, no. 7 (Aug. 1952); *Seraph* 10, no. 9 (Oct. 1952).

61. *Seraph* 10, no. 9 (Oct. 1952): 9.

62. *Seraph* 9, no. 10 (Nov. 1951): 47.

63. *Seraph* 12, no. 4 (Apr.-May 1954): 11.

64. *Seraph* 14, no. 6 (June 1956): 7.

65. *Seraph* 12, no. 2 (Feb. 1954): 5.

66. Author interview with Mildred Joyce.

67. *Seraph* 10, no. 2 (Mar. 1952): 9.

68. "Look at Your School," *Seraph* 2, no. 1 (Feb. 1944): 7.

69. *Seraph* 12, no. 4 (Apr.-May 1954): 11.

70. Author interview with Mildred Joyce.

71. *Seraph* 14, no. 2 (Feb. 1956): 21.

72. *Seraph* 14, no. 3 (Mar. 1956): 5

73. Author interview with Mildred Joyce.

74. Kantowicz, *Corporation Sole*, 185-88.

75. Parish Annual Report, St. Sabina, 1943.

76. *Seraph* 7, no. 10 (Nov. 1949): 39.

77. *Seraph* 7, no. 10 (Nov. 1949): 39.

78. Author interview with Mildred Joyce.

79. "Legion of Decency Crusade," *Seraph* 16, no. 1 (Jan. 1959): 29; "The Legion of Decency," *Seraph* 16, no. 9 (Nov. 1959): 3.

80. See Dolan, *Catholic Revivalism*, 195, for more discussion.

81. Author interview with Robert McClory.

82. Parish Annual Reports, St. Sabina, 1941-59.

83. "Sacred Heart League," *Seraph* 16, no. 12 (Dec. 1959): 25.

84. "The Sacred Heart League," *Seraph* 17, no. 14 (Feb. 1960): 23.

85. *Seraph* 9, no. 4 (May 1951): 6-7.

86. Ibid.

87. Ibid.

88. *Seraph* 10, no. 12 (Dec. 1950): 31.

89. "Memories Number Three," *Seraph* 10, no. 5 (June 1952): 21.

90. "Public School Children," *Seraph* 15, no. 9 (Sept. 1958): 7.

91. Author interview with George Hendry.

92. Author interview with Joseph Nelligan.

93. "Pastor Reports on Your School," *Seraph* 19, no. 5 (May 1962): 17.

94. E.C. Tocci, "Finance Your Children's Education through Your Credit Union," *Seraph* 19, no. 6 (June 1962): 11.

95. Author interview with Rev. Thomas S. McMahon.

96. Author interview with Joseph Nelligan.

97. Author interview with George Hendry.

98. St. Sabina Annual Reports, 1942, ACA.

99. "Mothers' Club," *Seraph* 12, no. 7 (July 1954): 15.

100. Author interview with George Hendry.

101. "The Younger Set Speaks," *Seraph* 12, no. 3 (Mar. 1954): 3.

102. "The Mothers' Club," *Seraph* 13, no. 5 (May 1955).

103. "The Pastor Reports on Your School," *Seraph* 19, no. 1 (Jan. 1962): 11.

104. Author interview with Joseph Nelligan.

105. Sanders, *Education of an Urban Minority*, 165.

106. Ibid., 167, 192.

107. "The Younger Set Speaks," *Seraph* 9, no. 3 (Apr. 1951): 29.

108. Greeley, *Irish-Americans*, 111, 112, 117.

109. Greeley, *American Catholic*, 58-59, 62.

110. "Parish Library," *Seraph* 7, no. 10 (Nov. 1949): 41.

111. "Library Notes," *Seraph* 15, no. 5 (May 1957): 11; *Seraph* 13, no. 4 (Apr. 1955), 13; *Seraph* 14, no. 9 (Sept. 1956): 29.

112. "Parish Library," *Seraph* 16, no. 9 (Sept. 1959): 31.

113. "New World 100% Plan," *Seraph* 7, no. 10 (Nov. 1949): 35.

114. "Let's Face It," *Seraph* 14, no. 8 (Aug. 1956): 1.

115. "Family Rosary," *Seraph* 13, no. 10 (Oct. 1955): 3.

116. "The Rosary," *Seraph* 15, no. 8 (Sept. 1957): 3.

117. Author interview with Rev. Thomas S. McMahon.

118. Author interview with Dee Foertsch.

119. Author interview with Helen O'Connor.

120. Author interview with Terence O'Rourke.

121. Author interview with George Hendry.

122. Author interview with Dee Foertsch.

123. Author interview with Rev. Thomas S. McMahon.

5. The Saints Come Marching In

1. Author interview with Bernard DesChatelets.

2. Edward Gilbreth, "It was a Great Day for All," *Southtown Economist*, 16 Mar. 1955, 1.

3. Advertisements in *Seraph*.

4. Author interview with Joseph Nelligan.

5. Author interview with George Hendry.

6. Kitagawa and Taeuber, *Local Community Fact Book*, 156.

7. Author interview with Terence O'Rourke.

8. Author interview with Bernard DesChatelets.

9. Author interview with George Hendry.

10. Author interview with Terence O'Rourke.

11. "March Festivals," *Seraph* 10, no. 2 (Mar. 1952): 47.

12. Author interview with Rev. Thomas S. McMahon.

13. Ibid.

14. Author interview with George Hendry.

15. Author interview with Rev. Thomas S. McMahon.

16. "Thousands View St. Pat's Parade," *Southtown Economist*, 18 Mar. 1953, 2.

17. Author interview with Bernard DesChatelets.

18. Author interview with Rev. Thomas S. McMahon.

19. "St. Patrick's Day Observed," *Southtown Economist*, 17 Mar. 1954, 2.

20. Author interview with Nathalie Hagerty.

21. Author interview with Terence O'Rourke.

22. Author interview with Rev. Thomas S. McMahon.

23. "St. Patrick's Day Parade," *Seraph* 13, no. 2 (Mar. 1955): 5.

24. "Shamrocks on Trinity Sunday," *Seraph* 14, no. 5 (May 1956): 5.

25. Sister M. Dorine, "Chicago-Cincinnati-Layfayette-Rockford Unit," in Sinsinawa Dominican Education Conference Procedings and Addresses, Third Triennial Meeting, 14 July 1955, vol. 9, no. 1, 67. Sinsinawa Dominican Archives.

26. Author interview with Rev. Jerome Riordan.

27. Author interview with Terence O'Rourke.

28. Skerrett, *Catholic Dimension*, 44, 47.

29. Lizabeth Cohen, *Making a New Deal: Industrial Workers in Chicago, 1919-1939* (New York: Cambridge Univ. Press, 1990).

30. Biles, *Big City Boss*, 11-13; Funchion, "Political and Nationalist Dimensions," 83-93.

31. Author interview with George Hendry.

32. Author interview with Dee Foertsch.

33. Author interview with George Hendry.

34. Ibid.

35. *Community of God and People*, 29.

36. Kantowicz, *Corporation Sole*, 152-53, 195.

37. Ibid.; Cohen, *Making a New Deal*, 83.

38. *New World*.

39. Kantowicz, *Corporation Sole*, 173-83.

40. Ibid., 180.

41. Cohen, *Making a New Deal*, 83.

42. Kantowicz, *Corporation Sole*, 180.

43. St. Sabina Annual Reports, 1940, ACA.

44. *Seraph* 9, no. 12 (Jan. 1952): 45.

45. Author interview with Rev. Thomas S. McMahon.

46. Rader, *American Sports*, 97-98.

47. McMahon, *Father Tom*, 81-82.

48. Author interview with Joseph Nelligan.

49. McMahon, *Father Tom*, 85, 102; author interview with Rev. Thomas S. McMahon; St. Sabina Annual Report, 1939, ACA.

50. McMahon, *Father Tom*, 85, 162; author interview with Rev. Thomas S. McMahon.

51. McMahon, *Father Tom*, 139; author interview with Rev. Thomas S. McMahon.

52. Author interview with Rev. Thomas McMahon.

53. Ibid.

54. Ibid.; McMahon, *Father Tom*, 139; *Seraph* 7, no. 11 (Nov. 1949): 11; *Seraph* 8, no. 12 (Dec. 1950): 41.

55. *Seraph* 8, no. 11 (Dec. 1950): 39, 41.

56. Author interview with Rev. Thomas S. McMahon; McMahon, *Father Tom*, 137-48; *Seraph* 7, no. 11 (Nov. 1949): 11.

57. Author interview with Rev. Thomas S. McMahon.

58. Ibid.

59. Ibid.

60. McMahon, *Father Tom*, 121-22.

61. Author interview with Rev. Thomas S. McMahon.

62. McMahon, *Father Tom*, 121.

63. Author interview with Rev. Thomas S. McMahon.

64. Author interview with George Hendry.

65. Author interview with Bernard DesChatelets, 6 Oct. 1986.

66. Author interview with George Hendry.

67. Author interview with Bernard DesChatelets.

68. Ibid.

69. Author interview with George Hendry.

70. Author interview with Terence O'Rourke.

71. McMahon, *Father Tom*, 121-22.

72. Merlin X. Mungovan, *Seraph* 9, no. 10 (Nov. 1951): 37.

73. Author interview with Rev. Thomas S. McMahon.

74. Ibid.

75. McMahon, *Father Tom*, 162.

76. Author interview with Rev. Thomas S. McMahon.

77. Author interview with Rev. James Kill.

78. Author interview with Rev. Thomas S. McMahon.

79. Author interview with Helen O'Connor.

80. "Where Are They Dancing?" *Seraph* 14, no. 2 (Feb. 1956): 23.

81. Author interview with George Hendry.

82. Author interview with Rev. James Kill.

83. Author interview with Kate Clair.

84. McMahon, *Father Tom*, 96-97.

85. Author interview with Joseph Nelligan.

86. McMahon, *Father Tom*, 97-98.

87. Ibid., 102-3.

88. "Mr. and Mrs. Club," *Seraph* 7, no. 10 (Nov. 1949): 31.

89. "Young People's Club," *Seraph* 10, no. 4 (May 1952): 3.

90. McMahon, *Father Tom*, 112-13; *Seraph* 12, no. 5 (Sept. 1954): 5-6; *Seraph* 10, no. 6 (July 1952): 5-7; *Seraph* 9, no. 8 (Sept. 1951): 5-7.

91. Kantowicz, *Corporation Sole*, 178-79.

92. Author interview with Bernard DesChatelets.

93. Marguerite Kane, "Scouting at St. Sabina," *Seraph* 9, no. 12 (Jan. 1952): 49.

94. "Girl Scouts, Brownie and Intermediate Scouts," *Seraph* 17, no. 14 (Mar. 1960): 11.

95. Author interview with Dee Foertsch.

96. Author interview with Joseph Nelligan.

97. James R. Barrett, "Why Paddy Drank: The Social Importance of Whiskey in Pre-Famine Ireland," *Journal of Popular Culture* 11, no. 1 (summer 1977): 161/23.

98. Author interview with John O'Leary, 18 Oct. 1987; see also Duis, *Saloon*, 152-53, 165, 168-69.

99. Duis, *Saloon*, 153.

100. Author interview with Dee Foertsch.

101. Author interview with Bernard DesChatelets.

102. Barrett, "Why Paddy Drank," 162/24.

103. Allsop, *Bootleggers*, 45, 50-52, 55-56, 66, 77, 100, 145.

104. Author interview with Joseph Nelligan.

105. Farrell, *My Baseball Diary*, 187-93; author interview with Joseph Nelligan.

106. Author interview with Joseph Nelligan.

107. Author interview with Dee Foertsch.

108. Author interview with Joseph Nelligan.

109. Author interview with George Hendry.

110. Author interview with Joseph Nelligan.

111. Author interview with George Hendry.

112. Author interview with Rev. Thomas S. McMahon.

113. *Seraph* 9, no. 11 (Dec. 1951): 5.

114. Author interview with Mildred Joyce.

115. Author interview with Helen O'Connor.

116. Bender, *Community*, 5-10.

117. Author interview with Terence O'Rourke.

118. Bender, *Community*, 43.

119. Bodnar, *Transplanted*, xv-xxi.

6. The Troubles

1. Koenig, *History of the Parishes*, 330.

2. Kantowicz, *Corporation Sole*, 65.

3. Kantowicz, "Church and Neighborhood," 354-55.

4. "Bridgeport," *Chicago Tribune*, 18 Jan. 1864, 1.

5. Slayton, *Back of the Yards*, 146, 148.

6. Author interview with Dee Foertsch.

7. William Gremley, "Social Control in Cicero," CIC Papers, Box 2, File July-Sept. 1951, 38, 40.

8. Confidential Memorandum to the File Regarding Rev. P. J. Buckley, Pastor of St. Odilo, CIC Papers, 25 Sept. 1951; Koenig, *History of the Parishes*, 1027-28.

9. Koenig, *History of the Parishes*, 100.

10. Slayton, *Back of the Yards*, 208-11.

11. Spear, *Black Chicago*, 91, 130.

12. Spear, *Black Chicago*, 5-6, 11; Philpott, *Slum and Ghetto*, 116.

13. Spear, *Black Chicago*, 6-7.

14. Ibid., 29-38.

15. Ibid., 131-33.

16. Ibid., 129, 139-40.

17. Ibid., 201-18.

18. Ibid., 214-17.

19. Ibid., 223-29.

20. Philpott, *Slum and Ghetto*, 113-200.

21. Hirsch, *Second Ghetto*, 4-29; Lemann, *Promised Land*, 6-7.

22. Hirsch, *Second Ghetto*, 31.

23. Ibid., 32-33, 34-35.

24. Ibid., 106-7, 213, 219, 229, 241-45, 253.

25. Cook, *Bygone Days*, 7-8.

26. "Mobbing Negroes," *Chicago Tribune*, 13 July 1864, 1.

27. Ibid.

28. Cook, *Bygone Days*, 10.

29. Cogley, *Catholic America*, 51.

30. Royko, *Boss*, 36-37.

31. American Civil Liberties Union—Chicago Division, Report, 25 Nov. 1949, 1, CIC Papers.

32. Thomas E. Rook, ACLU Report, 17 Nov. 1949, 3, CIC Papers.

33. Hirsch, *Second Ghetto*, 7, 85.

34. ACLU Report.

35. Rook Report, 1.

36. "Reveal 'Lily-White' Landlords Spurred Chicago Hate Riots," *Daily Compass*, 21 Nov. 1949, 4, in CIC News Clipping File.

37. ACLU Report, 2.

38. "Reveal 'Lily' White' Landlords Spurred Chicago Hate Riots," *Daily Compass*, 21 Nov. 1949, 4.

39. ACLU Report, 4; Rook Report, 3; Byron S. Miller, "Chicago Jewry Learns a Lesson," *Congress Weekly*, 2 Jan. 1950, 5, CIC Papers.

40. ACLU Report, 4.

41. Miller, "Chicago Jewry Learns a Lesson," 7.

42. South Deering Methodist Church Newsletter, Thanksgiving 1957, Box #20, CIC Papers.

43. Author interview with Msgr. Daniel Cantwell.

44. Author interview with John McDermott, director of CIC from 1960 to 1968.

45. Report of the Organizational Committee, CIC Papers, Box 1, File 1932-45.

46. Minutes, CIC Board Meeting, 21 Mar. 1945, CIC Papers, Box 1.

47. "The Sane and Decent Solution," Newsletter, Mar. 1953, CIC Papers, Box 4.

48. "A Brief Report on Our Activities for the Year Past," CIC Papers, Box 1, File Apr.-Dec. 1949.

49. Letter from Edward Marciniak, 4 Feb. 1950, CIC Papers, Box 1, File Jan.-July 1950.

50. "A Brief Report on Our Activities for the Year Past," CIC Papers, Box 1, File Apr.-Dec. 1949.

51. Confidential Memorandum to the File Regarding Rev. P.J. Buckley, Pastor, St. Odilo, 25 Sept. 1951, CIC Papers, Box 2, File July-Sept. 1951.

52. Author interview with John McDermott.

53. "A Brief Report on Our Activities for the Year Past," CIC Papers, Box 1.

54. Author interview with John McDermott.

55. Author interview with Mary Kay McMahon.

56. Koenig, History of the Parishes, 245-49.

57. Kantowicz, Corporation Sole, 212-13.

58. "Commission Confers with Cardinal," Excerpts from Monthly Bulletin on Chicago Commission on Human Relations, CIC Papers, Box 1, File 1946-47.

59. Confidential Memorandum from Rev. George Beemsterboer of St. Frances of Rome, 13 Sept. 1951, CIC Papers, Box 2.

60. Letter to CIC from William D. O'Brien, Pastor, Old St. John's Church, CIC Papers, Box 20.

61. "Story of a Colorful Parish," CIC Papers, Box 2, File, undated items 1951.

62. Letter from Ed Marciniak, 4 Feb. 1950, CIC Papers, Box 1, File Jan.-July 1950.

63. Sharum, Strange Fire Burning, 6, 7, 42-46, 61.

64. Ibid., 65, 121, 124.

65. Ibid., 151, 292.

66. Lloyd Davis, Exec. Sec., Council Against Discrimination, to Thomas E. Colgan, Exec. Dir., Letter, 2 Nov. 1953, CIC Papers, Box 4.

7. Make No Small Plans

1. Fish et al., Edge of the Ghetto, 41; author interview with Rev. Jerome Riordan.

2. Koenig, History of the Parishes, 1643.

3. Author interview with Rev. Jerome Riordan.

4. Ibid.

5. "The Pastor's Page," Seraph 10, no. 6 (July 1952): 1.

6. Ibid.

7. Dolan, American Catholic Experience, 308-19; Cogley, Catholic America, 174-78, 191-93.

8. Kantowicz, Corporation Sole, 203-8.

9. Ibid., 194-96.

10. Ibid., 191.

11. Ibid., 197-201; Kotre, Simple Gifts, 41-42.

12. Kotre, Simple Gifts, 39-41.

13. Kantowicz, Corporation Sole, 201; ibid., 41-48.

14. Parish Annual Report, St. Sabina, 1945.

15. Author interview with Rev. Jerome Riordan.

16. Ibid.

17. Ibid.

18. Author interview with Julia Hagerty.

19. Author interview with Rev. Jerome Riordan.

20. Burns, "Christian Family Movement," 1-4, 6.

21. "Christian Family Movement," *Seraph* 14, no. 5 (May 1956): 11.

22. Burns, "Christian Family Movement," 3-4.

23. Ibid., 10.

24. Ibid., 11-12.

25. Ibid., 6-7, 10-11.

26. Ibid., 9, 17, 31.

27. "Young Men Wanted," *Seraph* 14, no. 7 (July 1956): 19.

28. "Opportunity," *Seraph* 15, no. 4 (Apr. 1958): 17.

29. Author interview with Rev. Jerome Riordan.

30. "The Holy Name Society," *Seraph* 10, no. 9 (Oct. 1952): 21.

31. "St. Sabina Credit Union," *Seraph* 10, no. 10 (Nov. 1952): 17.

32. "Credit Union and Parish Conservation," *Seraph* 15, no. 15 (May 1958): 17.

33. "St. Sabina Altar and Rosary Society," *Seraph* 15, no. 8 (Aug. 1957): 21.

34. "Illegal Conversion," *Seraph* 15, no. 12 (Feb. 1958): 23.

35. "Talk," *Seraph* 15, no. 5 (May 1957): 3.

36. "Truth," *Seraph* 13, no. 8 (Sept. 1955): 3.

37. Steven M. Avella, *"This Confident Church": Catholic Leadership and Life in Chicago, 1940-1965* (Notre Dame: Univ. of Notre Dame Press, 1993), 249-87.

38. Author interview with Msgr. John J. Egan; *New World,* 6 Sept. 1961, sec. 2, 15; Horwitt, *Let Them Call Me Rebel,* 305, 323.

39. Author interview with Peter Martinez, volunteer with OSC 1960-62, became staff organizer in 1962.

40. Harold Cross, "Cardinal Indorses Organization of Southwest Community," *Southtown Economist* 17 Jan. 1960, 1.

41. "Planned Dispersion of Negroes," *Chicago Daily News,* 6 May 1959; Horwitt, *Let Them Call Me Rebel,* 324-25; Avella, *"This Confident Church,"* 249-87.

42. Author interview with Peter Martinez.

43. Donald O'Toole, "Why New Civic Group Was Formed," *Southtown Economist,* 21 Oct. 1959, 1.

44. M.W. Newman, "S.W. Side Neighborhood Works for Racial Peace," *Chicago Daily News,* 1 Sept. 1960.

45. Fish et al., *Edge of the Ghetto,* 11.

46. Lemann, *Promised Land,* 79.

47. Horwitt, *Let Them Call Me Rebel,* 329, 354-55

48. "Southwest Community Congress Meets Saturday," *Southtown Economist* 21 Oct. 1959, 1.

49. Horwitt, *Let Them Call Me Rebel,* 356-58.

50. Ibid., 356.

51. Stanley A. Koven, "The Day the Chicago Racists Lost," *Catholic World,* Egan Papers, Box 38, n.d., 313.

52. Author interview with Msgr. John Egan.

53. Fish et al., *Edge of the Ghetto,* 9.

54. Author interview with Peter Martinez.

55. Author interview with Rev. Jerome Riordan.

56. Donald O'Toole to Edward Chambers, OSC, Letter, Egan Papers, Box 38.

57. Eric Lund, "Urges Negro Quota in White Areas Here," *Chicago Daily News*, 6 May 1959, 1.

58. M.W. Newman, "S.W. Side Neighborhood Works for Racial Peace," *Chicago Daily News* 1 Sept. 1960, 1.

59. Author interview with John McDermott; A quota system was implemented in the western suburb of Oak Park. By the late 1960s and early seventies blacks from the Chicago neighborhood of Austin began moving into Oak Park and, while fearful of what integration might bring, residents did not want their village to follow the Chicago pattern of white flight and decay. In 1968 the suburb adopted a fair-housing ordinance; however, its liberal impulses were curbed later and they adopted a block exemption plan, whereby each block within the suburb was allowed a 30 percent ceiling on its black population. Property owners who rented or sold to blacks once the ceiling was attained risked being fined up to $1,000. Blacks who were refused access to housing in an exempted area were referred to the Oak Park Housing Center to find accommodations elsewhere in the community. This practice has been repeatedly criticized as discriminatory toward blacks because it curtails their right to freedom of movement. While a questionable practice, the exemption program has kept Oak Park a racially stable and integrated community. Wesley Hartzell, "Focus on Our Suburbs," *Chicago Today*, 4 Jan. 1974; J. Madeleine Nash, *Tribune Magazine*, 17 Feb. 1974; both in Chicago Historical Society, Oak Park Neighborhood Clipping File.

60. Fish et al., *Edge if the Ghetto*, 17.

61. Harold Cross, "Fate of Rev. Reed to Be Told Sunday," *Southtown Economist*, 6 Jan. 1960, 1; Robert Christ, "The Local Church in a Community Organization," Egan Papers, 8.

62. "Two Priests Get Apology Over 'Pink' Charges," *Chicago's American*, 19 Apr. 1960.

63. "Everingham Tells His Side of Story," *Southtown Economist*, 24 Apr. 1960.

64. Harold Cross, "Msgrs. Quit Council," *Southtown Economist*, 17 Apr. 1960, 1.

65. "Msgrs. Quit Council," *Southtown Economist*, 17 Apr. 1960, 2.

66. Harold Cross, "Ministers Back Msgrs. in Dispute Over Speaker," *Southtown Economist*, 27 Apr. 1960, 1.

67. Ibid.

68. Harold Cross, "Monsignors Get Apology for Slur by Speaker," *Southtown Economist*, 20 Apr. 1960, 1.

69. "Msgrs. Blast Critic," *Southtown Economist*, 8 May 1960, 1.

70. Fish et al., *Edge of the Ghetto*, 16.

71. Stanley A. Koven, "The Day the Chicago Racists Lost," *Catholic World*, n.d., Egan Papers, 313.

72. Christ, "Local Church," 11.

73. Fish et al., *Edge of the Ghetto*, 13.

74. Christ, "Local Church. "

75. Horwitt, *Let Them Call Me Rebel*, 333.

76. Author interview with Peter Martinez.

77. Interview with Rev. Jerome Riordan.

78. Author interview with Grace Benzig and Terence O'Rourke.

79. Edward T. Chambers to Rt. Rev. Msgr. John Egan, Letter, 18 Oct. 1962, Egan Papers.

80. Louise Ryan, "Father Lawlor Exiled," *Southtown Economist*, 7 Feb. 1968, 1; Bonnie Vinaccia and Louise Ryan, " 'Fugitive'—Fr. Lawlor," *Southtown Economist*, 27 Mar. 1968, 1.

81. Fish et al., *Edge of the Ghetto*, 13-14.

82. Christ, "Local Church," 4, 17.

83. Author interview with Peter Martinez.

84. Robert Christ, "The Local Church," 9.

85. Fish et al., *Edge of the Ghetto*, 14.

86. "Religious Groups Plan Meet on Racial Problems," *New World,* 22 June 1962, 20; interview with Msgr. Daniel Cantwell, Aug. 1985.

87. Christ, "Local Church," 10.

88. Horwitt, *Let Them Call Me Rebel*, 334.

89. Christ, "Local Church," 11.

90. Author interview with Peter Martinez.

91. Horwitt, *Let Them Call Me Rebel*, 334.

92. Christ, "Local Church," 9.

93. Fish et al., *Edge of the Ghetto*, 14-15.

94. Rev. Robert Christ to Msgr. John Egan, Letter, 21 Mar. 1963, Egan Papers, Box 38.

95. Christ, "Local Church," 13.

96. Author interview with Peter Martinez.

97. Ibid.

98. Christ, "Local Church," 12.

99. Ibid., 13.

100. Author interview with Peter Martinez.

101. Parish Annual Report, St. Sabina, 1960.

102. Author interview with John McDermott.

103. Author interview with Msgr. John J. Egan.

104. Newman, "S.W. Side Neighborhood Works for Racial Peace."

105. Parish Annual Reports, St. Sabina, 1960-65.

106. Author interview with Robert McClory; ibid., 1958-65.

107. Harold Cross, "Cardinal Indorses Organization for the Southwest Community," *Southtown Economist,* 17 Jan. 1960, 1.

108. Author interview with Msgr. John J. Egan.

109. Author interview with John McDermott.

110. Author interview with Peter Martinez.

111. Author interviews with Irvin and Eileen Schultz.

112. St. Sabina Parish Census, 1957-63; Fish et al., *Edge of the Ghetto*, 3, 12.

113. Author interview with Rev. Jerome Riordan.

114. Donald O'Toole, "Remarks on the Organization for the Southwest Community," 4 Feb. 1960, Egan Papers.

115. Harold Cross, "Panic Sales of Homes at End Here," *Southtown Economist,* 27 Jan. 1960, 1.

116. "Flight to Suburbs Slowed, Says OSC," *Southtown Economist,* 8 Jan. 1961, 1.

117. "OSC Home Loans Mark Fourth Year," *Southtown Economist,* 25 Dec. 1963, 1.

118. "Panic Sales of Homes at End Here," *Southtown Economist,* 27 Jan. 1960, 1.

119. "Experiment, O'Toole Tells OSC," *Southtown Economist,* 30 Oct. 1960, 1.

120. M.W. Newman, "What Happens When White Neighbors Refuse to Panic?" *Chicago Daily News,* 3 Sept. 1960.

121. "Panic Sales of Homes End Here," *Southtown Economist,* 27 Jan. 1960, 1.

122. M.W. Newman, "S.W. Side Gets Tough in War on Panic Peddlers," *Chicago Daily News,* 2 Sept. 1960; "OSC Will Continue 'War' on Blockbuster Tactics," *Southtown Economist,* 13 July 1960, 1.

123. "Blockbusting is Prime Target of OSC Committee," *Southtown Economist,* 20 Mar. 1960, 1; "OSC Spring Goal: End Blockbusting," *Southtown Economist,* 3 Apr. 1963, 1.

124. Newman, "S.W. Side Gets Tough," 1.

125. Ibid.

126. Harold Cross, "Threaten Civic Leader," *Southtown Economist,* 7 Aug. 1960, 1.

127. Harold Cross, "Two Get Fraud Sentences," *Southtown Economist,* 12 Nov. 1961, 1.

128. Harold Cross, "Blockbuster Fined," *Southtown Economist,* 29 July 1962, 1.

129. "Experiment, O'Toole Tells OSC," *Southtown Economist,* 30 Oct. 1960, 1.

130. Wm. Arthur Rogers, "Home Funds Available," *Southtown Economist,* 25 May 1960, 1.

131. O'Toole, "Remarks on the Organization for the Southwest Community."

132. "OSC Reports Rise in Remodeling," *Southtown Economist,* 15 Aug. 1962, 1.

133. Harold Cross, "OSC Rows Over Issue," *Southtown Economist,* 19 Mar. 1961, 1; "Quit S.W. Side Group in Open Occupancy Row," *Southtown Economist,* 3 Mar. 1961, 1; "Monsignor: 'Come Back Highland,' " *Southtown Economist,* 30 Mar. 1961, 1.

134. Harold Cross, "See OSC Floor Fight," *Southtown Economist,* 5 Nov. 1961, 1.

135. "Memorandum for File," 25 Aug. 1962, Egan Papers.

136. Harold Cross, "Congress 'Duel' Looms," *Southtown Economist,* 1 Nov. 1961, 1; Rev. Gordon Irvine, "Analysis of the Roll Call Vote on a Constitutional Change at the Third Annual Congress of the Organization for the Southwest Community," May 1963, Egan Papers.

137. Harold Cross, "OSC Election Upset," *Southtown Economist,* 8 Nov. 1961, 1, 6; Irvine, "Analysis of the Roll Call Vote," 2-4.

138. Irvine, "Analysis of the Roll Call Vote, 3.

139. Cross, "OSC Election Upset," 6; Irvine, Analysis of the Roll Call Vote, 3.

140. Cross, "OSC Election Upset," 6.

141. Irvine, "Analysis of the Roll Call Vote," 4; Harold Cross, "Threaten Bolt From OSC Ranks," *Southtown Economist,* 24 June 1962, 1; "Highland C.C. Rejoins OSC," *Southtown Economist,* 29 Oct. 1962, 1.

142. Horwitt, *Let Them Call Me Rebel,* 430-31.

143. Ibid., 431.

8. Where Two or Three Are Gathered

1. Author interview with Robert McClory.

2. Author interview with Terence O'Rourke.

3. Author interview with Rev. Daniel Sullivan.

4. Author interview with Terence O'Rourke.

5. Author interview with Nathalie Hagerty.

6. Lemann, *Promised Land,* 68.

7. "An Informal Analysis of Changing Parishes," *Community* (July-Aug. 1956): 1, 5; author interview with Dee Foertsch.

8. Agnes Podolinsky, "Blueprint for Changing Neighborhood," *New World,* 3 Aug. 1962, 12; author interview with Dee Foertsch.

9. Author interview with Dee Foertsch.

10. Author interview with Mary S. Dunne.

11. St. Sabina Communion Register, 1950-60; Hirsch, *Second Ghetto,* 6-8.

12. Author interview with Mildred Joyce.

13. Author interview with Robert McClory.

14. Author interview with Terence O'Rourke.

15. Author interview with Rev. Jerome Riordon.

16. Author interview with Terence O'Rourke.

17. Author interview with Julia Hagerty.

18. "Count Your Blessings," *Seraph* 19, no. 8 (Aug. 1962): 5.

19. Ibid.

20. "Slander," *Seraph* 18, no. 8 (Aug. 1961): 5.

21. Author interview with Mary S. Dunne.

22. Author interview with Robert McClory.

23. Author interview with Terence O'Rourke.

24. Author interview with Bernard DesChatelets.

25. Ibid.

26. Author interview with Terence O'Rourke.

27. Author interview with Robert McClory.

28. Interview with Ethel Lawrence by author and Ted Karamanski.

29. Author interview with Dee Foertsch.

30. Author interview with Mildred Joyce.

31. Author interview with Grace Benzig.

32. Author interview with Dee Foertsch.

33. Author interview with Robert McClory.

34. Annals of the Sisters of the Third Order of St. Dominic, St. Sabina, 1963, 59. Sinsinawa Dominican Archives.

35. Author interview with Robert McClory.

36. Author interviews with Irvin and Eileen Schultz, Dee Foertsch, and Mildred Joyce.

37. Burns, "Christian Family Movement," 30.

38. Sharum, *Strange Fire Burning*, 493.

39. "Whites Meet Negroes at Home, Change Attitudes," *Community* (Dec. 1960): 3.

40. Sharum, *Strange Fire Burning*, 494-95.

41. Ibid., 501-8.

42. Sharum, *Strange Fire Burning*, 514-15; Friendship House, Minutes of Meeting, 1 Feb. 1965, Friendship House Papers.

43. "Report to Staff," 7 Jan. 1965, Friendship House Papers, Box 37.

44. Author interview with Mildred Joyce.

45. Author interview with Dee Foertsch.

46. Author interview with Irvin and Eileen Schultz.

47. Author interview with Mildred Joyce.

48. Author interview with Terence O'Rourke.

49. Edward Chambers and Nick von Hoffman to Msgr. John J. Egan, Memorandum, "Police activity in connection with race violence on the Southwest Side," Egan Papers, Box 35.

50. "OSC Says Crime Down," *Southtown Economist* 30 Aug. 1961, 1.

51. Interview with Ethel Lawrence by author and Ted Karamanski.

52. "Crime Rate Increases in August," *Southtown Economist*, 27 Sept. 1961, 1; "Crime Up in Gresham," *Southtown Economist*, 20 May 1962, 1; "Crime Up in Gresham," *Southtown Economist*, 22 Apr. 1962, 1; "Gresham Crime is Up," *Southtown Economist*, 22 Aug. 1962, 1; "Gresham Crime is Up," *Southtown Economist*, 28 Nov. 1962, 1; "Demand More Police," *Southtown Economist*, 12 June 1963, 1; "Gresham Police Back," *Southtown Economist*, 16 June 1963, 1; "Gresham Crime Up," *Southtown Economist*, 18 Aug. 1963, 1.

53. Author interview with Joseph Nelligan.

54. Author interview with Mildred Joyce.

55. Author interview with Terence O'Rourke.

56. Author interview with Robert McClory.

57. Author interview with Mary S. Dunne.

58. Kitagawa and Taeuber, *Local Community Fact Book*, 157.

59. Author interview with Mary S. Dunne.

60. Author interview with Bernard DesChatelets.

61. Author interview with Robert McClory.

62. "Three Youths Admit Killing Youth, Wounding Girl," *Southtown Economist*, 18 Aug. 1965, 3.

63. Author interview with Rev. Daniel Sullivan.

64. Ibid.
65. "Slain Youth's Pals Give Mom $2,780," *Southtown Economist*, 25 Aug. 1965, 1.
66. Author interview with Robert McClory.
67. Author interview with Rev. Daniel Sullivan.
68. Ibid.
69. Author interview with Bernard DesChatelets.
70. Interview with Ethel Lawrence by author and Ted Karamanski.
71. Author interview with Ann Gaskin.
72. Author interview with Mary S. Dunne.
73. Author interview with Dee Foertsch.
74. Author interview with Robert McClory.
75. Author interview with Msgr. John J. Egan.
76. Author interview with George Hendry.
77. Horwitt, *Let Them Call Me Rebel*, 432.
78. Author interview with Mary S. Dunne.
79. Author interview with Msgr. John J. Egan.
80. Author interview with Ann Gaskin.
81. Author interview with Robert McClory.
82. Author interview with Bernard DesChatelets.
83. Ibid.
84. Author interview with Terence O'Rourke.
85. Author interview with Mary S. Dunne.
86. Ben Joravsky, "A Moment of Truth," *Chicago* (Aug. 1986), 99; "Murray Defends Law," *Southtown Economist*, 15 Sept. 1963, 1.
87. Joravsky, "Moment of Truth," 99; "Murray Defends Law," 1.
88. Joravsky, "Moment of Truth," 100.
89. Ibid., 101.
90. Author interview with John McDermott.
91. Author interview with Charles Marble.
92. *Community Area Data Book*.
93. Author interview with Terence O'Rourke.
94. Author interview with Joseph Nelligan.
95. Author interview with Mary S. Dunne.
96. Author interview with Mildred Joyce.
97. Author interview with Dee Foertsch.
98. Author interview with Mildred Joyce.
99. Author interview with Dee Foertsch.
100. Author interview with Robert McClory.
101. Ibid.
102. Author interview with Kris Kopcinski.
103. Author interview with Robert McClory.
104. Author interview with Charles Marble, 24 May 1993.
105. Author interview with Robert McClory.
106. Author interview with Ann Gaskin.
107. "Ban Liquor: Auburn," *Southtown Economist*, 31 Mar. 1968, 1; "Auburn Dry Vote Considered," *Southtown Economist*, 3 Mar. 1968, 12.
108. Author interview with Bernard DesChatelets; Duis, *Saloon*, 153.
109. Author interview with Charles Marble.
110. Author interview with Robert McClory.
111. Ibid.
112. Author interview with Charles Marble.
113. Interview with Ethel Lawrence by author and Ted Karamanski.
114. Author interview with Robert McClory; "See High School Jam," *Southtown*

Economist, 21 Aug. 1963, 1; Vic Watia, "Cook School Jammed," *Southtown Economist,* 24 Mar. 1968, 1; "Demand More Room," *Southtown Economist,* 17 Mar. 1968, 1.

115. Author interview with Charles Marble.
116. Annals, 1966-1967, 65.
117. *Criteria for Evaluation of Catholic Elementary Schools. 1965.* St. Sabina (Washington, D.C.: Catholic Univ. Press, 1965), 39.
118. Author interview with Margaret Ortman.
119. Author interview with Ann Gaskin.
120. Author interview with Charles Marble.
121. Author interview with Mildred Joyce.
122. Author interview with Bernard DesChatelets.
123. Author interview with Charles Marble.
124. Author interview with Grace Benzig.
125. Author interview with Mildred Joyce.
126. Author interview with Bernard DesChatelets.
127. Author interview with Dee Foertsch.
128. Author interview with Mary S. Dunne.
129. Author interview with Mildred Joyce.
130. Author interview with Dee Foertsch.
131. Author interviews with Terence O'Rourke and Rev. Daniel Sullivan.
132. Author interview with Rev. Jerome Riordan.
133. Author interview with Mildred Joyce.
134. Author interview with Mary S. Dunne.
135. Author interview with Dee Foertsch.
136. Author interview with Mildred Joyce.
137. Author interview with Msgr. John J. Egan.
138. Author interview with Ann Gaskin.
139. Author interview with Rev. Daniel Sullivan.
140. Author interview with Dee Foertsch.
141. Author interview with Rev. Daniel Sullivan.
142. Horwitt, *Let Them Call Me Rebel,* 433.
143. Jackson, *Crabgrass Frontier,* 213-15.
144. Horwitt, *Let Them Call Me Rebel,* 434-37.
145. Ibid., 437.
146. Author interview with Dee Foertsch.
147. Author interview with Charles Marble.
148. Fox and Haines, *Black Homeowners,* 18, 29, 31-32, 167.
149. Ibid., 57, 66-67, 117-19.
150. Author interview with Charles Marble.
151. Author interview with Rev. Daniel Sullivan.
152. Fox and Haines, *Black Homeowners,* 61-63.
153. Author interview with Terence O'Rourke.
154. Author interview with Rev. Daniel Sullivan.
155. Author interview with Robert McClory.
156. Author interview with Ann Gaskin.
157. Author interview with Charles Marble.
158. Parish Annual Reports, St. Sabina, 1968.
159. Author interview with Rev. Daniel Sullivan.
160. Author interview with Robert McClory.
161. Author interview with Rev. Daniel Sullivan.
162. Ibid.
163. "Golden Jubilee Set for Msgr. John McMahon," *New World,* 10 Sept. 1976.
164. Interview with Ethel Lawrence by author and Ted Karamanski.

165. "St. Sabina Pastor Dies," *Chicago Catholic,* 24 Oct. 1980.

166. Author interview with Charles Marble.

167. Interview with Ethel Lawrence by author and Ted Karamanski.

168. Author interview with Charles Marble.

169. Carol Jouzaitis, "Billboards a Battleground," *Chicago Tribune,* 30 Mar. 1990, sec. 4, p. 1; Susan Kuszka, "St. Sabina Scores a First in Drug War," *Chicago Tribune,* n.d.

170. Author interview with Dee Foertsch.

171. Koenig, *History of the Parishes,* 100.

172. Author interview with Dee Foertsch.

173. Author interview with George Hendry.

174. Author interview with Rev. Jerome Riordan.

175. Author interview with Bernard DesChatelets.

176. Author interview with Julia Hagerty.

177. Author interview with Joseph Nelligan.

178. Author interview with Dee Foertsch.

179. Author interview with Robert McClory.

180. Author interveiw with Charles Marble.

181. Author interview with Mildred Joyce.

182. Author interview with Dee Foertsch.

183. Ibid.

184. James N. Trant to Rev. Michael Pfleger, Letter, *Seraph* (summer 1986).

185. Author interview with Julia Hagerty.

Conclusion

1. Farrell, *Studs Lonigan,* 373.

2. Ibid., 374.

3. Fanning, "Literary Dimension," 131-32.

4. Hansberry, *Raisin in the Sun,* 97-99.

5. Ibid., 99.

6. Lasch, *True and Only Heaven,* 410-12; Lemann, *Promised Land,* 239-40.

7. Gremillion and Castelli, *Emerging Parish,* 194.

8. Ibid., 196-98.

9. Ibid., 200-202.

10. Author interview with Rev. William Hogan.

11. Fanning, "Literary Dimension."

Bibliography

Archival Sources

Archdiocese of Chicago Archives and Records Center, Chicago, Ill.
  Parish Anniversary Histories
  Parish Annual Reports
  St. Sabina Parish File
Archives of the Sinsinawa Dominicans, Sinsinawa, Wisc.
  Sinsinawa Dominican Education Conference Proceedings and
  Addresses
  Annals
  Criteria for Evaluating Catholic Elementary Schools, 1965, St. Sabina.
Catholic Interracial Council. Papers. Chicago Historical Society.
Friendship House. Papers. Chicago Historical Society.
City of Chicago. Board of Election. Presidential Returns. Nov. 6, 1928. Chicago Municipal Reference Library.
Egan, Msgr. John J. Papers. University of Notre Dame, Southbend, Ind.

Other Primary Sources

Chicago City Directory. 1916-27.
A Community of God and People: St. Sabina Church, 1916-1966, Anniversary History. Private Printing, 1966.
Hagerty, Cornelius J., C.S.C. *The Hagerty Family History*. Private Collection.
McMahon, Rev. Thomas S. *Father Tom, Associate Priest*. Chicago: Franciscan Herald Press, 1973.
St. Sabina Parish Census. 1957-63.
St. Sabina Parish Sacramental Records. 78th Street, Chicago, Ill. Marriage, Baptism, First Communion, and Funeral Registers.
The Seraph (St. Sabina Parish Bulletin)

Periodical Sources

American Historical Review
American Sociological Review
Chicago
Chicago Daily News
Chicago History
Chicago Today
Chicago Tribune

Chicago's American
Community
Daily Compass
Ethnicity
Journal of Popular Culture
The New World
Records of the American Catholic Historical Society
Southtown Economist

Interviews

Benzig, Grace. Lockport, Ill. 22 Oct. 1986.
Cantwell, Msgr. Daniel. Chicago, Ill. 18 Aug. 1985.
Cavanaugh, Lucille. Chicago, Ill. 9 Sept. 1985.
Cecilian, Sister. Sinsinawa, Wisc. 5 Jan. 1989.
Clair, Emmett. Crestwood, Ill. 30 Sept. 1986.
Clair, Kate. Crestwood, Ill. 30 Sept. 1986.
DesChatelets, Bernard. Hometown, Ill. 3 Oct. 1986.
Dunne, Mary S. Oak Lawn, Ill. 12 Nov. 1986.
Egan, Msgr. John J. Chicago, Ill. 29 July 1985.
Foertsch, Dee. Chicago, Ill. 21 Nov. 1986.
Gaskin, Ann. Chicago, Ill. 5 Nov. 1986.
Hagerty, Julia. Chicago, Ill. 7 Nov. 1986.
Hagerty, Nathalie. Hometown, Ill. 15 Sept. 1985.
Hendry, George. Chicago, Ill. 11 Feb. 1987.
Hogan, Rev. William, S.J. Chicago, Ill. 15 July 1993.
Joyce, Mildred. Wilmington, Ill. 15 Nov. 1986.
Kill, Rev. James. LaGrange Park, Ill. 21 Oct. 1986.
Kopcinski, Kris. Chicago, Ill. 1 Sept. 1986.
Lawrence, Ethel. Chicago, Ill. 23 May 1993.
Marble, Charles. Chicago, Ill. 24 May 1993.
Martinez, Peter. Chicago, Ill. 4 Feb. 1986.
McClory, Robert. Evanston, Ill. 6 Jan. 1986.
McDermott, John. Chicago, Ill. 11 Sept. 1985.
McMahon, Mary Kay. Oak Lawn, Ill. 5 Nov. 1987.
McMahon, Rev. Thomas S. Oak Lawn, Ill. 10 Nov. 1986.
Nelligan, Joseph. LaGrange Park, Ill. 14 Jan. 1987.
O'Connor, Helen. Chicago, Ill. 6 Jan. 1986.
O'Leary, John. Oak Park, Ill., 15 Oct. 1985.
O'Rourke, Terence. Chicago, Ill. 29 Aug. 1985 and 30 Sept. 1986.
Ortman, Sister Margaret. Sinsinawa, Wisc. 5 Jan. 1989.
Riordan, Rev. Jerome. Hanover Park, Ill. 10 Aug. 1987.
Schultz, Eileen. Chicago, Ill. 8 Feb. 1986.
Schultz, Irvin. Chicago, Ill. 8 Feb. 1986.
Sullivan, Rev. Daniel. 12 Dec. 1986.

Secondary Sources

Allsop, Kenneth. *The Bootleggers: The Story of Chicago's Prohibition Era.*
   New Rochelle, N.Y: Arlington, 1968.

Avella, Steven M. *This Confident Church: Catholic Leadership and Life in Chicago, 1940-1965*. Notre Dame: University of Notre Dame Press, 1993.

Barlow, Carrie Mae. *Auburn-Gresham: The Survey of a Local Community*. Ph.D. diss., University of Chicago, 1934.

Bender, Thomas. *Community and Social Change in America*. Baltimore: Johns Hopkins Univ. Press, 1978.

Biles, Roger. *Big City Boss in Depression and War: Mayor Edward J. Kelly of Chicago*. DeKalb: Northern Illinois University Press, 1984.

Bodnar, John. *The Transplanted: A History of Immigrants in Urban America*. Bloomington: Indiana Univ. Press, 1985.

Branch, Edgar M. *James T. Farrell*. Minneapolis: Univ. of Minnesota Press, 1963.

Brewer, Eileen Mary. *Nuns and the Education of American Catholic Women, 1860-1920*. Chicago: Loyola Univ. Press, 1987.

Brown, Thomas N. *Irish-American Nationalism, 1870-1890*. Philadelphia: Lippincott, 1966.

Burns, Jeffrey M. "The Christian Family Movement." Working Paper Series. Spring 1982. Cushwa Center for the Study of American Catholicism. University of Notre Dame.

Chinnici, Joseph P., O.F.M. *Devotion to the Holy Spirit in American Catholicism*. New York: Paulist Press, 1985.

Cohen, Elizabeth. *Making a New Deal: Industrial Workers in Chicago, 1919-1938*. New York: Cambridge University Press, 1990.

Cook, Frederick Francis. *Bygone Days in Chicago: Recollections of the "Garden City" of the Sixties*. Chicago: McClurg, 1910.

Clark, Dennis. *Hibernia America: The Irish and Regional Cultures*. New York: Greenwood, 1986.

Cogley, John. *Catholic America*. Garden City, N.Y: Image, 1973.

Community Area Data Book. Chicago Association of Commerce and Industry, 1970.

Connolly, S.J. *Priests and People in Pre-Famine Ireland, 1780-1845*. New York: St. Martin's, 1982.

Dolan, Jay P. *The American Catholic Experience: A History from Colonial Times to the Present*. New York: Doubleday, 1985.

————. ed. *The American Catholic Parish: A History From 1850 to the Present*. New York: Paulist, 1987.

————. *Catholic Revivalism The American Experience 1830-1900*. Notre Dame: Univ. of Notre Dame Press, 1983.

————. *The Immigrant Church: New York's Irish and German Catholics, 1815-1865*. Notre Dame: Univ. of Notre Dame Press, 1983.

Duis, Perry R. *The Saloon: Public Drinking in Chicago and Boston, 1880-1920*. Urbana: Univ. of Illinois Press, 1983.

Ellis, Elmer. *Mr. Dooley's America: A Life of Finley Peter Dunne*. New York: Knopf, 1941.

Fanning, Charles, ed. *Mr. Dooley and the Chicago Irish: An Anthology*. New York: Arno, 1976.

Fanning, Charles, Ellen Skerrett, and John Corrigan. *Nineteenth Cen-*

tury Chicago Irish. Chicago: Center for Urban Policy, Loyola University, 1980.

Farrell, James T. *My Baseball Diary*. New York: Barnes, 1957.

———. *Studs Lonigan*. New York: The Modern Library, 1938.

Finke, Roger, and Rodney Stark. *The Churching of America, 1776-1990: Winners and Losers in Our Religious Economy*. New Brunswick: Rutgers Univ. Press, 1992.

Fish, John, Gordon Nelson, Walter Stuhr, and Lawrence Witmer. *The Edge of the Ghetto: A Study of the Church Involvement in Community Organization*. New York: Seabury, 1966.

Fox, Roger, and Deborah Haines. *Black Homeowners in Transition Areas*. Chicago: Urban League, 1981.

Fried, Lewis F. *Makers of the City*. Amherst: Univ. of Massachusetts Press, 1990.

Glazer, Nathan, and Daniel P. Moynihan. *Beyond the Melting Pot: The Negroes, Puerto Ricans, Jews, Italians, and Irish of New York City*. Cambridge, Mass.: The MIT Press.

Greeley, Andrew M. *The American Catholic: A Social Portrait*. New York: Basic, 1977.

———. *The Irish-Americans: The Rise to Money and Power*. New York: Harper and Row, 1981.

Gremillion, Joseph, and Jim Castelli. *The Emerging Parish: The Notre Dame Study of Catholic Life Since Vatican II*. San Francisco: Harper and Row, 1987.

Halsey, William M. *The Survival of American Innocence: Catholicism in an Era of Disillusionment, 1920-1940*. Notre Dame: Univ. of Notre Dame Press, 1980.

Hansberry, Lorraine. *A Raisin in the Sun*. New York: Signet, 1987.

Hauser, Philip, and Evelyn M. Kitagawa. *Local Community Fact Book for Chicago, 1950*. Chicago: Univ. of Chicago Press, 1953.

Hirsch, Arnold R. *Making the Second Ghetto: Race and Housing in Chicago, 1940-1960*. New York: Cambridge Univ. Press, 1983.

Historic City: The Settlement of Chicago. Chicago: Department of Development and Planning, 1976.

Holli, Melvin, and Peter D'A. Jones, eds. *Ethnic Chicago*. Grand Rapids: Eerdmans, 1984.

Holt, Glen E., and Dominic A. Pacyga. *Chicago: A Historical Guide to the Neighborhoods, The Loop and Southside*. Chicago: Chicago Historical Society Press, 1979.

Horwitt, Sanford D. *Let Them Call Me Rebel: Saul Alinksy—His Life and Legacy*. New York: Knopf, 1989.

Jackson, Kenneth. *The Ku Klux Klan in the City, 1915-1930*. New York: Oxford Univ. Press, 1967.

———. *Crabgrass Frontier: The Suburbanization of the United States*. New York: Oxford Univ. Press, 1985.

Jentz, John B., and Irene Hansen, ed. *Rethinking the History of Religion in Chicago: A Symposium*. The Newberry Papers in Family and Community History. Paper 1.

Kane, Paula Marie. "Boston Catholics and Modern American Culture, 1900-1920." Ph.D. diss., Yale University, 1987.

Kantowicz, Edward R. *Corporation Sole: Cardinal Mundelein and Chicago Catholicism.* Notre Dame: Univ. of Notre Dame Press, 1983.

Kitagawa, Evelyn M., and Karl E. Taeber, ed. *Local Community Fact Book: Chicago Metropolitan Area, 1960.* Chicago: Univ. of Chicago Press, 1963.

Koenig, Rev. Harry C., S.T.D., ed. *A History of the Parishes of the Archdiocese of Chicago.* Chicago: The New World, 1980.

Kotre, John. *Simple Gifts: The Lives of Pat and Patty Crowley.* New York: Andrews and McMeel, 1979.

Lasch, Christopher. *The True and Only Heaven: Progress and Its Critics.* New York: Norton, 1991.

Lemann, Nicholas. *The Promised Land: The Great Black Migration and How It Changed America.* New York: Knopf, 1991.

McCaffrey, Lawrence J. *Ireland: From Colony to Nation State.* Englewood Cliffs, N.J: Prentice-Hall, 1979.

McCaffrey, Lawrence J. *The Irish Diaspora in America.* Bloomington: Indiana Univ. Press, 1975.

McCaffrey, Lawrence J., Ellen Skerrett, Michael F. Funchion, and Charles Fanning. *The Irish in Chicago.* Urbana: University of Illinois, 1987.

Meagher, Timothy J., ed. *From Paddy to Studs: Irish-American Communities in the Turn of the Century Era, 1880 to 1920.* New York: Greenwood, 1986.

Miller, David W. *Church, State, and Nation in Ireland, 1898-1921.* Pittsburgh: Univ. of Pittsburgh Press, 1973.

Novak, Michael. *The Rise of the Unmeltable Ethnics: Politics and Culture in the Seventies.* New York: Macmillan, 1972.

Orsi, Robert Anthony. *The Madonna of 115th Street: Faith and Community in Italian Harlem, 1880-1950.* New Haven: Yale University Press, 1985.

Pacyga, Dominic A., and Ellen Skerrett. *Chicago: City of Neighborhoods.* Chicago: Loyola Univ. Press, 1986.

The People of Chicago, Who We Are and Who We Have Been: Census Data on Foreign Born, Foreign Stock, and Race, 1837-1970. City of Chicago: Department of Development and Planning, 1976.

Pierce, Bessie Louise. *A History of Chicago: The Beginning of a City, 1673-1848.* Vol. 1. New York: Knopf, 1937.

Philpott, Thomas Lee. *The Slum and the Ghetto: Neighborhood Deterioration and Middle-Class Reform, Chicago, 1880-1930.* New York: Oxford Univ. Press, 1978.

Rader, Benjamin G. *American Sports: From the Age of Folk Games to the Age of Spectators.* Englewood Cliffs, Prentice-Hall, 1983.

Royko, Mike. *Boss: Richard J. Daley of Chicago.* New York: New American Library, 1971.

Sanders, James W. *The Education of an Urban Minority: Catholics in Chicago, 1833-1965.* New York: Oxford Univ. Press, 1977.

Schaaf, Barbara C. *Mr. Dooley's Chicago.* Garden City, N.Y.: Anchor, 1977.

Shanabruch, Charles. *Chicago's Catholics: The Evolution of an American Identity.* Notre Dame: Univ. of Notre Dame Press, 1981.

Sharum, Elizabeth Louise. *A Strange Fire Burning: A History of the Friendship House Movement.* Ph.D. diss., Texas Tech University, 1977.

Slayton, Robert. *Back of the Yards: The Making of a Local Democracy.* Chicago: Univ. of Chicago Press, 1986.

Spear, Allan H. *Black Chicago: The Making of a Negro Ghetto, 1890-1920.* Chicago: Univ. of Chicago Press, 1967.

Sullivan, Gerald E. *The Story of Englewood, 1835-1923.* Chicago: Foster and McDonnell, 1924.

Taves, Ann. *The Household of Faith: Roman Catholic Devotions in Mid-Nineteenth Century America.* Notre Dame: Univ. of Notre Dame Press, 1986.

Thernstrom, Stephen. *The Other Bostonians: Poverty and Progress in the American Metropolis, 1880-1970.* Cambridge: Harvard Univ. Press, 1973.

Wakin, Edward, and Father Joseph F. Scheuer. *The De-Romanization of the American Catholic Church.* New York: New American Library, 1966.

Wirth, Louis, and Margaret Furez. *Local Community Fact Book, 1938.* Chicago: Chicago Recreational Commission, 1938.

Index

CPSIA information can be obtained at www.ICGtesting.com
Printed in the USA
LVOW12s1031260814

400847LV00001B/25/P